Social Lives of Medicines

Medicines are the core of treatment in biomedicine, as in many other medical traditions. As material things, they have social as well as pharmacological lives, with people and between people. They are tokens of healing and hope, as well as valuable commodities. Each chapter of this book shows drugs in the hands of particular actors: mothers in Manila, villagers in Burkina Faso, women in the Netherlands, consumers in London, market traders in Cameroon, pharmacists in Mexico, injectionists in Uganda, doctors in Sri Lanka, industrialists in India, and policymakers in Geneva. Each example is used to explore a different problem in the study of medicines, such as social efficacy, experiences of control, skepticism and cultural politics, commodification of health, the attraction of technology and the marketing of images and values. The book shows how anthropologists deal with the sociality of medicines, through their ethnography, their theorizing, and their uses of knowledge.

SUSAN REYNOLDS WHYTE is Professor at the Institute of Anthropology of the University of Copenhagen. Previous publications include *Questioning Misfortune* (Amaury Talbot Prize 1997), *The Context of Medicines in Developing Countries* (co-edited with Sjaak van der Geest, 1988) and *Disability and Culture* (co-edited with Benedicte Ingstad, 1995).

SJAAK VAN DER GEEST is Professor of Medical Anthropology at the Department of Sociology and Anthropology of the University of Amsterdam. Previous publications include *The Art of Medical Anthropology: Readings* (co-edited with A. Rienks, 1998) and *Health Reforms and the Quality of Health Care in Zambia* (with J. Kamwanga and M. Macwan'gi, 1999).

ANITA HARDON is Professor of Care and Health Anthropology and Director of the Amsterdam School for Social Science Research at the University of Amsterdam. Previous publications include *Drug Policy in Developing Countries* (with Najmi Kanji *et al.* 1992), *Reproductive Rights in Practice* (co-edited with Lisa Hayes, 1997) and *Confronting Ill Health: Medicines, Self-Care and the Poor in Metro Manila* (1991).

Cambridge Studies in Medical Anthropology

Editor

ALAN HARWOOD *University of Massachusetts, Boston*

Editorial Board

WILLIAM DRESSLER *University of Alabama*
RONALD FRANKENBERG *Brunel University, UK*
MARY JO GOOD *Harvard University*
SHARON KAUFMAN *University of California, San Francisco*
SHIRLEY LINDENBAUM *City University of New York*
MARGARET LOCK *McGill University*
CATHERINE PANTER-BRICK *University of Durham, UK*

Medical anthropology is the fastest-growing specialist area within anthropology, both in North America and in Europe. Beginning as an applied field serving public health specialists, medical anthropology now provides a significant forum for many of the most urgent debates in anthropology and the humanities. It includes the study of medical institutions and health care in a variety of rich and poor societies, the investigation of the cultural construction of illness, and the analysis of ideas about the body, birth, maturity, ageing and death.

This series includes theoretically innovative monographs, state-of-the-art collections of essays on current issues and short books introducing main themes in the subdiscipline.

1. Lynn M. Morgan, *Community Participation in Health: The Politics of Primary Care in Costa Rica*
2. Thomas J. Csordas (ed.), *Embodiment and Experience: The Existential Ground of Culture and Health*
3. Paul Brodwin, *Medicine and Morality in Haiti: The Contest for Healing Power*
4. Susan Reynolds Whyte, *Questioning Misfortune: The Pragmatics of Uncertainty in Eastern Uganda*
5. Margaret Lock and Patricia Kaufert, *Pragmatic Women and Body Politics*
6. Vincanne Adams, *Doctors for Democracy*
7. Elisabeth Hsu, *The Transmission of Chinese Medicine*
8. Margaret Lock, Allan Young and Alberto Cambrosio (eds.), *Living and Working with the New Medical Technologies: Intersections of Inquiry*
9. Daniel Moerman, *Meaning, Medicine and the 'Placebo Effect'*

Social Lives of Medicines

Susan Reynolds Whyte
University of Copenhagen

Sjaak van der Geest
University of Amsterdam

Anita Hardon
University of Amsterdam

CAMBRIDGE
UNIVERSITY PRESS

CAMBRIDGE UNIVERSITY PRESS
Cambridge, New York, Melbourne, Madrid, Cape Town, Singapore, São Paulo, Delhi

Cambridge University Press
The Edinburgh Building, Cambridge CB2 8RU, UK

Published in the United States of America by Cambridge University Press, New York

www.cambridge.org
Information on this title: www.cambridge.org/9780521804691

First published 2002
Reprinted 2006

A catalogue record for this publication is available from the British Library

ISBN 978-0-521-80025-9 hardback
ISBN 978-0-521-80469-1 paperback

Transferred to digital printing 2009

Contents

V Conclusion

Illustrations

Part I

Introduction

1 An anthropology of materia medica

'Materia medica' is the Latin term for medical material, the remedial substances usually called medicines or drugs. It is an old-fashioned term, slightly pedantic, but let it stand, to remind us that medicines are material things. In scholarly works 'materia medica' often refers to the assemblage of drugs available in a particular society or historical period, so it invites comparative assessment. It also designates a branch of academic study. At European and American universities there were departments and courses in materia medica until they were replaced in the nineteenth and early twentieth centuries by the new science of pharmacology. Whereas the study of materia medica ranged over the sources, preparation and use of all kinds of therapeutic substances, pharmacology focused on their effects upon bodily tissues. The emergence of the new discipline coincided with important developments in biochemistry and the beginning of drug synthesis in Europe.

This book is about materia medica in the sense that it takes medicines as the material *things* of therapy. But we propose to see them as things with social lives; we are more concerned with their social uses and consequences, than with their chemical structure and biological effects. The medicines with the most active social lives in the world today are the commercially manufactured synthetic drugs produced by the pharmaceutical industry. They have vigorous commodity careers; their dissemination to every part of the globe has far-reaching implications for local medical systems. They have become part of the materia medica of every local society – an eminent example of globalization. At the same time they are the most personal of material objects, swallowed, inserted into bodies, rubbed on by anxious mothers, used to express care and intimately empower the uncertain individual.

The global spread of biomedical drugs casts another light on the botanical and mineral substances that have constituted the materia medica of most peoples throughout human history. The different kinds of medicines provide context and meaning for one another. At the same time, all medicines have certain social and cultural characteristics in common.

3

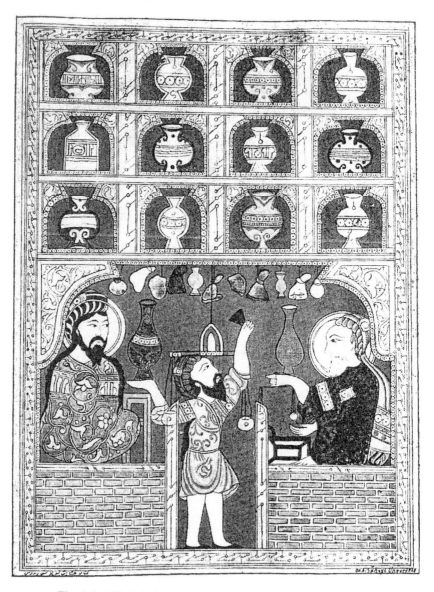

Fig. 1.1 A Baghdad pharmacist's shop in 1224, illustrated in an Arabic manuscript.

So the chapters to follow touch upon the whole range of medicines, although they emphasize commercial pharmaceutical drugs. Thus we explore a field of study distinct from ethnopharmacology, which focuses primarily on the biochemical properties and effects of 'indigenous' medicines (while recognizing the importance of people's own conceptions about these medicines).

In this introduction, we set out our assumptions about medicines as social and cultural phenomena. We briefly review the ancient tendency of medicines to move, as a background for appreciating the amazing spread of biomedical pharmaceuticals. We trace the development of anthropological interest in medicines, and explain our framework for the book.

What are medicines?

Medicines are substances with powers to transform bodies. Prayer, and rest, and exorcism may also have therapeutic powers, but they are not objectified or crafted or commodified as medicines are. The centrality of medicines for medicine is apparent in the identity of the words used in English. The same word, related to the Latin *mederi*, to heal, is used for the science or practice of treating and preventing disease, and for the substances used in that practice. Medicines are the primary means by which most medical traditions work upon disease and their use is the fundamental technology of biomedicine as an applied science. At a time when intellectuals and media in countries of the North are debating the new medical technologies, it is worth stepping back to consider the old medical technology, the use of medicines, as a general phenomenon.

1. Medicines are substances. Their materiality, their thinginess, is a property of great analytical importance for anthropology. As things they can be exchanged between social actors, they objectify meanings, they move from one meaningful setting to another. They are commodities with economic significance, and resources with political value. Above all they are potent symbols and tokens of hope for people in distress.

2. Medicinal substances have powers to transform. At least, such powers are attributed to them by social actors. Assumed efficacy is a defining property; a substance that no one believed efficacious would generally not be considered a medicine. They are supposed to do something, to change the body in a discernible way.

3. Transformative powers can be put to different purposes. Prototypically, medicines are meant to heal. They should do something about disease. Some medicines, such as vaccines, are meant to prevent particular diseases, or, like vitamins and tonics, to strengthen the body. Where intense awareness has been created about the factors that increase

chances of getting certain diseases, people even take medicines against risks. Medicinal powers can be used to injure as well as to heal. The term for medicine in many African languages refers to harmful as well as wholesome substances (Whyte 1988:218).

4. Medicines can be simultaneously noxious and beneficial. The ambiguity of medicinal potency is recognized in many cultures. The old Greek word *pharmakon*, from which 'pharmaceutical' derives, also meant poison. The eighteenth-century European pharmacopeia contained toxic drugs like belladonna and compounds of arsenic and mercury. The development of the science of toxicology was intimately linked with those of materia medica and pharmacology (Weatherall 1993:919). Today, package inserts in pharmaceuticals must warn of possible adverse effects and contra-indications. Beneficial as they are, medicines can harm accidentally ('Keep all medicines out of the reach of children') or be used for suicide. The potentially noxious effects of medicine are a key concern in the biomedical tradition: 'There is...no known drug that is not harmful or even poisonous at high doses, and much of the scientific work on drugs has attempted to widen the gap between effective and toxic doses' (Burger 1986:1).

5. Medicines are used intentionally to achieve an effect in some *body*. One of the themes of this book is that they have other effects as well. They change minds and situations and modes of understanding.

Medicines on the move

Medicines are mentioned in some of the oldest documents of ancient civilizations. Clay tablets incised with cuneiform script record medicines used in Sumeria 2,000 years before our era. The 60-foot-long Ebers Medical Papyrus has a section on ancient Egyptian medicinal remedies. The Rg Veda, dating from the latter part of the second millennium BC in South Asia, refers to specialists who knew the mysteries of healing herbs. Foundational texts of the Ayurvedic tradition, such as the Caraka Samhita, from the first millennium of our era, contain hundreds of medicinal recipes that can be related to nosologies of disease. In China, Shen-nung's Scripture on Materia Medica, from the first century AD, contained as many descriptions of therapeutic substances as there were days in a solar year – 365 (Unschuld 1988:181).

It seems reasonable to assume that at least some medicines were exchanged from place to place from early times. In south Asia, for example, it is suggested that herbs from mountain or jungle areas were traded into other ecological zones (Basham 1976:30). In any case, knowledge about medicines was transmitted across geographic and temporal distances, as research on historical texts has shown. The Greeks, full of admiration for Egyptian medicine, transcribed their prescriptions (Wilson 1962). Hittite scribes in Anatolia copied tablets of Babylonian medical texts from Mesopotamia with their herbal mixtures, suppositories and lotions (Oppenheim 1962). Whole books of materia medica were translated; indeed whole traditions of medical and medicinal knowledge diffused. One of the most striking examples is the spread of the classic Greek tradition to the Arab world, on to South Asia as Unani medicine (from the Arabic 'Yunani' meaning Ionian) and in time back to Europe again (Bürgel 1976).

In Greece the use of a range of botanical and inorganic substances was documented in the writings of Hippocrates of Cos and his followers about 400 years BC. However, the use of medicines was limited, emphasis being given to dietetics (Ackerknecht 1962:391). The great manuscript known as 'De Materia Medica' by Dioscorides, from the first century AD, contained an exhaustive description of plants, animal products and chemical substances (like mercury and arsenic), including those he had learned about during his travels as a surgeon with the Roman armies. His successor in the second century, the physician and prolific writer Galen, reorganized these listings but also sought out new medicines. 'He travelled widely in Egypt, learning about the drugs imported from India, Africa and elsewhere from the shippers who brought them' (Conrad et al. 1995:61).

This text-based tradition underwent a great revival as the Greek manuscripts were translated into Arabic around the third century. The flowering of formal medicine in the expanding Arab–Islamic world included systematic work on materia medica as Arab armies overran new territories with different assemblages of medicinal plants, animals and minerals. The expansion in medicinal knowledge is evident in the seventh-century manuscript on materia medica by Ibn al-Baytar which listed over 3,000 items, whereas that of Dioscorides had included only about 850. Arab–Islamic medicinal knowledge was written down and transmitted in a book trade that stretched from Spain to India. It was made available to literate lay people in popular introductory texts (Conrad 1993:703–7). Much of this corpus was translated into Latin in the eleventh century, introducing to Europe the wealth of Arabic knowledge of drugs.

In early modern Europe (1500–1700) the lively movement of medicines (as well as texts about them) is well documented. Enormous efforts were made to retrieve the drugs described in Dioscorides' Materia Medica. 'Venice . . . ordered its diplomats, physicians, and traders in the Middle East and in the Mediterranean to be on the look-out for the plants that grew in Dioscorides' stamping ground' (Conrad et al. 1995:305). Seeds and specimens were transported, some to be planted in the first botanical gardens at Pisa and Padua.

New remedies were brought to Europe from Asia and the New World, of which one of the most famous was the 'Peruvian bark', brought back to Rome in the early 1630s by Jesuit missionaries. Tried out successfully in Rome and Genoa against the 'intermittent fevers' of those malarial areas, it quickly spread throughout Europe. Physicians debated its fit into the Galenic system of humours (Jarcho 1993:19), just as Latin Americans would discuss the hot and cold properties of penicillin three centuries later. The bark was so esteemed that royalty made gifts of it. Supplies shipped back by merchants were stolen from warehouses or captured at sea by pirates (Jarcho 1993:201–2). The exotic drug challenged medical thinking and enjoyed a long cultural career in which it developed from being a specific against 'the intermittents' to being used as a panacea (Maehle 1999:223–90). It was not until 1820 that the active principle quinine was isolated from the bark of the tree named *Cinchona* by Linnaeus. Its travels were to continue as plantations were established by the Dutch in Java in the nineteenth century (with seeds smuggled out of Peru and Bolivia); they provided almost the entire world supply of commercial quinine up until the Second World War.

More mobile medicines

Throughout most of history medicines have been made from plants, animal parts and minerals through drying, grinding, decoction. This was certainly true in Europe as attested by the pharmacopoeias, books of standard drug recipes, published by medical academies in Florence, Lyons and London from the late Renaissance. After the time of Paracelsus (1482–1546) the methods of medical (iatro-) chemistry spread a new kind of drug production through much of Europe. The new technology came to be associated with those who challenged the dominant Galenic methods of established medicine and also with social reform (Temkin 1964:5; Conrad *et al.* 1995:318–23). Yet although iatrochemistry gained wider currency, herbal medications were still the most commonly used in Europe right up through the eighteenth century.

The revolution in drug production came in the nineteenth and twentieth centuries and laid the ground for a truly exponential increase in the movement of medicines. It built on advances in physiology, chemistry and pharmacy in France, and most dramatically in Germany. From the early 1800s, methods for extracting pure drugs, or active principles, from crude natural products were developed. At the same time, the new science of pharmacology was being professed (Weatherall 1993).

From the mid-nineteenth century, the 'fine chemical' industries in Germany began to synthesize drugs and produce them on a large scale. With World War I, American, English and French companies began their own industrial production to ensure supplies. Then, in the late 1930s the first sulfa drugs were developed and this set off a flurry of activity as the potential of anti-infective drugs became apparent. But it was not until after the Second World War, when antibiotics, including the new drug penicillin, were made widely available, that 'the great drug therapy era' opened. The pharmaceutical scene was transformed. Teams of scientists in industrial laboratories developed new drugs as well as 'me-too' products that duplicated existing ones but were marketed as different. Thousands of synthetic products replaced the limited number of natural origin available before 1935. Both prescription medicines and the increasing number of over-the-counter (OTC) drugs were heavily promoted (Silverman and Lee 1974:5–22). The movement of medicines that had long existed on a modest scale became a mighty current as drugs were pumped out onto national and international markets.

Mass produced biomedical pharmaceuticals spread to Asia, Africa and Latin America with remarkable speed. By the 1960s, antibiotics were being incorporated in the materia medica of Ayurvedic practitioners in India (Taylor 1976). By the 1970s one critical observer was writing about 'the drugging of the Americas' (Silverman 1976). While the vast majority of pharmaceuticals were and are manufactured in Western industrialized countries, some developing countries established their own production. By 1980, about 11 per cent of pharmaceutical production (by value) was located in Third World countries, mainly India, Egypt, Brazil, Argentina, Mexico and South Korea (Melrose 1982:28–9). The globalization of synthetic pharmaceuticals made a vast array of products available in poor countries, and prompted a growing concern about the dangers of misuse and waste of scarce resources. It was in the 1980s that the concept of essential drugs, inexpensive and safe medications for the most common diseases, gained notice, mainly through promotion by the World Health Organization (Mamdani and Walker 1985; Kanji et al. 1992: 28–41).

It is against this historical background of mobile medicines that we can set the development of an anthropological interest in materia medica. However, it is important to note that while historians and activists focus on the movement of medicines, anthropologists combine that interest with questions about why medicines are so attractive to people. What do they mean that could explain their movement from hand to hand and place to place? How is their movement shaped by social relations and how does it in turn shape those relations?

Anthropology takes up the study of medicines

The cultural (symbolic) logic of transformative substances was discerned by early anthropologists in 'primitive' societies. Since the publication of *The Golden Bough* by Sir James Frazer in 1890 (see chapter 3), anthropologists have attended to the way people conceive of forces as incarnate in, susceptible to the influence of, or powerfully represented by, material objects. They emphasized the possibilities this opens for communicating and controlling in an uncertain world. Studies of magic and fetishism showed how people manipulated things, including substances made for the purpose, to transform people and situations. In his classic treatment of magic, Malinowski wrote about 'material objects ... substances best fitted to receive, retain, and transmit magical virtue, coverings designed to imprison and preserve it until it is applied to its object' (Malinowski 1948:72). 'Magic is the quality of the thing, or rather, of the relation between man and the thing ... It implies the performing magician quite as much as the thing to be charmed and the means of charming' (1948:75). The questions to be asked concerned how substances carried meaning within a cultural world and how people used them for their particular purposes.

Several generations of anthropologists theorizing cosmology, ritual and symbolism explored these relationships. Lévi-Strauss was one giant in the landscape, explicating the 'science of the concrete' (Lévi-Strauss 1966) and the effectiveness of symbols (Lévi-Strauss 1963). A key landmark was the work of Victor Turner, pointing to the way symbols condense and unify different meanings. Before medical anthropology was established as a field, he was already writing of the overlap between 'medicine' as 'drug' and as 'ritual symbol' (Turner 1967:335). He showed how the meaning of Ndembu materia medica was mobilized as herbalists took ritual steps to awaken 'the powers hidden and slumbering in herbs' (1967:350).

With the growth of medical anthropology as a specialized field in the 1970s, the approaches already developed for studying rituals and symbols were widely applied to illness, healing and medicines. Building on the tradition of fieldwork in local communities, much medical anthropology concentrated on showing how seemingly exotic healing practices made sense. Within the 'ethnomedicine' approach, indigenous medicines were placed in relation to the cosmology, ritual and knowledge of a local (usually ethnic) group, as Turner had done. It was an approach whose great value was contextualization; healing practices made sense in relation to the shared meanings and social arrangements of the setting. Its weakness was that context was often presented as integrated tradition, a homogeneous, static view of local culture and society.

An alternative approach was rapidly gaining prominence. The notion of medical pluralism focused attention on the co-existence of different healing traditions within the same society. This was clearly useful in complex societies such as India, where different kinds of sacred and secular, professional and popular traditions flourished side by side (Leslie 1975). But with the spread of biomedicine in the wake of colonialism and international trade, the concept served to underline that all societies had several modes of conceiving illness and practising treatment. The development of a research interest in medical pluralism was a precondition for the medical anthropological work on pharmaceuticals.

A few early pioneers drew attention to the spread of pharmaceuticals that accompanied the worldwide dissemination of biomedicine. Alland's study of Abron healing (1970) in the Ivory Coast contained a clear statement of the attraction of Western medicines (in contrast to Western medicine). Michael Logan (1973) showed how pharmaceuticals fit into Guatemalan humoural concepts. Cunningham's work on 'injection doctors' in Thailand (1970) drew attention to the popularity of hypodermic injections. However, these studies were exceptions to the dominant interest of anthropology in exotic cosmologies and ritual practices.

In the 1980s, fieldworkers were beginning to de-exoticize the study of medicines in non-Western settings (Van der Geest 1984). Research on the meaning and use of aspirin and penicillin was becoming just as legitimate as studies of fetishes and purifying herbal enemas. This was probably due in part to the simple fact that biomedicine, and particularly 'biomedicines', were genuinely popular and heavily used in many societies of Africa, Asia and Latin America (Foster 1984). Moreover, Illich's (1976) attack on biomedicine's expropriation of health and radical critiques of the pharmaceutical invasion of the Third World (Silverman 1976; Gish and Feller 1979; Medawar 1979; Medawar and Freese 1982; Melrose 1982; Muller 1982; Silverman *et al.* 1982) had caught the attention of some academics.

Researchers documented the local realities in which medicines were actually made available and used (Nichter 1980; Haak 1988; Nichter and Nordstrom 1989; Etkin *et al.* 1990). They showed the significance of the transaction of medicines through commercial and informal channels (Ferguson 1981; Van der Geest 1982a, 1982b; Fassin 1987), and emphasized that most pharmaceuticals, even regulated 'prescription only' drugs, were taken as self-medication, that is, without the supervision of a formally trained health worker (Haak and Hardon 1988; Hardon 1991). The first edited volume on the topic wove together themes concerning transactions of pharmaceuticals and considerations of the meanings attached to them (Van der Geest and Whyte 1988). These topics were followed up in a second anthology (Etkin and Tan 1994) that included more articles on the practical problems of ensuring biomedically effective use of medicines in the conditions obtaining in countries of the global South.

Analytical moves

As older paradigms of modernization and development were supplemented by analyses of transnational cultural flows (Appadurai 1990; Hannerz 1992), anthropologists focused on the way that political ideals, entertainment, institutional forms, fashions and commodities both transformed and were transformed by the contexts through which they moved. Biomedicine is one of the best examples of globalization; it is truly cosmopolitan, not Western, medicine (Leslie 1976). In diverse social settings it provides a particularly appropriate empirical base for addressing newer theoretical issues concerning cultural globalization (Parkin 1995).

The older interest in 'medical pluralism' (Leslie 1975; Janzen 1978) took on new facets with the appreciation that oppositional identities are one possible outcome of globalization. Attending to pharmaceuticals facilitates understanding of how 'traditions' come to appear distinctive while simultaneously influencing one another deeply. Pharmaceuticals and 'indigenous' medicines take on meaning in contrast to one another (Sussman 1988; Nichter 1989:195–6). At the same time, pharmaceuticals may provide a prototype in terms of packaging and marketing for 'indigenous' medicines (Afdahl and Welsch 1988; Leslie 1989; Tuchinsky 1991). One outcome of this process was an emphasis on the medicinal aspect of other systems of healing as 'traditional' medicines gained ideological weight in opposition to synthesized pharmaceuticals, and became increasingly commercialized.

Pharmaceuticals may also be directly incorporated in a medical tradition notionally distinguished from biomedicine, as has been reported from South Asia (Bhatia et al. 1975; Burghart 1988; Wolffers 1988). The model of medical pluralism is further problematized by the appearance of pharmaceutical specialists who belong neither to the tradition of biomedicine as practised in formal health institutions, nor to the tradition of indigenous medicine. These 'quacks' or 'charlatans' or 'bush doctors' or 'injectionists', as they are called by the professional ideology, suggest that notions like 'creolization' (Hannerz 1987; Whyte and Van der Geest 1994:138–9) or 'counterwork' (Fardon 1995) which emphasize the creative revision of forms and ideas may be more useful than the idea of pluralism for grasping the dynamics of pharmaceuticals in complex health care systems.

In recent decades, an increasing interest in Western culture and its products meant that biomedicine came to be seen as a cultural phenomenon worthy of study. As the 'exotic bias' diminished, more anthropologists from both the North and the South did fieldwork in their own societies on aspects of popular culture and everyday life. Capsules, tablets and hypodermic syringes were no longer taken for granted and ignored; they could be defamiliarized (denaturalized) and analysed in terms of the meanings people attributed to them in settings as different as Uganda (Birungi 1998), the Philippines (Tan 1999), the United States (Vuckovic 1999) and France (Fainzang 2001).

A renewed interest in material objects (Miller 1995) and their consumption cast older Marxist approaches to commodities and fetishism in a new light (Douglas and Isherwood 1979; Appadurai1986; Ellen 1988; J. Ferguson 1988) and provided a bridge between culture and economy. The 'thinginess' of medicines and their tendency to become commodities suit them extremely well to this perspective. Seeing medicines as material culture opens up two sweeping vistas. One has to do with processes of commoditization, globalization and localization. The 'zations' (Anderson 1996:296, quoting L. Cohen) view is the broad one of social and political economic history, in which medicines not only move, as they always have done to some extent, but where their movement has implications about influence, dependence and transformation.

The other vista has to do with the positions of medical materials in technologies of health care. If we think of technologies as 'practical arts' with purposes, and consider the relations between people and objects in accomplishing these purposes, then we will be led to examine the ways in which artefacts are extensions of people in some situations, and fiercely contested in others (Pickstone 1994). It is possible to ask questions about powerful substances as part of a complex of institutions, technologies and practices characterized by styles of reasoning (Cambrosio et al. 2000:5). We can look 'at how [people] perform things, rather than at the frozen products of those performances' (2000:8).

The social lives of medicines

In Appadurai's introduction to the anthology *The Social Life of Things* (1986) and in Kopytoff's contribution to the same book, the notion is proposed that things have biographies. That is, it is useful analytically to trace the careers of material things as they move through different settings and are attributed value as singularities or as commodities for exchange. We used this idea to organize a review of the literature on pharmaceuticals: their production and marketing, their prescription, their distribution through intertwined formal and informal channels, their deaths through one or another form of consumption, and finally their lives after death in the form of efficacy in modifying bodies (Van der Geest *et al.* 1996).

In reality of course, things alone do not have a social life. At most they can be seen as agents in the sense argued by actor-network theorists: they form parts of complexes that co-produce effects in particular situations; things and people both can be seen as actors in that they mutually constitute one another (Prout 1996). But even if one does not accept the radical position that things and people are equally agents, it is essential for anthropologists to describe the lives that medicines have with people and between people. These lives are imbued with the practical artfulness and purpose that characterize technology. They are lived in relation to problems and contexts.

It is these qualities that we want to capture in the chapters that follow. Each builds on an ethnographic description of medicines in a specific place in Europe, Asia, the Americas or Africa. Each shows medicine in the hands of particular types of actors, moving between persons in certain kinds of social relations. The first four chapters take the perspective of consumers of medicine and the following four give more weight to the providers. Finally, we focus on the strategists who manufacture and market medicines, and those who attempt to regulate them. Thus we move from the intimate relations of mothers and children, to the global ones of the World Health Organization and the member states for which it formulates policy. Each chapter concentrates on a different analytical problem in the study of medicines, one that seems well illustrated by the empirical case. Theoretical discussions and comparative material from other places are brought in to develop the main point. As each issue unfolds, it comes to overlap with some of the others. We hope in this way to give a sense of coherence, without forcing material and concepts into one tight paradigm.

The consumers: meaningful medicines at work

We begin with mothers and children in Metro Manila and the problem of efficacy – a logical starting point since drugs are used for their effects. In poor neighbourhoods of Manila, women say that cough and cold remedies dry up or 'ripen' colds, drive out phlegm and stop coughing. But there is a strong element of habit in their use of these remedies. They do not posit causes of colds, or experiment empirically to choose the most effective medicine. This 'habitual' form of therapeutic practice, noted many years ago by one of the ancestors of medical anthropology

(Ackerknecht 1946), suggests that we need to consider efficacy very broadly. Drugs have effects on the mindful bodies of individuals; in speaking of the 'meaning response' (Moerman 2000) or the 'placebo effect', we recognize that social and psychological factors contribute to these individual effects. But drugs also have social and performative effects in the way they confirm sickness, and demonstrate the character and intentions of those who administer them. Using a commonly recognized treatment in a habitual (unarticulated, unconscious) way has this kind of social efficacy.

The problem of efficacy relates to perceptions of the powers of medicinal substances. This brings us to the symbolic nature of medicines and the question of not what, but how, medicines mean. In chapter 3 we move from the slums of Manila to the Sahel plains of Burkina Faso. Whereas Manila mothers use medicines from the local shop, Mossi people prepare remedies from plants and animals in their locality. The logic they use is one of connections between causes, symptoms and treatments of illness. A disease that makes a child's skin stiff and shiny like that of a snake may have been caused by its mother stepping over one, and should be treated with snake skin. Among the users of biomedicines, as among the Mossi users of plant and animal substances, symbolic associations may be metaphoric (analogies of likeness) or metonymic (connections of part and whole, for example). When medicinal substances with such meaningful associations are applied to ailing bodies, they concretize the problem and thus make it accessible to therapeutic action of a fitting symbolic nature. Suggesting connections and making disorder and its correction tangible is the symbolic and very practical work of medicines, even those synthesized in factories and prescribed by doctors.

This insight leads on to the next analytical problem, that of control. The materiality of medicines makes them graspable tools in the effort to control disease. But control is a tricky matter. In chapter 4, we see this illustrated in the case of distressed Dutch women controlling their anxiety with benzodiazepines. Whereas medical professionals speak of controlling or managing a disease with medication, the users of medicines are usually trying to control not just their physiological symptoms, but their situation. That is, they are trying to make adjustments so that they can manage their lives and projects. Medicines are empowering in that they offer users a means of control. In making this assertion, we place medicines within the lifeworlds of situated actors. But we must distinguish between control in the short term, and longer-term consequences of using medicines to deal with problems. Control may lead to being controlled. Drug dependence is the most obvious form of subjection. Social scientists point to others as well. Defining a problematic situation as tractable through medicines may eventually increase the control of medical professionals and ideology – the process called medicalization. This may leave people feeling dependent on doctors and drugs to understand and deal with their problems.

Scepticism about biomedical drugs is the theme of chapter 5. We listen to patients in London who express their doubts about pharmaceuticals and their resistance to biomedical hegemony. Some see them as dangerous to health. Many contrast the artificiality of pharmaceuticals to the authenticity of nature and natural medicines. This kind of oppositional thinking about medicines, so pronounced in the alternative, or complementary, medicine movement of our day is found in other versions where biomedicine is seen as an imported medical tradition. Despite the global popularity of pharmaceuticals, resistance to certain kinds of biomedical drugs, or critically characterizing the whole category of Western or allopathic medicines, is reported from many developing countries. We suggest that scepticism be seen as a kind of cultural politics, in which medicines are used to express issues of identity, control and power. Oppositions may be implied more than explicated. For the users of drugs, the personal is political in that they critically evaluate the larger connotations of putting medicinal substances into their bodies.

The providers: medicinal commodities and social relations of therapy

Turning towards the providers of drugs in the next section, we begin with drug vendors and their customers in a West African market. Commodification is the theme of chapter 6. The example from Cameroon illustrates how antibiotics are sold like other commodities, having effectively escaped the regulation that was intended to restrict their free exchange. This situation is common in many developing countries. It works to the advantage of those who make their living by selling medicines and it is also welcomed by the customers. Commodification can be understood in two different senses: medicines are commodified; and in a larger sense, so is health. Following Appadurai and Kopytoff, we show how the things themselves are diverted from the enclave of professional control and made common. That is, they are freely accessible and available to anyone with money; they are familiar and popular. The commercial interests in these valuable items ensure that they reach the remotest villages. They have lively commodity careers. This must be seen in terms of the other meaning of commodification: the idea that health can be purchased in the form of medicines or even that recovery from any illness requires buying medicines.

In the following chapter, we continue with the topic of selling drugs, but use it as a way of examining the articulation of sectors in health care systems. The ethnographic setting is Mexico and Central America. The actors are pharmacists and their customers. Ideally pharmacists are professionals who fill prescriptions written by doctors. They are part of the formal and professional sector of biomedical health care. In reality they bridge sectors. Pharmacists often function like physicians, providing advice along with medicines, even suggesting diagnoses. In Latin America, as in many parts of the world, the attendants in drug shops are often not trained pharmacists. Restrictions on sales of prescription drugs are not necessarily observed; that is, pharmacy shops function like part of the informal sector. As members of the local community, 'pharmacists' may share local ideas about medicines, rather than adhering strictly to standard biomedical guidelines. They may thus bridge the distinction between biomedical and indigenous or traditional medicine, perhaps selling both kinds. In a sense, commodification is the dynamic here, mixing, bridging and breaking through notional boundaries.

One kind of provider of medicines well known in many developing countries is the injectionist. Chapter 8 sets out the history of injection provision in Uganda as a basis for discussing the issue of technology. Injections are extremely popular ways of administering medicines; in fact most households own their own needles and syringes. With injectable chloroquine and penicillin for sale in local shops, 'high tech' medicine is readily available. In order to understand the use of injectable medicines today, we must analyse technology in the broad sense of material culture linked to knowledge, procedures, social roles and meanings. Like all technologies, injection practices in Uganda have purposes (injection is a practical art) and institutional histories. They became routinized as the highest standard of care in formal biomedical facilities. They gained social efficacy as the recognized token of 'best treatment' carrying a moral connotation about the quality of therapeutic relationships. In time they were commodified, made common, as providers offered them for sale outside of formal health facilities. Their meanings are shaped by local ideas of illness and the body, but in turn injections form those ideas by symbolically localizing illness in the flesh and blood. In the era of AIDS, new meanings concerning trust and personal relations have been attributed to injection equipment.

Physicians are the prototypical providers of medicines in professional medical traditions. In writing prescriptions, they communicate instructions about medicating disease. Chapter 9, about prescribing doctors, takes the theme of communication and unfolds it to show the many ways, in addition to inscription, that physicians communicate with patients about medicines. In fact, they communicate with and through medicines, as well as about them, as shown in the example from Sri Lanka where verbal communication is minimal. In a busy clinic, where high-caste doctors were treating poor, low-caste patients, there was limited verbal exchange about symptoms and diagnosis. The two parties had different perceptions of illness, and there was no time for dialogue. Both had great confidence in the medicines, however, and the act of prescribing functioned as a positive gesture that allowed them to avoid discussing their differences. Writing a prescription is an effective way of ending a consultation, and conveying authority and concern. Yet in other situations, the doctor does try to communicate with the patient about symptoms, and here medicines with their concreteness provide effective ways of pointing up elusive sensations. Adjusting prescriptions is a procedure that helps doctors to communicate about pathological processes. A patient consulting a doctor of Chinese medicine may become more attentive to changes in her mindful body knowing that she must monitor them in order to report to her practitioner who adjusts the medication in follow-up visits. Thus prescribing, with its writing, its dialogue about materia medica and its unspoken (mis)understandings is a rich communicative practice with implications for the patient's experience of illness and the doctor's ability to reach out to patients.

The strategists: marketing images and regulating practice

In the third section of the book, we turn away from the immediate concerns of ill people and the practices of passing medicines from providers to users. We focus on the strategists, who plan and direct the movements and uses of medicines from more distant positions. Chapter 10 is about the manufacturers of commercial medicines who market their products to both users and providers. The example of companies making 'traditional' Ayurvedic and Unani medicines in India shows that manufacturers are producing images as well as material things. In many ways the companies are modelled on those that manufacture biomedical pharmaceuticals. They test their products and make scientific claims about their efficacy. At the same time, they distance themselves from biomedicine by underlining the superiority of the Indian tradition with its values of purity and harmony with the environment. Ethnographic studies of pharmaceutical companies are extremely rare. But by studying marketing practices (advertising, package inserts, the activities of sales representatives), it is possible to trace the cultural economy of the manufacturers. The market, culture and medicine form three sides of a triangle. Commercial aims are clothed in cultural values of scientific integrity and humanitarian concern. They play on local values and images, while claiming the legitimacy of a universal science.

In the headquarters of international organizations, in national ministries of health, at conferences in big hotels, in the offices of donor agencies, other strategists are concerned with medicines. Chapter 11 focuses on health planners concerned to improve the availability and effective use of medicines. It presents the case of the attempt by the World Health Organization to establish and implement an Essential Drugs Policy that would encourage rational and economical choices concerning drugs. Limited resources should be spent on drugs that are necessary, effective, safe and affordable for use against the most common treatable diseases. In many ways the policy was seen as inimical to the commercial aims of the drug industry. It encouraged health managers to evaluate the market critically and to choose on the basis of objective health needs, rather than demands nurtured by the pharmaceutical companies. Two analytical issues emerge clearly in connection with the analysis of medicines in the hands of health planners. One has to do with the process of policy formation, in which different interest groups contend. The drug industry, doctors and AIDS activists lobby against some or all of the limitations on drugs to be purchased in the public sector. Private sector commercial interests are reluctant to accept regulation on what drugs they may sell. The second issue concerning the planners has to do with the effects of policies. Health planners produce papers, and dispute about the contents of the papers. But translating paper policies into action is a complicated affair. For in reality drugs are in the hands of all the kinds of actors highlighted in this book. Assumptions about efficacy, symbolic associations, hopes for control, scepticism, commodification, lack of strict regulation in health systems, the seduction of technology, communication by prescription, and commercial interests all play in to the circulation and use of medicines.

The book concludes by considering a category of actors that has been implicit throughout: anthropologists who describe and analyse the social lives of medicines. Through participant observation we too are caught up in the sociality of medicines and take stances on the kinds of knowledge we produce and the ways it is used.

Part II

The consumers

2   Mothers and children: the efficacies of drugs

When mothers treat their children's common health problems with medicines, they assume that medicines work. In this chapter we examine that assumption, suggesting that they work in more ways than one. They have pharmacological effects on the bodies to which they are applied – effects deriving from the biochemical properties of their ingredients. They also have healing effects arising from the meanings they contain for people – the placebo effect or 'meaning response' (Moerman 2000:56). Both these forms of efficacy relate to the outcome of treatment for the individual mindful body. But medicines can also have social efficacy – that is, effects on the relations between those enacting illness and treatment. These different forms of efficacy reinforce one another. Moreover, in real life efficacies are assessed not by pharmacologists but by social actors, who have their own criteria and expectations. Thus drug efficacies must be studied not only through random controlled trials, as biomedical researchers do, but also through analysis that places the problem of efficacy within a particular social and cultural context.

Treating children's coughs and colds in Manila

In the sprawling urban conglomerate known as Metro Manila, mothers have an enormous array of medicines from which to choose treatment for their children. They are bombarded daily with advertisements about the virtues of pharmaceutical products. How do they decide which to choose and how do they judge the efficacy of these remedies? In two poor communities in the city, Hardon (1991) carried out a study of self-care for everyday health problems, describing mothers' concerns, their rationales for action and their evaluations of medicine efficacy. Combining qualitative and quantitative methods, the study documented health care practices in families with pre-school children during a five-month period, recording details of perceived cause, therapy choice and efficacy of medications in 1,411 illness events, mainly diarrhoea episodes, coughs, colds and fevers.

Fig. 2.1 Medicines have social efficacy: young mother with sick child in the Philippines.

Self-care with modern pharmaceuticals was found to be the dominant form of therapy. On average, out of every ten pre-school illness episodes, only one was treated on advice of a health professional; four were treated with modern pharmaceuticals in self-care; one was treated with traditional remedies only; and four were left untreated. As coughs and colds are the most common conditions confronting children, we concentrate on the way mothers treat these disorders, and the notions of efficacy that they apply.

What a mother does when her child suffers a cough or a cold depends on the symptoms. If the child has a runny nose (*sipon*) and the mother is not afraid that the condition will worsen, she will wait and see, and occasionally give lime (*kalamansi*) juice. Otherwise she usually gives a cough-cold remedy which she believes prevents the disorder from becoming worse. If the episode is accompanied by fever, however slight, the mother immediately gives an analgesic to help the heat come out.

The most common cough-cold remedies used in these poor urban communities are the branded drugs Neozep, Tuseran and Allerin, and the herbal remedies *kalamansi* juice and oregano. The most common analgesics are the branded drugs Aspilet, Biogesic, Medicol, Alaxan and Tempra. Doctors are rarely consulted for common colds. Mothers seek a doctor only if the child does not improve, if the condition worsens rapidly or if the fever becomes very high. When consulted, doctors usually prescribe a combination of medicines, including antibiotics, a cough syrup and an analgesic.

The tendency to use pharmaceuticals even for non-severe self-limiting disorders is related to people's anxiety over health and the trust they have in the power of medicines. One out of five families has lost a young child owing to a severe illness. High childhood mortality and morbidity are related to the insanitary living conditions and poverty that cause many children to be malnourished. Many families have difficulty feeding their children three times a day. In talking about their children's disorders mothers often use notions of illness progression, indicating their concern with the possibility of the disease becoming severe. Common expressions are: 'that is a result of the cold'; 'brought by the cold'; 'the cold turned directly into fever'. Reference is also made to recurring symptoms and chronicity of ill health: 'that recurs'; 'it does not leave anymore'; 'that is a relapse'.

The mothers tend to relate coughs and colds to disturbances in hot–cold balance and weather. Examples of such disturbances are: 'hot weather', 'felt hot and bathed' and 'tired, was sweating, then took a bath'. Another common aetiological notion is *pilay*. *Pilay* is literally translated as 'lameness' (Panganiban 1970) and occurs when a child has fallen, as children often do. The fall results in a literal or symbolic sprain, or broken bone. Usually mothers suspect the cause to be *pilay* only if the illness does not improve after initial self-medication. Then they believe that the help of a *hilot* (a traditional midwife/healer who uses massage to treat *pilay*) is needed. Underlying these narratives on causation are ideas about vulnerability of the child – children have to be protected against sudden changes of temperature and against falling and spraining/breaking bones. Coughs and colds can be prevented by responsible parents who avoid these imbalances and threats to the child. Consequently, if children are ill often, women tend to talk about their mothers as negligent.

Cough, as Tan observes, is considered undesirable and blameworthy in urban poor communities. He cites a young mother who describes this graphically: 'If the cough is continuous, (the child's) father is disturbed. When he comes back from work, and is hot headed, then he hears the child coughing . . . Because I am the mother, if the child is sick, I am blamed' (Tan 1999:90). Tan argues that it is not surprising that the manufacturers of cough and cold medicines emphasize a hacking dry cough in their advertising. The dry cough conveys not just the image of lungs bursting from the strain, but also the potential of social disruption.

Fixed treatment strategies

Hardon found that in their first response to coughs, colds and other common childhood disorders people follow 'fixed' treatment. Intending to describe people's explanatory models for childhood disorders, in much the same way as Kleinman had done for Taiwan, she anticipated that explanations of sickness and treatment would guide choices among available therapies and therapists (Kleinman 1980:104–18)[1] and that expected outcomes would form the basis for evaluations of efficacy. But she found that mothers initially do not seem concerned about the aetiology of common disorders, and do not actively choose therapies. They do what they are used to doing.[2] The fixed treatment strategies are in fact performative – by keeping to them, mothers show that they care for their children. They do what is expected of them when the children are ill. The fixed treatment strategies reflect the social efficacy of medicines. Pharmacologically the medicines calm down the child's cough, diminish fever and stop the nose from dripping. This pharmacological effect reinforces the social efficacy of medicines, as it proves that the care is appropriate. Mothers, children, fathers and others are reassured that the cough is under control.

Treatment options are numerous in the Philippines. The Philippine health care system is flooded by 14,000 different modern pharmaceutical preparations produced mainly by multinational companies. Many of the medicines can have risks when taken without expert advice, are of questionable pharmacological efficacy and are relatively expensive (Tan 1999). In the urban poor communities, the most common source of medicines (accounting for 40 per cent of the medications used during Hardon's study) is small grocery stores, which legally are not supposed to sell drugs. These shops sell people's day-to-day household needs, such as soap, rice, a few vegetables, Coca-Cola, beer, cigarettes and a limited stock of around ten different medicines.

These ten medicines account for around 50 per cent of the medications used in common cough and cold cases in the communities – they have become part of people's fixed treatment strategies in common childhood illnesses. They have in common that they have been on the market for a long time and are advertised heavily on a local radio station during prime time, that is, when women listen to the radio while doing household chores in the mornings.[3] An average of three or four drug advertisements are aired per hour. The advertisement jingles are well known in the community – when asked to complete sentences of jingles like the one on Neozep nearly all children could do so. Such jingles reinforce the idea that you need a pill for every ill. Medicines are projected as 'cure alls'.

Advertisements typically start with a problem statement: a family member suffers from cough, cold or headache. Then comes the message, 'take a drug', followed by a reassurance, 'the drug is safe' or 'the drug is effective' or 'the doctor prescribes the drug'. The following advertisement for the most common cold remedy serves as an example:

MALE CHILD: Mom, what do you take at a first sign of cold?
FEMALE ADULT: Not just anything, I take Neozep. I know it works and most importantly, Neozep has no harmful ingredients.
MALE ADULT: No wonder more people who take proprietary cold tablets rely on Neozep, more than all others combined.

Thus the fixed treatment strategies are part of a shared system of symbols that make sense to people who chat together, use the same shops and listen to the same radio programmes. They know what it means when a neighbour gives her child Neozep.

Evaluating efficacy of medicines

Hardon found that respondents in the weekly illness recalls generally evaluate efficacy of medicines positively. They assert that symptoms disappear when they give their child cough and cold medicines or that the child's health improves. Only in around one out of ten of the treatments do they report that there is no effect. Tan, in his study of the power of medicines in the Philippines, notes that people expect not only that the medicine alleviates symptoms; it should also restore ability to function. The child should start playing again, the adult can return to work (Tan 1999:210–11).

More insights on efficacy were recorded during small-group interviews in which people were asked to sort commonly used cough and cold medicines, including herbal remedies, into piles (a so-called drug-sorting exercise). Mothers were asked to explain why they sorted cough and cold drugs into certain piles. Their explanations usually are related to differential efficacy of the medicines. A commonly mentioned effect of cough and cold remedies is the 'coming out' of mucus/phlegm (*lumalabas ang plema*). This is attributed to both pharmaceuticals (for example the expectorants Citrex and Allerin) and plant remedies (for example oregano, lime and *sambong* (*Blumea balsamifera*)). Among several cough remedies known to 'stop' the cough, a popular example is Tuseran, a drug that contains a cough suppressant. People also distinguish cold remedies that 'dry up' (*natutuyo*) – such as Vicks and Neozep. Drying up is not an effect that is attributed to plant medicines. Some mothers also expect cold remedies to 'ripen the cold' (*nahihinog ang sipon*): a cold is considered nearly cured when nasal discharge is yellow. So efficacy is not only about whether or not a medicine works, but about how it works – what particular changes it brings about.

Perceived efficacy of medicines is further found to be related to price and provenance: more expensive drugs are more powerful, according to the mothers in these communities. During the drug-sorting exercise Hardon often heard people say: 'That drug is expensive, but it has a strong (*malakas*) effect' or 'That drug is inexpensive, but it is not so effective.'[4] In group discussions it became clear that modern medicines' efficacy is related to their metonymic associations – made in the United States – tested by doctors – made in clean laboratories. It is this symbolic value of medicines that evokes the 'meaning response'. Herbal remedies, advocated by community health workers as alternatives to expensive medicines, were not seen to have such 'powers' and were thus considered less effective.

The 'meaning response' is further affected by cultural views on appropriate shape, colour and form of medicines. In the Metro Manila slums Hardon found that administration form was pivotal in the treatment of childhood disorders: drops are for infants, syrups for slightly older children and tablets for adults. Capsules should be taken with care as they are relatively powerful drugs.

Although medicines are rarely reported to be ineffective, it does sometimes happen that people perceive a treatment to have failed. Then they use the concept of *hiyang*, which literally means 'compatible,' to point up the match between patient and medicine. Efficacy depends on the suitability of a drug for a particular person. *Hiyang* explains why the drug works for one patient, and not for another. For example in an interview on the efficacy of cough and cold remedies the mother of Marc Joseph tells Hardon:

One week ago I went to the doctor with him, in the provincial hospital. The doctor prescribed Ventolin. I bought it in a pharmacy in town. It cost me 32 pesos. Ventolin is expensive. I gave it to him, but he did not get better. Probably it is not *hiyang* for him. It is hard to find a suitable drug for this small boy. He suffered from allergy. So I stopped giving the drug.

Another informant, Gloria, comments on one specific drug called Rondec: 'Yes, that drug has the same effect. But, it is not *hiyang* for us.' The notion of *hiyang* underlines personal differences in the way medicines work upon illness.

The combination of efficacies

Most medicines mothers routinely give to their children contain pharmacologically 'active' ingredients that alleviate illness symptoms. Analgesics cause the fever to go down and cough syrups contain substances that suppress cough. These actions constitute what may be called pharmacological efficacy – the biochemical effects of drugs on the individual body. While biomedical researchers focus on these, they recognize that medicines have curative effects beyond their biochemical properties. Numerous double blind[5] random controlled trials have shown that inert substances ('medicines' with no pharmacologically active ingredients) can make the condition of the user improve, often nearly as much as that of a medicine that does contain an active ingredient. They work because people expect them to work and have confidence in their efficacy and/or in the person giving them. Medicines carry with them a powerful symbolic value – the promise of return to health. In biomedicine, symbolic healing is called the placebo (literally 'I shall please') effect. Daniel Moerman defines such effects as 'the desirable psychological and physiological effects of meaning in the treatment of illness' (2000:52). He writes: 'The placebo effect is of particular interest to anthropologists because it is a clear case of symbolic and meaningful events – involving relationship, discourse, form, belief, knowledge, commitment, history – having an apparently direct effect on human biology' (2000:56). Clinical studies have shown that the placebo effect is related to many different aspects of medicine use: patient and doctor expectations that the patient will recover, the setting in which the medicine is administered, the form in which it is administered (inert injections are more powerful than inert pills), the reason for which it is given and the expected outcome. It is argued that the attention and empathy of a caretaker or practitioner giving medicines has an effect on people's well-being – they are likely to feel less anxious and distressed (Spiro 1986; Roberts 1995; Moerman 2000).

The meaning response reinforces the pharmacological efficacy of medicines. The contribution of each type of efficacy to the 'total effect'[6] of the medicine can differ. When pharmacologically inert substances are given to patients as 'placebos' then the pharmacological efficacy is zero – and the 'total effect' is constituted of meaning response. Other medicines, such as antibiotics, have strong pharmacological actions – they kill bacteria and cure the disease. However, even the efficacy of such pharmacological cures can be reinforced by a meaning response. Some medicines may not be placebos in the sense of being inert, but their action is not directed to the disorder that is being treated. Spiro (1986) calls such medicines 'impure' placebos and defines them as drugs with some pharmacological action that is not immediately or seriously relevant to the clinical problem. Many harmless but active agents that doctors give fall in this category, including vitamins and antihistamines. Interestingly, the side-effects of these pills can evoke a meaning response, as they signal to the patient that the drug is working.

Most research on efficacy focuses on the effects of drugs upon the disease of an individual. However, it is known that the providers of drugs are affected by their meanings too: physician enthusiasm enhances the 'meaning response' of the patient. Patient and practitioner exchange views in a treatment encounter so that their assessments influence one another; the patient's expressions about the efficacy of a treatment affect the practitioner's judgement of it too (Waldram 2000:607).

As students of social relations, we can move out of the clinic and take this insight several steps further. The symbolic efficacy of medicines may work upon the givers as well as the receivers of medicine, adding conviction to their actions, and influencing the relationships that are important to them. Medicines are part of a therapeutic process that mothers enact when their children fall ill. As Frankenberg (1986) and Prout and Christensen (1996) assert, illnesses can be seen as repetitive performances through which children and adults experience, substantiate and confirm the social roles and relationships of everyday life. By giving medicines, mothers show that the child is in need of care (thus confirming the child's sick role) and that they are good mothers. At the same time, by doing something about the condition, they imply that they are in control. These implications of caregiving we label as 'social efficacy' to draw attention to the way that giving medicine works through suggesting something about the people involved.

Medicines are important tools in the therapeutic process that unfolds when children present symptoms of ill health to their parents. In conditions where there is much anxiety about children's health, as is the case in the poor neighbourhoods of Metro Manila, mothers use medicines to care and to prevent the health problems from deteriorating. Medicines provide women the reassurance that something can be done about the illness (a sense of agency if you like) and children with the recognition that they are ill and are entitled to good care. They also show others in the community that the child is being looked after – obviating judgements of parental negligence. Social and pharmacological efficacies are co-produced in the therapeutic process. Pharmacological efficacy contributes to symptom relief – fever diminishes, the child coughs less, and eats and plays again. The 'calming' down of the cough is desirable socially – the sound of cough signals poor care. It not only irritates the child's lungs, it also irritates others, like fathers and mothers-in-law, potentially leading to social distresses that go beyond the illness condition of the child.

Medicines are socially efficacious because people share a common set of images and ideas about them. Community studies on medicine use in many different settings (Logan 1983; Adome *et al.* 1996; Rasmussen *et al.* 1996; Reeler 1996; Senah 1997) suggest that people increasingly believe that they need a pill for every ill. Even in the remote Karakoram Mountains of Pakistan, where we would perhaps expect people to use traditional medicines, a heavy reliance on Western pharmaceuticals was found (Rasmussen *et al.* 1996). Mothers and fathers, convinced that medicines are essential in the treatment of common childhood disorders, expressed the following views:

> 'Medicine is needed for every illness. If medicine is not used, the illness will become serious.'
> 'All illnesses need medicine. No illness will be cured without medicine.'
> 'Medicine is to the sick, what water is to the thirsty.'
> 'If we don't get medicine, how will we get cured?'

The quotes illustrate how strongly people value the efficacy of medicines in childhood disorders. Such confidence in pharmaceuticals and expectations of positive outcomes lay the ground for the meaning response.

People do not seem aware that sick children will usually recover without drugs. They relate the power of medicines to their price, origin in American and European high tech laboratories, and attributes such as colour, consistency and dosage form. These aspects of the medicine contribute to their symbolic value, as we shall see in chapter 3, and strengthen the 'meaning response'. In the case of childhood disorders, the symbolic value of the medicines affects the meaning with which mothers endow the medicines, and as a consequence the meaning response evoked in their children. At a very young age children become aware of the 'power' of medicines.

The cultural construction of efficacy

This brings us to the point that meaning responses and social and pharmacological efficacies are embedded in culturally specific expectations of the healing process. Efficacy, as Etkin (1988, 1992, 1994) has argued, is culturally constructed. It is understood in the context of a larger healing process, including initial perceptions of symptoms, notions of causation and severity, subsequent treatment actions and expectations of outcome, as well as evaluations of efficacy and further treatment choice if outcome is unsatisfactory. Etkin's extensive ethnographic work among the Hausa in Nigeria describes how expected treatment outcomes change in the course of an illness. Proximate effects may be signs that the disease entity is leaving the body; these should be followed by the ultimate outcome of a restoration of health. For example, Hausa therapies for cough include the burning of plants and inhalation of smoke.

The desired proximate effect in this case is the discomfiture and chasing of the cough inducing agent (spirit, witch) or the dislodging of the disease substance (natural product)...The Hausa...expect as later outcomes in the sequence of treatments antitussive, inflammation suppressive, and decongestant effects. (Etkin 1988:308)

Asserting the need to view treatment and healing as processual, Etkin stresses that for the Hausa only a series of outcomes will fulfil expectations.

Etkin (1994) describes how pharmacologically defined side-effects can have important symbolic value. She explains that for the Hausa purgation is considered desirable in the first stages of the treatment of stomach disorders. Sodium bicarbonate is commonly used, and its side-effect of flatulence and belching is viewed positively as evidence of disease egress. 'Primary' and 'side' effects of modern pharmaceuticals are constructed in much the same ways as the outcomes of plant use traditionally have been (Etkin 1994). Generally, what is a primary and what is a secondary or side effect is not given, but is open to cultural interpretation.

An excellent example of the cultural construction of efficacy comes from a recent study (Bruun 2001) in a Malawi fishing village of the category of medicine called 'Ciba'. The term Ciba seems to have once referred to a brand of rifampicin, a drug used to treat tuberculosis that has the (biomedically defined) side-effect of turning the urine orange. Today Ciba includes a range of pharmaceuticals taken to prevent and treat sex-related diseases. People remark that Ciba changes the colour of urine (though not always to orange); others note that they urinate more than usual when they take Ciba. Drawing on Etkin's work, Bruun (2001:46–7) shows how people understand such signs. They are taken to show that Ciba is having the desired effect of purifying the body of the 'bad blood' and pollution caused by 'wrong' sex, that is, sexual relations with a woman who is menstruating or who has recently delivered or miscarried, sex with many different partners, or sex with 'someone you doubt', who might have a sexually transmitted infection, even HIV/AIDS.

In another sense too, assumptions about efficacy are culturally constructed. In the description from Manila, we pointed to the lay notion of *hiyang*. When a medicine does not work, people attribute this to the relation between the drug and the individual; the drug is not *hiyang*, not compatible with the patient. *Hiyang*-like concepts, although not studied systematically, have been reported from elsewhere as well. In Indonesia, Sciortino (1987) describes a concept, *cocok*, that people use to refer to compatibility between a patient and a therapy. *Cocok*, she explains, determines not only whether a patient can use Western medicines, but also which Western medicines suit a particular individual. Her respondents used *cocok* as an *ad hoc* explanation for the success or failure of a therapy, and at the same time *cocok* was a guide for future therapy choice. In Sri Lanka, Nichter and Nordstrom report that people used a similar concept, *behet ahanava* (medicine answering), to evaluate the effect of a medicine. 'Reference to "that medicine answering" specifies that a type of medicine is suitable for one's body and interacts in a healthy way' (Nichter and Nordstrom 1989:382). *Hiyang*-like concepts suggest that people interpret pharmacological efficacy differently than biomedical practitioners do. Biomedical treatment protocols are based on the principle that medicines have the same action in all patients: dosages are standardized by age-category, and effects are considered to be universal. The underlying assumption is that biological bodies are the same in all settings, and that pharmacological action is located in the medical substance that is ingested. *Hiyang*-like concepts emphasize individual differences in efficacy: bodies are not the same and pharmacological efficacy is relational – it depends on the compatibility between the pharmaceutical and the individual taking the drug.[7]

Applying a broader understanding of efficacy

In biomedicine the success of therapeutic efficacy is generally seen to be based primarily on pharmacological action. Acknowledgement of the multifaceted nature of efficacy requires reflection on how biomedicine contributes to the healing process, and how other medical systems and self-care practices can reinforce the pharmacological efficacy of therapies that are prescribed as part of what is now called 'evidence based medicine'. Doctors will have to respect that the antibiotic they prescribe to a child with pneumonia is reinforced by the maternal caretaking, and that a massage by a traditional midwife can further improve the condition of the child.

Recognition of the multifaceted nature of efficacy could lead to radical changes in medical practice. Such insights are being applied in child health programmes in developing countries, if only because maternal notions of medical efficacy have proved to be barriers to the adoption of pharmacologically effective treatment regimes. Young children are a target group for health programmes in developing countries; in conditions of poor sanitation and malnutrition they risk sickness and death from disorders like diarrhoea and pneumonia. Globally orchestrated child survival programmes target these common childhood illnesses. Oral rehydration solution (ORS) is promoted as the best treatment for diarrhoea; it saves life by preventing dehydration. However, medical anthropological studies show that acceptance of ORS tends to be limited. People often prefer antidiarrhoeal medicines, which have palliative effects, such as hardening the stools or stopping the diarrhoea. ORS is not considered an appropriate remedy.

This was the case in Nigeria's Oyo State, where Iyun found that parents used syrups, antibiotics and kaolin to treat children's diarrhoea even though they knew about ORS. The disinterest in ORS was related to a cultural construction of efficacy that linked disorders and their treatment to notions of hot and cold.

Many mothers believe that the development of 'stomach heat' (*kun gbigbona*) is the physical manifestation of childhood diarrhea – i.e., diarrhea is closely associated with 'bodily heat' (*igbona*) . . . The implication of this folk etiology is that children with diarrhea should not take anything hot. Rather, they should take cold food items as well as cold medicines to cool down the stomach that is suffering from hot impediment. Indeed, some mothers emphasized their children belong to a cold water (*olomi tutu*) family or lineage, and accordingly should not take hot medicaments. One mother said . . . 'We offer cold things because diarrhea is caused by body heat in the stomach. We should not offer the child anything hot, that is with similar temperature.' (Iyun 1994:43)

ORS is considered a hot treatment because health workers originally stressed the importance of boiling the water before use. The association with heat remains, even after it has cooled. If ORS is hot, then its efficacy for treating a hot disorder is questionable. Iyun recommends that health workers promote ORS by emphasizing the 'cooling or smoothing effect of salt, sugar solution' thus adjusting its image to local perceptions of efficacy. Such a culture-sensitive child health programme will not only facilitate the use of ORS; it is also likely to enhance the meaning response evoked by medications and enhance social efficacy – making both mothers and children feel better.

Conclusion

Most research on efficacy problematizes the outcome of medicinal treatment for the individual patient's disorder. But once it is recognized that 'meaning mends', as Moerman (1991:131) puts it, the problem of efficacy opens on to a broader cultural and social analysis that puts the sick individual into a context of shared meanings and social interactions. This chapter has examined two ways of proceeding from there.

One is to look at the culturally shaped expectations of medicinal effect, thus revealing the 'rationality' of people's assessments of efficacy. This approach focuses on the systematic and more or less conscious attention that social actors pay to illness etiology and bodily processes. It can offer convincing explanations of why, for example, Hausa people find the inhalation of smoke efficacious as a first step in treating cough. Or, as in the case from the Philippines, it can show how people come to believe that coughs need medicine, and that medicines have particular effects, such as making phlegm come out, 'ripening' or 'drying up' a cold. It can even be used to suggest to health workers in Nigeria's Oyo State that ORS should be presented as a cooling treatment rather than emphasizing the boiling of water. This is cultural analysis in the classic sense; it shows the different ways people have of reasoning about medicinal means and effects upon the 'mindful body'. Ethnoscience or ethnosemantic studies try to develop models of reasoning. Others, like Tan's and Hardon's work from the Philippines, emphasize how commercial marketing and advertising push particular images of efficacy and how these are appropriated by consumers.

Another approach to efficacy stresses the way medicines have effects on social relations. This approach allows us to take into account a rather uncomfortable fact: that users of medicines do not always seem to be monitoring efficacy. While researchers are obligated to explicate outcomes, social actors do not necessarily attend to results in the same way. Of course people do make empirical observations, and they are concerned when a treatment does not work, as we saw in the discussion of *hiyang*. But very often, they give the medicine that is usual in such cases without consciously reasoning about its effects (unless asked to do so by an anthropologist!). Many years ago, Ackerknecht wrote about 'instinctive' or 'automatic' treatment practices, distinguishing them from both supernatural and naturalistic ones:

They are actually habitual. Tradition determines certain almost automatic acts in certain situations which together are not important enough to theorize about . . . To call such attitudes 'naturalistic' or 'rational' seems to inject into the data contents they actually do not have. People in this case operate below the threshold of full consciousness. (Ackerknecht 1946:478)

The notion of social efficacy provides a way of understanding such habitual practices. They can be seen as the performance of treatment in a conventional and therefore recognizable way. People are acting in ways that make sense to them because they make sense to others. That sense is about exerting control, showing care, doing what is considered best. It is not necessarily about articulated models of illness or testing the effect of a substance on the sick body. It is often unspoken – that is, it is practised rather than discursive sense. And as Bourdieu has argued, such practices may be part of fundamental dispositions shared by people in similar social positions (see note 2).

Finally, it is important to remember that the different forms of efficacy, though distinguishable analytically, are experienced simultaneously. A double-blind random controlled trial is designed to isolate for purposes of analysis (to dissolve a whole into parts). But life is lived as a synthesis (a putting together of parts into wholes). Not only do efficacies tend to combine, but the acts of giving/taking medicine and looking to effects are integrated into larger processes of dealing with problems and living life.

3   Villagers and local remedies: the symbolic nature of medicines

'People act practically by acting symbolically', according to Sahlins (1976). This chapter is devoted to the practical utility of medicines as symbols.[1] People use medicines to do hermeneutic (as well as pharmacological) work. Within a given meaningful world, particular images make illnesses concrete and provide suggestions for applying medication. In turn medicines suggest perceptions of the condition for which they are used. To show how these associations play into one another, we begin with symbolic images employed by Mossi villagers in Burkina Faso. They see connections between symptoms and treatments, and the phenomena of their everyday surroundings such as forked sticks and tethered donkeys. In the same way, we argue, people in Western societies imagine illness in terms of enemy targets and 'magic bullets', or congested pipes to be unclogged. The distance from Mossi herbs to modern pharmaceuticals is shorter than expected. What Mossi users of local remedies and European consumers of biomedicine have in common is the practical strategy of concretizing inchoate bodily complaints through symbolic associations. Thus unpleasant experiences are made comprehensible and amenable to the practical, because meaningful, action of substances.

Medical images among Mossi villagers

The Mossi, who are the largest ethnic group in Burkina Faso, count over 3 million people. Most of them are peasants intimately familiar with the plants, animals and landscape of their surroundings. Their most important agricultural product is millet, which forms the basis of their daily diet. The Mossi are well known for their skills in the production of iron. Other handicrafts include leather work, cotton weaving and dyeing textiles.

Between November 1988 and April 1989 Adèle Meulenbroek did research among rural Mossi people in the Basma region in Burkina Faso.

Fig. 3.1 Everyday life is a rich source of symbolism: Mossi women pounding millet in Burkina Faso.

Her research focused on local names of illnesses and of herbal and other indigenous remedies. She asked people to explain to her the meanings of those names. When she went through the list of terms and people's explanations, she was struck by the abundance of symbolic associations. The terminology demonstrates the Mossi predilection for making symbolic connections to explain medical problems and to find suitable medicines (Meulenbroek 1989).

In the field of medicine Mossi people predominantly rely on their traditional knowledge and practice. For many of them modern medical facilities seem remote, in geographical but also in social and cultural terms. In most circumstances, local medical knowledge, both expert and popular, is closer to their perception of illness than biomedical explanation; however, traditional and modern therapies are sometimes used simultaneously. Some medical problems, meningitis for example, are considered to fall within the range of biomedicine, whereas others may be more effectively treated by a healer or by lay people themselves.

Nao-gada, *the sickness of feet string*

N is a young woman of sixteen. One morning, about six years ago, she woke up with stiff and painful legs. She could not walk. The family concluded that she was suffering from *nao-gada*, an illness that causes sore and stiff feet and may also lead to wounds on the feet. Biomedical observers suspect they can identify the illness as synovitis, arthritis or rheumatism. The relatives treated her for one year and then took her to a healer who gave her leather strips to tie round the feet. After the treatment, which went on for six months, she felt much better, but she still feels some pain, especially in the rainy season.

Nao-gada is derived from *naore*, which means 'feet', and *gada*, 'string' or 'bandage'. Some explain the name of the illness ('feet string') with a reference to the ropes that are tied around the front legs of a donkey and cause sore spots and wounds. These wounds resemble the wounds of the human illness. Others say that the term means that the one suffering from *nao-gada* cannot walk, like the tied donkey.

Informants did not know what caused the illness but questions about therapeutic treatment resulted in an inventive analogy. The strips of animal skin, which traditionally are used to pack salt when it is transported, are tied around the feet of the patient. The therapeutic analogy is that although the strips have remained around the salt blocks for a long time (the salt comes from far), they will eventually be removed when the salt is unwrapped and sold. It is hoped that in a similar way, the illness will go away from the feet, when the strips are removed.

Koadanga, *the partridge sickness*

Mossi people are aware that biomedicine has no effective therapy for hepatitis. Its treatment takes a long time and does not address the cause of the disease. It is merely concerned with alleviation of the symptoms. In the local pharmacopoeia there are medicines against hepatitis which are considered more effective. Their potency is also recognized by biomedical health workers who sometimes prescribe them to their own patients.

In the Mossi language, Moré, hepatitis is called *koadanga* which means 'partridge'. The name is related to the most popular treatment of the disease which involves the eating of partridge. A partridge is killed and its large feathers are plucked. The bird is cooked with a herb mixture containing the roots of the *sosoga* tree and the bark or branches of the *kod-pokka* tree. The patient suffering from *koadanga* drinks the decoction and eats the meat of the partridge. The crucial thing to note is that all these ingredients have a yellow colour: the roots, bark and branches of the two trees, and the skin and small feathers of the partridge. (The bark and branches of the *kod-pokka* tree are also used to paint leather yellow.)

Koadanga illustrates Mossi homoeopathic thinking: like cures like. The homoeopathic principle invites symbolic associations, in the description, explanation and cure of illness. In the case of *koadanga* it is the yellow colour that the ingredients of the cure and the symptoms of the disease have in common. Because of their similarity in colour the partridge gives its name to the disease and provides its medicine.

Mossi symbolic images

The links between illness, 'feet string' and partridges made by Mossi people provide examples of what Lévi-Strauss called 'the logic of the concrete'. He pointed to the rich variety of such associative thinking in the ethnographic record: in Siberia, for example, the Kalar use of frozen bear excrement to treat constipation, the Iakoute application of a woodpecker's beak to an aching tooth (1966:9).[2] But the Mossi material invites us to consider in more detail how such associations are used. Following Fainzang's (1986) study of medical views in another society in Burkina Faso, the Bisa, one can discern three directions in the way Mossi people use symbols: some provide a description, some offer an explanation and some refer to therapy. The third 'direction' is the most relevant for the discussion in this chapter: what role do symbolic images play in the way people select medicines for health complaints and select complaints for medicines? Some of these images are easy to understand; others are rather complex, at least for the outsider.

Descriptive terms may contain a phonetic imitation of a symptom or relate the (symptom of the) illness to an object, a tree or an animal on the basis of similarity or contiguity. Similar associations are made with regard to cause and cure. We shall present a few complex illness terms to highlight the symbolic vagaries which the Mossi follow to establish illness nomenclature, aetiology and cure.

Ra-yaka is a children's illness characterized by fissures around the anus. Folk etymology claims that the term is composed of *raoogo* (wood) and *yaka* (forked): the fissures resemble the shape of forked branches. This guides people to explain the illness as the result of the mother using a forked branch to poke up the fire while she was pregnant. The illness is treated by burning a forked branch (which resembles and has caused the fissures), mixing the black ash with butter and smearing the mixture on the anus.

People tend to link descriptive, causal and curative references and lump them together. The existing illness terms have no clear-cut and generally accepted meanings. They rather constitute invitations for improvising exegeses to people who are asked about their meaning. An illness term which contains a concrete reference to an animal or plant or to an object in daily life leads informants to link the illness to that particular animal, plant or object by pointing out similarity and/or contiguity and seeking the cause and cure of the illness in the domain of that same animal, plant or object. If in the Mossi nomenclature, a link is perceived between an illness and some concrete object, a causal connection is likely to be assumed as well.

Neoongo (lit.: 'ostrich') is a disease which causes clefts and cracks in hands and feet, resembling the feet of the ostrich. It sometimes leads to bleeding. The disease occurs mainly in the 'cold' season. The informants explained the name of the illness by pointing at the similarity between the symptoms and the legs of the ostrich. Most informants said that the cause of the illness is unknown, but a few held the opinion that someone suffering from the illness had stepped on an ostrich's nest and broken the eggs. The black powder to treat the illness has to be prepared with a feather or a bone of an ostrich. The powder, mixed with butter, must be smeared on hands and feet.

Tãnturi is the name of a wild pig, but it also is a term for an illness which causes itching pimples over the entire body. The illness may cause loss of hair. The skin of the patient, it is said, resembles the skin of the *tãnturi*. Various informants said they did not know the cause of the illness, but some believed it could be caused by hunters' killing of the animal. The relatives of hunters also run the risk of catching the disease when they touch the animal. In the treatment of the illness some people said a bone of the *tânturi* has to be used, but more specific information was not provided.

Rasem-piungo is an open space in the landscape, a spot where nothing grows. The term is also used for a children's illness which has as its most prominent symptom that the child loses hair. Biomedical observers suspect that the illness may be a fungus infection (*Tinea capitis*). Obviously, the origin of the term *rasem-piungo* is metaphorically descriptive. The child's bare head is compared with the bare spot in the landscape. But this is only the beginning of the associative ramification. Asked about the cause of the illness people are 'taken in' by the concreteness of the metaphoric picture and start to seek for causal explanations in the 'real' *rasem-piungo*. Some say that during her pregnancy the mother has walked over a bare spot in the land. After its birth the baby started to develop the signs of *rasem-piungo*. Others suggest that the child itself has walked over the spot. In both explanations the metaphoric relation has turned into literal truth. The free association has been 'naturalized', imprisoned in the factuality of natural conditions. A similar process takes place in people's reasoning about appropriate treatment of the illness. Again the metaphoric comparison proves its powerful hold over people's imagination: the treatment, too, is related to the natural *rasem-piungo*. People advise treating the illness by mixing some soil from a *rasem-piungo* with water and smearing it on the head of the patient. Finally, the metaphor extends its influence to preventive measures. Pregnant women are warned to avoid bare spots in the land and mothers are admonished to keep their children away from such places in order to prevent *rasem-piungo*.

Keesing (1987), in his critique of anthropological interpretation, reproaches his colleagues for taking metaphors and metonyms too seriously. Dead metaphors are resuscitated by anthropologists who hear them for the first time. Meaningless terms are charged with whatever informants are willing to say after being pressured to do so by the anthropologist. Symbolism is created in the ethnographic encounter. It should not be ruled out that some of the Mossi ethnographic data was indeed produced on the spot, with the researcher as catalyst (cf. Pool 1994:23) and that they should be regarded as 'negotiated fiction' (again Pool's term). Perhaps a more trustworthy answer to the anthropologist's questions would have been: I don't know (as in fact several informants did say). However, the mere fact that people did make the above associations, whether improvised for the occasion or based on common knowledge, shows the symbolic train of their medical thinking and acting. Few people can 'make up' stories out of nothing. Apparently, the concreteness of the symbolic images provided sufficient 'stuff' to enlighten the researcher about the causes and appropriate cures of the various illnesses.

Metaphors, metonyms and medicines

Symbolism is about making associations, often between perceptible images and concepts. Such associations can be analytically divided into metaphors and metonyms. That is, associations may depend on similarity or on contiguity.

Frazer's 'crude intelligence'

Such a distinction was made in Frazer's classic anthropological study of magic, *The Golden Bough*, first published in 1890. Frazer's discussion of magic has been widely criticized because of his derogatory remarks about magic as faulty thinking: 'a spurious system of natural law as well as an abortive art' (Frazer 1957:15). He refers to 'the crude intelligence not only of the savage, but of ignorant and dull-witted people everywhere' (1957:16). But when we 'clean' these sneers from his writing, we discover a highly imaginative account of the working of magical thinking. Two quotations illustrate this:

If we analyse the principles of thought on which magic is based, they will probably be found to resolve themselves into two: first, that like produces like or that an effect resembles its cause; and second, that things which have once been in contact with each other continue to act on each other at a distance after the physical contact has been severed. The former principle may be called the Law of Similarity, the latter the Law of Contact or Contagion. From the first of these principles, namely the Law of Similarity, the magician infers that he can produce any effect he desires merely by imitating it: from the second he infers that whatever he does to a material object will affect equally the person with whom the object was once in contact, whether it formed part of his body or not. Charms based on the Law of Similarity may be called Homoeopathic or Imitative Magic. (1957:14)

Both branches of magic, the homoeopathic and the contagious, may conveniently be comprehended under the general name of Sympathetic Magic, since both assume that things act on each other at a distance through a secret sympathy, the impulse being transmitted from one to the other by means of what we may conceive as a kind of invisible ether, not unlike that which is postulated by modern science for a precisely similar purpose, namely to explain how things can physically affect each other through a space which appears to be empty. (1957:16)

Frazer's 'homoeopathic magic' is what we would call metaphoric, an association based on similarity. His 'contagious magic', which is based on some kind of contiguity, will be called metonymic.

It is striking that Frazer succeeds so well in explaining 'the native's point of view' while rejecting it so squarely. His eloquence in presenting the magician's view gives rise to the suspicion that after all these views were not so alien to the Western scientist. Frazer was able to comprehend and appreciate them:

Thus the analogy between the magical and the scientific conceptions of the world is close. In both of them the succession of events is assumed to be perfectly regular and certain, being determined by immutable laws, the operation of which can be foreseen and calculated precisely. (1957:64)

Frazer's ideas about the logic of magical thinking are beautifully demonstrated in the ethnographic work of Victor Turner among the Ndembu people of Zambia. He writes: 'All the senses – sight, hearing, taste, smell, and touch – are enlisted in the service of association and analogy' (1967:343). Ndembu people have a tendency

to regard like or shared experiences as creating a mystical bond between all persons . . . things, and activities comprising the experience or closely associated with it . . . From the point of view of the Ndembu, persons and things which 'were together' in space and time at a moment of critical significance for an individual or group may acquire a deep and permanent relationship of 'mystical participation'. (1967:351–2)

The Mossi material, which we present in this chapter, suggests that people spontaneously group together phenomena which are similar or which relate to one another in terms of contiguity (nearness in place, time or otherwise). Frazer's concept of magic and Turner's idea of 'mystical bond' fit the Mossi way of medical reasoning. People tend to attribute causal principles to similarity and contact though they may not be able to account for their working in precise terms. Similarity and contiguity are magnets which attract name-giving, causal reasoning and therapeutic practice. In a variation on the well-known adage, *Post hoc ergo propter hoc* (After it, therefore because of it), one could say *Sicut hoc ergo propter hoc* (Like it, therefore because of it) and *Ad hoc ergo propter hoc* (Near it, therefore because of it).

Metaphors

Metaphors help us to grasp 'reality' in an intellectual sense, to see the world in a certain way and, consequently, to communicate about that intellectual experience. Metaphors have a practical value; they help people organize their lives. Fernandez (1986:8) applies Burke's definition of proverb to metaphor: a 'strategy for dealing with a situation'. But it is still not clear how that metaphoric assistance, that strategy, works. To explain this, Fernandez resorts to a spatial metaphor: metaphors 'take

their subjects and move them' (1986:12). To where? One of the most
popular 'movements' accomplished by metaphors in everyday life is from
inchoateness to concreteness. A metaphor, like a proverb, is a predication
upon an inchoate situation. It says that something much more concrete
and graspable – a rolling stone, a bird in the hand – is equivalent to
the essential elements in another situation we have difficulty in grasping
(1986:8). Lakoff and Johnson (1980) provide an abundance of examples of common metaphors which turn elusive concepts into objects of
substance. Time is money: it can be spent, saved, wasted, invested or
donated. The mind is a machine (with wheels that hum or get rusty) or
a brittle object (that can snap or shatter).

Let us apply this to the experience of not feeling well, a typical example
of a situation that is difficult to grasp. Although bodily sensations seem
very direct and concrete to the subject, they are elusive and obscure at
the same time. Pain, for example, is an indefinite experience. The subject
does not fully understand his own body and, worse, he finds it extremely
difficult to communicate the pain sensation to others. Pain, by definition,
is a lonely sensation and what cannot be shared by others cannot be
discussed or recognized by others and thus remains, in a sense, abstract,
a non-experience.

By likening the pain sensation to other experiences that are more tangible, we move, in Fernandez's terms, the inchoate to a domain where
things are easier to grasp. The metaphoric assistance in dealing with not
feeling well is that it makes the complaint specific, even palpable. Images
from the tangible world of nature and physics are applied to the elusive
experiences of nausea ('a wave') and pain ('a vice'). Illness assumes an
appearance of concreteness which makes it accessible for communication
and therapeutic action. Metaphors and metonyms show their practicality.

Terms transform illness into empirically verifiable phenomena. Victor
Turner, writing about the Ndembu, remarks that to make a disease accessible to therapeutic action, they make it visible by symbolic means
(1967:343). In biomedicine both doctors and patients use physical and
technical metaphors to describe the cause of the complaint: defect, tension, shock, rupture, stricture, pressure, perforation, stress, expulsion and
sedimentation. They speak of canals and vessels, flow and congestion, the
intestinal flora, growths and invasions. A diffuse subjective experience is
concretized and objectified and becomes an 'it' (Cassel 1976).

In industrialized countries, concrete and mechanistic images of illness
and health are also familiar in popular speech. The body, and the heart
('ticker') in particular, are referred to as an engine that may break down,
not run well, become worn out, and need to be checked. Terms like 'fuel',

'battery' and 'spare part' are frequently used to describe health problems. The plumber's model of the body, with its pipes, pressure, circulation, flushing and draining, has proved an apt and practical metaphor. Everywhere, people draw upon the images that are at hand in the world in which they live.

Metaphoric movements of medicines

It is not difficult to see that the concretization of illness brought about by metaphor prepares the ground for the use of medicines. If the problem is physical, then the remedy should be physical. Medicines appear the perfect answer to the problem.

Western pharmaceuticals, as substances, change the substance of the ailing body. Vitamins build strong bodies. Heart medicines thin the blood. Diuretics get rid of water. Psychiatric medicines clear the mind. Vaccines teach substances in the body how to fight invasions, as in this example from an urban resident of the eastern United States:

I think my most basic idea of how a vaccine works is that you put some dead or severely disabled germs, bad things, bacteria or viruses, into your body that in and of themselves do not pose a threat to disable you. And that your body sends again these little white blood cells to come and check 'em out, and they have some kind of a struggle with them, but they learn, through their struggle, what these bad things are about, so that . . . the next time they chance upon something like this, they're going to have no problem coping with it. (Martin 1994:197)

In every case there is a suggestion, by analogy, about the nature of the problem: thick blood, a cluttered mind, untrained guards. The medicines draw on the same storehouse of analogy and provide a neatly appropriate solution in concrete form.

In a medical system characterized by ideas of 'hot' and 'cold', medicines are also conceptualized as hot or cold and thus able to remedy a hot–cold imbalance (Logan 1973). Similarly, where likeness in colour occupies people's minds, medicinal efficacy is commonly related to colour (Turner 1967; Ngubane 1977; Bledsoe and Goubaud 1988). Peasants in the Northern Andes of Peru believe that black medicines are most effective in absorbing the heat (Oths 1992). In Rwanda, medicines are applied to restore the regular flow of bodily fluids (Taylor 1988). Among the Sakhalin Ainu (Ohnuki-Tierney 1981), as among the Mossi, medicines are selected on homoeopathic principles; an illness associated with a certain animal is treated with substances of that same animal. In all examples metaphoric concreteness sets the tone.

Metonyms

There are two closely related metonymic processes that are of great significance for making illness concrete and facilitating the use of medicines. These are 'part for whole' and 'localization'. Locating a health problem in some part of the body has mainly two effects – it makes the complaint more specific and allows for directed action. Locating the complaint in a part does not deny the suffering of the whole body or the whole person. The implied causal ordering of the metonym is that the illness of the (whole) person is brought about by the dysfunctioning of one body part. In northern Thailand, the pains of arduous physical labour are treated as located in an inflamed womb, as we shall see in chapter 4.

Locating the complaint is, as it were, providing a geographical map for therapeutic intervention. Medicines, as we have seen, are believed to work in a very concrete manner. They change the physical composition or restore the mechanics of a body part. They can be applied locally or sent to the troubled area through the canals of the metabolic and arterial system. Thus consumers in Europe and North America treat the symptoms of a cold with nasal sprays or cold capsules. The logic of localization may be applied quite stringently, as when African consumers of commercial pharmaceuticals empty capsules of antibiotics into wounds, or place aspirins on an aching tooth. The localizing metonym shows the way for medicines to be taken. Medicines, according to Willems (1998:114), not only follow the pathways in the bodily geography but – in a sense – also create those pathways.

Another metonymic style of explaining and dealing with illness is 'producer-product' or 'agent-effect'. Experiences can be made concrete and tractable by seeing them as conditions that have been brought about by some agency. Attributing illness to a certain person is transporting the elusive experience to the concrete world of social relationships where power, knowledge and specialized techniques of others can be marshalled to solve the problem. Medicines become metonymic substances in that they are treated as physical representations of a larger context of which they are a part. Greenway (1998) describes how *despatchos* (medicines used in ritual offerings) in the Peruvian Andes come to represent and objectify the identity of the patients. By manipulating these objects, the healer also works on the patient and his situation.

Metonymic movements of medicines

The 'charm' of medicines is that, even removed from a previous context, they retain a potential connection to it. The medicines have a metonymic association with medical doctors who prescribe them, with laboratories that produce them, with medical science that forms their ultimate ground. Through medicines people enjoy the fruits of medical expertise without the inconvenience of actually having to go to the doctor.

It is not only the case that medicines are associated with doctors, however. In many situations they represent a whole cultural context. This probably explains the frequently cited popularity of medicines with a foreign origin (cf. Whyte 1988:225 ff; Rekdal 1999). Hand in hand with the near universality of ethnocentrism goes a widespread belief in cultures throughout the world that extraordinary knowledge can be found elsewhere, far away usually. Supernatural (or rather super-cultural) capacities lie outside the domain of the familiar. An exotic provenance of medicines, therefore, is easily seen as a promise that these are indeed superior.

The way in which a medicine's connection to another cultural context may be emphasized to enhance its charm is beautifully illustrated by a Philippine television ad for Alvedon, a brand name for paracetamol, manufactured by Astra of Sweden. Pictures show a Swedish doctor taking the drug, while an announcer explains that Alvedon is the product of 'the same Swedish technology' that produced the Volvo. This is followed by pictures of the tennis champion Björn Borg, and the Nobel Prize ceremony in Stockholm (Tan in Van der Geest and Whyte 1989:360).

Conclusion

The meaning of medicines must be understood in terms of the experience and conception of illness. Metaphors are often used to concretize illness, which opens the way for therapy by *things*. But the very existence of medicines as a form of treatment motivates the conception of illness in appropriately concrete (and therefore treatable) terms. In providing concrete models for feeling ill, medical science provides many of the metaphors we live by.

Medicines, herbs as well as pharmaceuticals, predicate a graspable world of healing upon the sufferer, giving the imagined 'itness' of the disease the countering 'itness' of the medicine and vice versa. Discursive reasoning is inextricably bound up with symbolic associations. The 'linguistic embellishment' of aetiology and cure is part of the therapeutic efficacy.

Among the Mossi, names, causes and treatments of illness reveal a strongly metaphoric and metonymic style of reasoning. Cause, effect and cure are grouped together around powerful images derived from everyday life, such as tools and other objects of daily use, plants and animals. These images are 'good to think' in the sense that they not only help to name and classify the illness, but also provide the 'stuff' for its causal explanation and cure. Mossi associative reasoning amply demonstrates the appropriateness of Frazer's concepts of homoeopathic and contagious 'magic'. The existence of a concrete point of metaphoric or metonymic reference has a magic hold over aetiological and curative beliefs. Concreteness, in Lévi-Strauss' view, provides a logic which attracts people both intellectually and emotionally. Indeed, people derive intellectual and social satisfaction from linking illness concepts to key images which – paradoxically – are attributed pathological as well as curative action. This seeming contradiction is never explicitly discussed and does not seem to worry these home-herbalists. The contradiction simply dissolves in the 'heat' of the image, in the 'logic of the concrete'.

The Mossi 'order' seems far removed from the one of natural science classification and Aristotelian logic. Upon closer consideration, however, their and our styles of reasoning may be less far apart. Metaphoric and metonymic associations also underlie the everyday logic of people in 'modern' society. Notions of the hereditary and contagious nature of disease, for example, can be seen as attempts to provide a causal explanation through a metonymic connection. And an increasing number of studies show how much metaphor and metonym is jumbled up in the empiricist rationalism of natural science (cf. Martin 1987; Latour 1990). Seeing the symbolic in science constitutes what Sahlins has called anthropology's liberation from 'the prison house of naturalism'. It marks an increased awareness of the penetration of symbols into the analysis of the practical (Sahlins 1976:102).

4 Women in distress: medicines for control

As we have seen in the previous chapter, medicines hold out the promise of making disease graspable, casting the problem as something tangible and amenable to efficacious action. They offer a means of control, a way of making that condition tractable. In the hands of people in distress, medicines seem empowering. But their potential to define problems symbolically as appropriate for medicinal therapy means that those who produce and prescribe them have power to influence how people understand and deal with their life situations. Users of medicine may be both *in* control and *under* control. It is this ambiguity of control that we want to explore by considering how medicines are used to overcome day-to-day stresses in women's lives.

Medicines for women in distress

In her study *Rituals of Silence* Haafkens (1997) examines the use of benzodiazepines – medicines prescribed for mental distress – by women in the Netherlands. She describes how the medicines not only make it possible for women to live with their mental health problems, but also provide society with a means of controlling anxiety and stress. The ambiguous relation between self-control of female distress and medicalized social control of life problems is the main theme of this chapter.[1]

On the one hand, women use benzodiazepines like other medicines to enhance the quality of their individual lives. Medicines liberate them from bodily discomfort, and give them means to control natural bodily processes such as conception, menstruation and menopause. Medicines are part of day-to-day body regimes, in which women strive to fulfil societal expectations of work capability, appropriate fertility, attractive appearance and mental stability. Such self-control with medicines fits in with secularized twentieth-century Western culture, where health is seen to be the responsibility of individuals and families, and control of the body is a core cultural value. 'Wellness', indeed, is widely considered today as

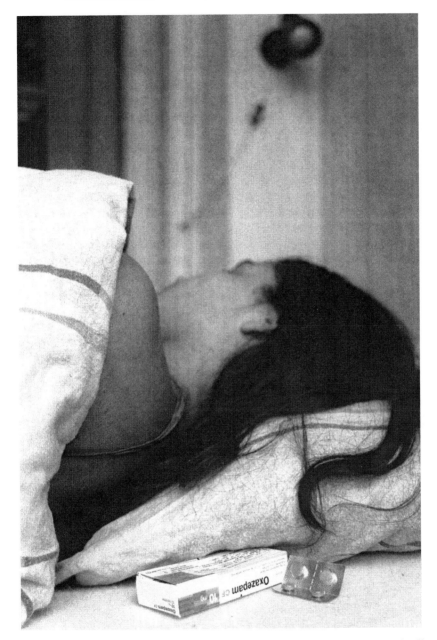

Fig. 4.1 'If I don't sleep, I am not able to do the things I want to do all day. So it's quite simple. I take sleeping pills.'

'virtue', and for some people has the aura of a secular path to salvation (Crawford 1984; Conrad 1994).

On the other hand, benzodiazepines and other medicines also function as a medical means of social control. In modern societies, where medicine has replaced religion as a dominant moral ideology and social control institution, more and more of everyday life has come under medical dominion, influence and supervision, a process known as medicalization (Zola 1972; Turner 1984:203–14, 1987; Conrad 1992). Medicalization critiques point out that these processes have negative effects in that they decrease autonomy, making people into patients and increasing their dependence on the medical profession and indirectly on the pharmaceutical industry (Stacey 1988; Gabe and Calnan 1989). Illich (1976) was one of the first to emphasize the iatrogenic effects of such forms of social control. He calculated in the late 1970s that every tenth night of sleep in England was controlled by a hypnotic drug; in the United States, central nervous system agents were the fastest growing sector of the pharmaceutical market, comprising 31 per cent of total pharmaceutical sales. He described the use of tranquillizers as 'medicalized addiction' (1976:78–9).

Benzodiazepines as means of controlling female distress

Benzodiazepines are the latest in a long line of drugs used to treat mental health problems like anxiety and insomnia. They were introduced in the 1960s and 1970s. The first brands to come on the market were Librium (containing the generic product chlordiazepoxide) and Valium (containing a related compound, diazepam). Then, a long list of benzodiazepines followed, including brands such as Mogadon, Ativan and Halcion. The benzodiazepines were promoted by their manufacturers as safe and non-addicting alternatives to the older generation of tranquillizers, notably the barbiturates (Medawar 1992). They were targeted specifically at female distress. Describing the content of advertisements for benzodiazepines and other psychotropic drugs, Stimson (1975) reports that in the adverts women's place in society was predominantly shown 'as one which generated stress, anxiety and emotional problems'. Images of the tired and tearful 'harassed housewife' in a cluttered kitchen, surrounded by crying children, were common. Images of women outnumbered men fifteen to one.

In the 1980s, benzodiazepines became the focus of widespread debate because of their potential to cause dependence. Until then, the risk of becoming addicted was considered remote. Manufacturers objected strongly to references to addiction, acknowledging only that there were very occasional problems with 'dependence-prone' patients. Slowly, however, the medical establishment became aware of the seriousness of dependence problems. Internationally, medical concern about benzodiazepines was reflected in the 1984 decision of the United Nations to put them on the list of controlled psychotropic substances. The British government introduced the 'Limited List' in 1984, requiring doctors working for the National Health Service to prescribe only a small number of benzodiazepines – and then at the lowest possible dosages, for limited periods of time. In 1992 controls were introduced in the Netherlands. Patients covered by national health insurance can only receive a prescription for thirty days at a time (Nederlandse Staatscourant 1991), but doctors may decide how often the thirty-day prescriptions can be repeated.

Long-term benzodiazepine use in the Netherlands

Around 1990, at the time of Haafken's study, about one in every seven women had a prescription for benzodiazepines filled annually in the Netherlands; men received such prescriptions much less often. Dutch medical guidelines acknowledged that the drugs were not as safe as initially thought, and recommended that the duration of benzodiazepine use be limited to one to two weeks, a few months at the most. Despite this advice, long-term use of benzodiazepines remained relatively common in the Netherlands, affecting an estimated 3 per cent of the Dutch population.

Haafkens, inspired by the symbolic interactionist tradition, aimed to explore, from their own point of view, how women's social relations contributed to long-term benzodiazepine use. She conducted open-ended life-history interviews with women who were current or former long-term users,[2] seeking to understand how the women's reactions to tranquillizers were mediated by the beliefs, expectations and knowledge they acquired through interaction with other people and through previous experiences. By describing women's embodied experiences with tranquillizers from prescription to cessation of use, Haafkens provides us with ethnographic materials which we can use to study the ambiguity between medicine as means of self-control and medicines as means for medical social control.

Medicalization critiques take as their point of departure that the autonomy of individual patients, in this case distressed women, is constrained by more powerful others – the doctors. Medicalized social control is seen to inhibit or deny rational, independent human action by allowing members of the medical profession to determine how others should behave. People's capacity for self-control is diminished. Doctors are seen as power-players who attempt to enhance their position in society and their status by demanding exclusive rights to define and treat illness and other problems, thereby subordinating the opinions and knowledge of lay people (Lupton 1997).

Haafkens' cases reveal the interpersonal aspects of the medical encounter, the mutual influences between doctors and patients, and the mix of emotions and desires that motivate their behaviour (Lupton 1997). In some of the encounters the doctor clearly takes control, and women uncritically accept the prescribed benzodiazepines as a solution to their distress. In other encounters women assert more self-control. They consider the doctor to be a gatekeeper for the medicines. They perform their illness in such a way that the doctor prescribes the medicines they want. The study shows that the relationship between the prescribing doctor and the tranquillizer user is not always one in which the doctor holds power and the woman plays a passive receiving role.[3]

Assertions of medical and self control in the initial medical encounter

Thirty-three of the fifty women interviewed by Haafkens said they started using benzodiazepines because their physician suggested they do so. Nineteen of these women said they were *unexpectedly* given a benzodiazepine prescription. When they went to see their doctors, these women were looking for someone to listen to their problems or to help them cope with their distress. The doctors responded with a prescription for benzodiazepines and the women accepted the advice. The following case illustrates the experiences of this group of respondents:

Motherhood was not easy for me at my age (41), especially under the circumstances. The father had very little time to help me with my baby. In the beginning I felt very isolated with my son. It's maybe my own fault but I am not exactly the type of mother who picks up her baby and goes. I was always worried. Does he need a bottle? Does he need this or that? And my financial situation was rough. Right before the end of my maternity leave, I was told by the advertising firm I used to work for that they had changed our previous arrangements and I could only come back if I was willing to work on a full-time basis. I contested this decision with the help of a lawyer, but all I ended up with was a small payment and a monthly unemployment allowance. But what I wanted was a job. So I had a lot of tension and I cried a lot, but in private. I always felt I had to hide my sadness from my baby. Babies need smiles, no tears. I cried a lot but basically at night. In 1991, two years after my son was born, I became very tense, to the extent that I would sometimes have an irregular pulse, and I decided to go to my family doctor to see what I could do. Immediately after I got into his office, I began to cry. He said, 'Oh I see what the problem is', and he prescribed six Serestas for me. He also advised me to take it easy for a while.

Around half of the thirty-three women for whom benzodiazepine use was initiated by a physician had had prior experience with psychotropic drugs. They took for granted that pharmaceutical treatment was indicated. The doctor told them to take benzodiazepines as replacement for the p medication and they accepted the advice.

Around one-third (seventeen) of Haafkens' respondents said t requested the benzodiazepines themselves. Nearly all of these women had prior experience using psychotropic drugs, many of them *without* previous medical supervision. They acquired information about tranquillizing agents through advertisements, from popular medical literature and from talking to relatives, partners or good friends. Some of them recalled how, when turning to their doctors for a benzodiazepine prescription, they asserted their need for the drug by presenting symptoms of distress that they hoped would prompt the doctor to prescribe the drugs they wanted. For these women the tranquillizers were a means for self-control and the doctor was merely a gatekeeper. One woman recalled:

When I finished my first Mogadon (obtained through an acquaintance, a nurse) I went to my family doctor and told him I was an insomniac, I was already taking care of the problem with counselling, but I wanted Mogadon in the meantime. He said: 'I don't think it is a very good idea to prescribe Mogadon. If you really need something, nowadays you can get much better medication.' I replied: 'That might be true, but I know how to use Mogadon and I have not tested this other medicine. I had very good experiences with Mogadon. Please give me Mogadon. I am not an addict and I will not become one either. I know how to handle this kind of pill.' So he prescribed 10 Mogadon.

An interesting comment that Haafkens makes on the medical encounters is that the physicians usually failed to inform the women about potential side-effects of the drugs. Why did they not do so? Were they afraid that women would then resist their advice? Unfortunately Haafkens did not interview the doctors to get their point of view, but the most likely explanation is that doctors, at that time, were simply not aware of the severity of dependence-related problems. The general practitioners probably prescribed benzodiazepines because they did not see an alternative way to deal with women's distress. Consultations in general practice are short and prescriptions are a convenient way to reassure women that something can be done, and to end the consultation (see chapter 9).

Women turn to their general practitioners as universal healers, and expect them to solve their problems. Indeed, both Dutch doctors and their patients are part of a culture in which biological reductionism reigns. Social problems become redefined as medical-biological disturbances. Moreover, most information doctors get about benzodiazepines is produced by manufacturers of the drugs, who tend to overvalue benefits, and disclaim possible side-effects and dependence problems (see chapter 10). Thus, to doctors and their patients, pharmaceutical interventions make sense (Montagne 1991).

Self-controlled continued use

No matter how medication was initiated, the first prescription for benzodiazepines in this group of long-term users marked the beginning of a drug-using career enshrouded in silence. In the Netherlands many doctors issue repeat prescriptions which are filled at the pharmacy, so doctors may not necessarily be aware of the exact amounts of benzodiazepines that their patients take, or the duration of use. Many women in fact actively avoided contact with their doctors about their continued benzodiazepine use, fearing that s/he would stop prescribing the valuable drug. People in their social networks who were aware of their benzodiazepine use kept quiet about it. Haafkens suggests that the silence surrounding their drug use gives women the freedom to continue taking benzodiazepines, which they feel are necessary for them to cope with their problems and maintain control of their lives.

About half of the women deviated from the prescribed drug regime, sometimes decreasing the dosage in order to control side-effects of the drugs, or increasing it, possibly to counteract the effects of increased tolerance to the drug, or otherwise to manage their day-to-day lives. These adaptations are further assertions of self-control. One woman reported:

I had promised my doctor to only use it when I really needed to. But very soon, I was taking it every night. It worked much better than those relaxation exercises. I immediately became hooked. That was clear. By the end of the first two weeks I had finished off 20 pills. My doctor has a joint practice with another woman. If one of them is not in, you can go to the other. The other one gave me a new prescription. I also found out that I could get refill prescriptions from the nurse, if the doctors were too busy. So that was easy.

Another woman, who had been using OTC drugs, described her use of Valium as follows:

INTERVIEWER: What was it like to take Valium? After all it is a more potent drug than the drugs you used before.
RESPONDENT: In fact I liked it, it made me a little bit stoned. And when I expected a busy day, I would often take one preventively, so that I wouldn't be bothered by nerves or headaches. I would also take the pills with me in my purse. During the day, I would take small bites, not an awful lot, just bites, especially when I began to feel stressed out.

Losing control

An analysis which focuses on women's agency in self-control of psychological stress with benzodiazepines can easily fail to acknowledge the power of medical technologies. Since the mid-1980s, it has been clear that benzodiazepines can cause physical dependence. Haafkens' study allows us not only to understand the micro-relations of power between women and their prescribing physicians and the dynamics in actual use; it also draws our attention to the power of the medicines. While many women perceived benzodiazepines to be liberating agents, others pointed to feelings of 'loss of control' over their drug taking – especially women who had taken increasing doses for some time. It was these women who attempted to regain control by quitting the drugs.

Haafkens found that women who were confronted with feelings of loss of control over their drug taking were tempted to increase the dosage of the drug. Some creatively found ways to increase the dosage without going back to their doctors for more; for example one woman got her supplies from a friend. She reported:

At present I get my prescriptions for Seresta once a week at the Community Health Clinic. They give me 32 pills, which is 4 a day. But I take 6 a day. So on the weekend I am often in trouble, and I have to go to my girlfriend, who is 18 years old and also uses Seresta. She gets more than I do. They want me to go to a clinic to stop using Seresta and take other pills instead. I know I have to do this eventually. But, what I am going through right now is unbearable. I find there is very little understanding for Seresta users. It's not a drug like others you know.

Others dealt with the feelings of lack of control over drug taking by daily routines to limit use. For example one woman explained:

If I hyperventilate in bed at night, I never go downstairs to take a Seresta. Then I sit up against a pillow, and tell myself 'Cut it out', and that helps. But I can't do that during the day. So over the past few months I have taken two pills a day, which comes down to sixty pills a month.

The tendency to increase the dosage is related to the pharmacological effects of benzodiazepines. Some long-term users experience increased tolerance to the drugs, needing more and more of the drug to achieve the original effects. This increase in dosage makes women dependent, indeed addicted to the drugs. Stopping the use of benzodiazepines is not easy for this group of women.

Resisting benzodiazepines

In Haafkens' group of fifty women, fourteen managed to quit after long-term use. They describe the process as long (lasting an average of 3.6 years) and arduous, as illustrated in the following cases.

RESPONDENT: I called my family doctor, made an appointment and told her, 'I want to stop using my medication.' She said, 'Fine.' So I stopped right away because that seemed the least roundabout way to do it.

INTERVIEWER: Didn't she give you any advice about how to cut down?
RESPONDENT: No, she didn't tell me anything. The woman must have been completely out of her mind. Later it made me very mad. After six days without Temesta, I had to call her again. I had never been that sick in my life. I was lying on the couch and my whole body was itching and shaking. My muscles were terribly sore. I couldn't walk. I could hardly get to the bathroom. I was hyperventilating. It is hard to describe what I was going through. You have no idea how sick I was. So I called her again and told her, 'This is too much for me.' And she said, 'Well, if it is too much for you, then you ought to start taking it again.' But, I thought: 'Now that I have gone through this hell of six days, I am not going to give up.' So I told her, 'No I don't want to start again. After all I have not gone through this agony for the fun of it.' So she said: 'Well in that case call the Community Mental Health Centre, I can't help you.'

This case occurred in 1991, when Dutch physicians had been informed about the side-effects of benzodiazepines, including the withdrawal symptoms. Doctors who were aware of these difficulties could have advised women to cut down *gradually* on their daily dosage of benzodiazepines and told them about the typical withdrawal symptoms to be expected. However, this second case illustrates that, even when properly informed, women still found it difficult to cope with the effects of quitting.

Many times I was convinced I had become seriously ill. I had terrible pains, heart problems, intestinal problems. My doctor was very understanding. Every time I panicked, he had me examined at the hospital to reassure me that these were withdrawal symptoms. I didn't know what it was like to have feelings after 17 years of taking pills. At first I was so overwhelmed by these feelings I would be completely focused on them and it made me lose perspective. It was so hard, for instance at work when I had to deal with people... It would scare me... In the past, every time I had feelings, I would take a pill. While cutting down, there were many times when I thought I really needed Oxazepam again. But my doctor knew how to talk me out of it. As I said, he somehow made me believe in my own potential.

The detailed descriptions of how women experience and use benzodiazepines are a unique feature of Haafkens' study. The narratives show how women's experiences are social products shaped in their day-to-day social worlds by their interactions with physicians and exposure to mass media and pharmaceutical marketing. Haafkens' respondents appear to be subject to the forces that promote medicalized social control in the form of a 'pharmaceuticalization' of their suffering. In accepting a medicinal solution, they seem to acknowledge that their problems are medical and amenable to a doctor's prescription. Yet as a long-term solution, benzodiazepines are not socially approved. Thus women may take their medicines for years in silence, quietly finding ways to keep themselves supplied. Many of these women view their medicines as empowering in that they help them to cope with the stresses of day-to-day life. However, the extent of physical dependence on the drug becomes clear when some women go through long arduous processes of giving up their medicinal means of control. For them, quitting is an act of resistance to the medical regime.

Day-to-day stress and the power of medicines

Benzodiazepines are just one category of medicines used to manage day-to-day life. Many Europeans use a whole plethora of medicine in self-care to treat bodily discomforts and disease. Medicines are increasingly used for health maintenance purposes as well: to control weight, reduce the effects of stress, lower blood pressure and minimize cancer risks. One of the most noted examples of this trend is the definition of menopause as a condition to be relieved by medication. Yet here, too, the charge of medicalization overlooks the complexities of agency and control. In spite of forceful efforts to medicalize the menopause, women have not become willing consumers of the medicines promoted to ease their discomfort.

Medicalization of the menopause has been traced to developments in American medical science in the late 1930s and 1940s, when endocrinologists started defining the menopause as a 'deficiency disease', which could be treated with the synthetic oestrogen, DES, first synthesized in 1938 (Bell 1987). Until the 1970s, however, hormonal treatment was mainly recommended for women suffering an especially difficult menopause in clinical practice; otherwise the 'turn' in life was seen to be a natural process (Topo 1997).

In the current era, the menopause is described in the medical literature more in terms of a disease, or as unnatural, and the use of hormonal drugs during this phase of life as a natural way of saving a woman from her imperfectly functioning body. Proponents of hormonal intervention argue that women nowadays live longer, and that their diminishing sex hormone production is therefore dysfunctional (Topo 1997). The pharmaceutical industry markets newer oestrogen-progestin combinations not only to increase the quality of life of women going through the menopause, but also to reduce the risks of ill-health in later life – specifically for the prevention of osteoporosis and cardiovascular diseases (Stampfer et al. 1991). For these purposes long-term use of hormone replacement therapy (HRT) is recommended.

Studies in actual menopause management show that despite these medical arguments, 'compliance' with HRT is low in terms of both uptake and subsequent adherence rates (Hunter et al. 1997; Topo 1997). For example, in England only 10 per cent of women aged 45–55 use the treatment (Oddens *et al.* 1992). Market research shows that over two-thirds of those starting HRT have stopped nine months later. The reasons given are unacceptable side-effects, doctor's advice, concerns about HRT, treatment being ineffective and feeling better. Qualitative studies on women's experiences with HRT reveal that they mainly use the drugs for the prevention of hot flushes, because they have a negative effect on their social lives (Hunter *et al.* 1997; Griffiths 1999).

The empirical evidence from these HRT-user studies shows that women resist being controlled medically. They actively make their own decisions about taking the therapies and challenge medical discourses. They resist medicalization, wanting to avoid taking medication except as a last resort, when menopausal symptoms are severe. Despite the medical assertions that HRT is good for health, women are concerned about side-effects and unknown risks; they worry about disturbing natural processes and the possible contaminating effects of putting chemicals into their bodies (Hunter *et al.* 1997). The views on HRT, according to Hunter and colleagues, reflect an overall distrust of hormonal interventions in the UK. Women felt the same concerns about the contraceptive pill.[4] Ambivalence about medicines reflects the paradox that women experience: taking control with medicines can imply being controlled. They did not want to be dependent on hormones promoted by industry and prescribed by doctors, fearing that medicinally controlling menopause could be detrimental to their health.

In non-Western settings, most discussions of medicalization have focused on the issue of the commodification of health (see chapter 6). Very few problematize the ambiguities of women's medicinal self and social control of daily distress. An interesting study among women in north-east Thailand by Sringernyuang (2000) shows how women in rural communities use antibiotics to manage day-to-day bodily complaints related to hard work. In Sringernyuang's study women were commonly found to complain about abdominal and waist pain and backache, symptoms they label as *mot luuk ak seep*. The literal translation is inflamed womb. Women in north-east Thailand relate the occurrence of *mot luuk ak seep* to the strenuous work that is common during the harvest and planting seasons. To manage these day-to-day stresses most women self-medicate, taking medicines called *ya kae ak seep*, for one or two days. *Ya kae ak seep* are locally produced antibiotics which the women can buy over the counter in small village grocery stores. The medicines symbolically point to the womb as the locus of distress, while providing the means to control the life condition of strenuous labour that is made tangible in the inflamed womb. Social control is not so much in the hands of doctors, who play a limited role. Rather it is the pharmaceutical industry which markets *ya kae ak seep* for womb-disturbances direct to consumers, that exerts influence as it seeks to make women dependent on its products.

Conclusion

Medicines play ambiguous roles in women's lives. On the one hand, they may act as agents of medicalized social control, as stressed in medicalization critiques. Medicines are used to treat non-medical problems of women, such as anxiety, insomnia, ageing, irregular menstruations and hard physical work. They increase women's dependence on medical practitioners and medicine manufacturers. At the same time, for women in distress, medicines clearly are important resources of power. They give them means to control their lives, in the absence of other possibilities for more structural change. In the ongoing interactions between distressed women and tranquillizers, it can be argued that both women and medicines have agency. The social well-being of women and the efficacy of the technologies are constantly negotiated, and mutually constitute each other.[5]

The ambiguous role of medicines as means of both (self-)control and being controlled is a consequence of the fact that power is not a possession of particular social groups, like doctors, but that it is relational and dispersed (Foucault 1980). In medicine-use trajectories, power can in fact shift between actors, as we have seen in Haafkens' detailed descriptions of benzodiazepine use. Initially, doctors exert power by prescribing the drugs – though the distressed women may manipulate this event by performing their problems in such a way as to get the medicines they want. In the period of continued use, women appear to be in control. They decide when and how to take their medicines, and they make sure they get sufficient supplies of the medicines, from the doctors' assistants or from other sources. Continued use is not questioned by medical professionals, nor by family and friends. Their silence gives women autonomy. Some long-term users, especially those who have increased dosages, suffer from feeling a loss of control – in that stage the medicine itself appears to have most power. When quitting, some women suffer withdrawal from physical and psychological dependence on the drug, but if they succeed, they regain control in their resistance against the power of the technology.

The evidence in this chapter requires us to rethink medicalization. Women clearly are not docile bodies acted on by medical doctors, nor are they overwhelmed by pharmaceuticalizing forces of industry, as we have seen in the case of the low uptake of hormone replacement therapy. They exert agency which, to paraphrase Giddens (1984:9), implies that at any stage in the clinical encounter or in the act of self-care they could have acted differently. However, the choices they have are not unlimited. The actions of Haafkens' respondents were conditioned by a health culture in which pharmaceutical treatment of mental distress is almost taken for granted. Medical structures constrain our choices and the range of thinkable ideas and conceivable behaviours (Singer and Baer 1995).[6]

5 Sceptical consumers: doubts about medicines

In contrast to the wide popularity of medicinal substances, there is also a growing distrust of and aversion to medicines. In the last chapter we saw how some people who welcomed medicines as a way to control their life situations, later came to reject them. Now we examine doubts about medicines more systematically with a view to the personal and cultural politics that are at stake when people refuse medicines. Reasons for resistance to the use of medicines vary. Some people reject the substances themselves as being toxic, unnatural, aggressive and debilitating for the natural immunity of the body. Others object to the way medicines are used as a substitute for personal concern by doctors or become a means of control exercised through medicines. Sometimes these concerns are expressed in an individual idiom, as personal decisions by men and women trying to take charge of their own lives. Sometimes objections to medicines are phrased in terms of what might be called cultural idioms, where biomedical drugs are compared unfavourably to natural medicines or indigenous medicines. Certain pharmaceutical techniques and products, such as injections and contraceptives, may be singled out for criticism as too strong and too dangerous. This chapter deals with scepticism about biomedical drugs revealed in the phenomena of 'non-compliance', the growing popularity of 'natural medicines' and the selective rejection of 'Western' drugs.

Sceptics in London

'I think nature has its own way of mending things in many cases . . . I'm always slightly wary of drugs of any sort really, I mean other than paracetamol . . . If I don't feel need to take them, I won't take them.' This remark by a man in his mid-forties in London represents the growing unease with pharmaceuticals among consumers. The man had been prescribed painkillers for joint pains but he decided not to take them because of their side-effects.

Fig. 5.1 'I'm always slightly wary of drugs of any sort really... If I don't feel the need to take them, I won't take them.'

Britten (1996), from whom this quotation has been taken, carried out a qualitative study among thirty adult patients from two general practices in London. One was in a socially deprived area and one in an affluent suburb. Most interviews were held in people's homes. She used a semi-structured schedule but encouraged her informants to talk freely. The conversations were recorded and transcribed. She wanted to know to what extent these people were subject to medicalization. By medicalization she meant the process by which people 'lose faith in their own knowledge and information, and in their own powers of judgement' and come to rely on what others – medical professionals – tell them to do. She was particularly interested in those who resisted medicalization.

Britten distinguished two types of attitudes among her informants. Some gave an 'orthodox account' about disease and medicine. These people had a positive appreciation of the role of their physician and the medicines he/she prescribed. They claimed they always complied with what the doctor told them to do. As one of them said, 'I can't see the point of coming to the doctor if you're not going to use what he suggests you, you know, that is a total waste of time' (Britten 1996:56).

Trust in medicines has been the dominant picture in the chapters so far, but the number of those who are more sceptical about doctors and, in particular, medicines is growing. Britten paid special attention to those who presented her with 'unorthodox' accounts. What objections had these people to medicines and why?

One type of account by the sceptics was 'aversion to medicines'. They described medicines as artificial, chemical and unnatural. The fact that they had been made in a factory was in itself a reason to suspect them. They were reluctant to put something manufactured into their bodies. Some of them stated that they preferred natural products such as homoeopathic or Bach Flower remedies: 'It's the chemicals I suppose . . . I just don't like artificial things . . . [Natural remedies] are not chemically made, like flowers are naturally grown things. I prefer to take those than factory made chemicals' (1996:60).

Pharmaceuticals were described as 'foreign to the body', an 'alien force' or 'intruding on the body'. One person thought that all medicines cause cancer:

I have a belief, whether I am right or wrong, that all medicines to an extent are carcinogenic. It's like everything else, if you take enough of it and overdose over a long period of time, you are always prone to perhaps . . . advancing the nature of things like cancer. (1996:61)

Britten's informants mentioned various mechanisms by which pharmaceuticals cause damage. Medicines, some said, lowered the body's resistance to infection and disease. One man, for that reason, rejected antibiotics: 'I think antibiotics do actually harm the body in some way... maybe it knocks out the... body's ability to create the necessary chemicals or white corpuscles or whatever they are to deal with the situation' (1996:61).

Another line of criticism concerned the ways synthetic medicines worked and were used. Some objected that pharmaceuticals only fight the symptoms and not the causes: 'You are only dulling the senses that are telling you you've got a headache... not actually getting to the root of the problem.' Others noted that pharmaceuticals offered uniform treatments that did not consider the specific problems of the individual patient.

A more moderate attitude was the preference for not taking medicines if it could be avoided. That concern was particularly aired with regard to strong or long-term medication. One man, a building labourer, who was suffering from chest pain and had been prescribed long-term medication, said he was reluctant to take the medicines: 'I don't want to be stuck with them for the rest of my life.'

In contrast to those who had a more positive attitude to medicines, these people often decided not to fill a prescription, without informing their physician. They criticized the doctor for over-prescribing and experienced his prescription as an easy way out of the consultation. Many of the women in Haafkens' study of benzodiazepine use (chapter 4) made a similar remark; they went to see the doctor to *talk* about their problems, hoping he/she would *listen* and give them advice. But to their surprise the doctor's reaction was a prescription for benzodiazepine. Britten's respondents emphasized that they wanted more attention to their problem instead of medicines and said it was difficult to get away from a consultation without a prescription. Some showed understanding for the doctor's love of prescription, however:

It's probably quite understandable for the doctor when he sees Mrs B for the fifteenth time that year with some ridiculous ache or pain and he just gives her something to get rid of her... that's probably cost effective from his point of view to see her out of the way. (1996:66)

Some interviewees said they were pleased when the doctor had *not* prescribed any medicine but had given them personal advice on how to go about the problem.

Whether the scepticism about pharmaceuticals is part of a larger complex of critique of science in general could not be concluded from this exploratory study, but seems likely.

In her conclusion Britten points out that patients rarely discuss their rejection of medicines with their doctor in order not to antagonize him or because they were in a hurry and did not want to enter into a debate. Even critical patients behaved quite passively in medical consultations. This leads her to the suggestion that research into 'non-compliance' should not be carried out in medical settings but in the sphere of everyday life because it is there that people take – or do not take – their medicines. Returning to her initial question about the extent to which people are being medicalized in their views and daily practices, she concludes: 'The challenge to medical dominance may occur not in the public but in the private realm, in the guise of non-adherence to prescribed medication' (1996:71).

Doubts, resistance and non-compliance

The views of Britten's interviewees are shared by two broad and very different categories of people: critical consumers in industrialized societies where biomedicine is the established orthodoxy and anxious patients in societies where biomedicine competes with older well-established traditions of treatment. The former are likely to have a relatively high level of school education, the latter not. The reasons for their resistance are almost one another's opposite. The former base their doubts on what they think they know about medicines, the latter on what they do not know. Both categories are somewhat exceptional. Research suggests that – certainly in global terms – people are overwhelmingly in favour of medicines. The resisters are therefore particularly deserving of our attention.

Scepticism towards medicines in industrialized countries gained momentum in the 1970s when criticism of biomedicine in general grew under the influence of publications about doubtful medical practices such as those of Illich (1976) and R. Taylor (1978). The coining of the term 'medicalization' (see chapter 4) constituted the beginning of a sharp awareness that biomedicine was going beyond its territory and imposing itself on numerous non-medical domains of life. Pharmaceuticals proved one of the most effective ways by which this process of medicalization took place. Both Illich and Taylor devoted considerable attention to the harmful consequences of prolific prescription of medicines. Several publications (Silverman 1976; Medawar 1979; Silverman et al. 1982; Melville and Johnson 1982) not only pointed at the possible iatrogenic effects of medicines but also criticized the commercial character of their production and distribution. Pharmaceutical companies – and in their wake, medical doctors – were accused of putting profits before health (chapter 10). Thus, the critical attitude towards medicines as potentially dangerous substances was reinforced by the argument that pharmaceuticals were made for profit as much as for therapy.

This criticism grew particularly pungent with regard to the delivery of expensive medicines to low-income countries (e.g. Melrose 1982; Muller 1982; Silverman *et al.* 1982). It was during that period that the WHO launched its Essential Drug concept (WHO 1977), a list of about 200 drugs which were considered effective, safe, indispensable and affordable (see chapter 10).

'Non-compliance'

The more critical stance of consumers towards medicines and those who prescribe them shows itself most convincingly in studies of non-compliance. Before the critical turn of the 1970s/1980s, non-compliance had been mainly studied from the doctor's point of view and was considered a medical problem due to 'deviant' behaviour by patients. Supposed reasons for their deviance were an 'irrational' view, ignorance, misunderstanding, poverty or lack of access to drugs, all on the part of the patient. The viewpoint of the doctor was not questioned. The traditional doctor-centred picture of compliance was thus summarized by Trostle (1988a:1,305): 'The physician is the proper ultimate authority over the actions of his or her patients; in exchange for a physician's services a patient owes fees, cooperation, and compliance; non-compliance is usually the patient's fault.'

Trostle, however, argued that compliance should be regarded not as the only right therapeutic route but as an ideology supporting the authority of medical professionals. Non-compliance, therefore, could be regarded as an attempt by patients to assert themselves against or outside the control of the medical professionals and should be studied from the opposite angle: from the patient's point of view (Verbeek-Heida 1983). In their overview of 'non-compliance' studies in the Third World, Homedes and Ugalde (1993) distinguish between patients who lack knowledge and motivation and those who consciously non-comply because they decide against the doctor's prescription. Indeed, so-called 'non-compliance' is often the outcome of scepticism about the doctor and his medicines.

In a study of medicine use by epileptic people in the United States, Trostle (1988b) found that almost 60 per cent of 127 adults did not take their anticonvulsive medications according to doctors' instruction. Some stopped taking them for a few days, others stopped taking them altogether and again others changed the dosage. In his discussion of these data Trostle takes as his starting point that 'understanding "non-compliance" as a series of strategies requires assuming that at least some types of non-compliance are inherently rational and logical' (Trostle 1988b:58). Managing epilepsy, people tested different types and dosages of medicines and their effects on seizures in the different situations of their daily life, trying to find the most comfortable solution for themselves. The following quotation from a middle-aged woman is illustrative:

> On my own I decided to decrease my dosage by half. I figured if the seizures are in my sleep who am I gonna hurt anyhow? You weigh one value against another: is it worth feeling protected from seizures to feel like THIS every day? It was more of a handicap walkin' around drugged up than having a seizure while sleeping. If my seizures had been in daytime I'm sure I would have taken it more seriously. I decided I would try on my own to stop and see if I had them. How will I ever know I can handle it, if I don't quit the meds and give it a try? I didn't tell the Clinic doctors because they'd just tell me to keep on. (Trostle 1988b:63)

Another study which, coincidentally, also focuses on people with epilepsy comes to similar conclusions, but puts more emphasis on the social implications of both the disease and the medication. Conrad (1985), who based his article on eighty in-depth interviews in the USA, argued that so-called non-compliant behaviour should first of all be seen as a form of self-regulation that allowed people to test their condition, control dependence, minimize stigmatization and ensure practical convenience.

Conrad points out that although medicines can increase self-reliance by reducing seizures, they are at the same time experienced as a threat to self-reliance: 'Medications seem almost to become symbolic of the dependence created by having epilepsy' (1988b:34). The drugs, in other words, have come to represent the disease and – paradoxically – recall what they are supposed to suppress. In epilepsy, the awareness of the disease, with its unforeseen seizures, is particularly worrying.

Epilepsy is also a stigmatizing disease. Although there are no visible stigmata, there are four signs which Conrad's interviewees experienced as marking their being different: a seizure in the presence of others, job or insurance applications, not having a driving licence and taking medicines. It is this last consideration that motivated some of them to alter or stop their medication entirely. Conrad writes: 'For some it is as if the medication itself represents the stigma of epilepsy.' One person felt 'if she could stop taking her medications she would no longer be an epileptic' (Conrad 1985:35).

Trostle's and Conrad's conclusions are confirmed by an increasing number of authors. Hunt and colleagues, who conducted a diachronic qualitative study among nineteen women being treated for vague and non-specific symptoms (such as headache, fatigue and dizziness, etc.) in an unnamed American city, found that three-quarters of them stopped following the doctor's instructions after a certain period of time. They did so, not because they did not understand the doctor's advice, nor because they disagreed with it, but because of reasons of 'convenience': 'their desire to control symptoms within the constraints of their daily routines' (Hunt *et al.* 1989:315).

Van Dongen, who describes the ambiguous meaning of medications in a psychiatric ward for chronic patients in the Netherlands, presents a different type of 'non-compliance'. Medicines replace words in the communication between staff and patients (see also Rhodes 1984). For some they are tokens of concern but for others a means of oppression. Medicines provide for staff members the power to maintain order in the ward. Medicines quell the disturbing symptoms of a psychosis or depression. One of the staff puts it frankly: 'When we get very difficult clients, we have medicines.' In reaction, some patients resist thus being controlled by medicines. They complain of unpleasant side effects – physical, psychological and social. Medicines become hostile substances, means of oppression, 'poison'. One of the patients said:

I don't want anti-psychotics. They make me psychotic! They give me a big head. They steal my mind. An injection is a scorpion, it shoots poison into you. At the moment, I don't take medicines anymore. I have found my mind back. In the morning I wake up with a clear head. (Van Dongen 1990:43 [our translation])

Medicines in this statement represent a social regime and become a means of both control and rebellion.

Estroff makes a similar point in her work on the significance of medications for psychiatric patients in an American community. She stresses the ambiguity of medicines that suppress disturbing symptoms and simultaneously produce disturbing side-effects. She casts the issue in political terms when she writes:

these long-term intrusions into clients' inside space may represent exercises of power, legitimated by medical affiliation of the treatment system, which underscore to clients their lack of control of themselves in relation to others... It is commonplace for power struggles between patients and staff to be acted out in the medications area. (Estroff 1981:116)

The ambiguity of medicines balancing between oppressive social control and voluntary self-control is beautifully illustrated in relation to the drug Antabuse, the primary means of treating alcoholism in Denmark. Antabuse interferes with the breakdown of alcohol in the body, causing unpleasant symptoms. People struggling to control their alcohol problems may decide to go onto a regimen of Antabuse voluntarily; others are pressured into doing so by family, employers, or judicial or welfare authorities. Steffen (n.d.) describes how people relate to this medication, whose primary purpose is not really cure but control. Antabuse is usually given under strict surveillance, but there are innumerable accounts of cheating and of testing the limits in order to drink one's way through the unpleasant effects. 'Antabuse is a reminder – a challenge', as one of her informants said. By objectifying control so starkly, it provides the means for experimenting with limits, tricking the mechanism, and testing possibilities. At stake is a personal politics that is about relations to others and, most importantly, to oneself.

These examples of non-compliance illustrate the way that not taking medicines can be an assertion of autonomy on the part of sick people, who feel that medications or doctors impinge on their lives in undesirable ways. This kind of personal politics may be more or less explicitly articulated.

Resistance and rejection

Consumers can also be sceptical because biomedical products do not tally with their cultural perception of illness and cure or because they are uncertain and worried about their effects. Medical anthropologists have reported many such cases from different societies. Although there seems to be an overwhelmingly positive appreciation of manufactured medicines which then may or may not be integrated into a local medical cosmology, the opposite reaction also occurs: people reject modern pharmaceuticals, or, more commonly, reject some of them for some types of patients or health conditions. One reason for rejection is that they are thought to be too strong and aggressive. Nichter and Nichter (1996:213) report that villagers in south-west India consider 'English' (or 'allopathic') medicines as powerful yet dangerous. In contrast to Ayurvedic medicines which are believed to maintain or restore balance, English medicines are seen as heating and liable to have dangerous side-effects. Injections, in particular, are believed to be very hot and are therefore not given to children. Pregnant women may for the same reason avoid injections, as they fear that the medicine will harm the foetus or cause an abortion. They may also reject pills because they think that these are difficult to digest and thus share the same space with the foetus for some time, causing it damage. Pregnant women, therefore, often prefer medicines in liquid form.

Injections, as we will see in chapter 8, enjoy wide popularity because of their perceived potency and 'high tech' foreign origin, but their power and foreignness may at the same time constitute their menace. Reservations about the value of injections are reported, for example, from a study among Dagomba people of northern Ghana. Injections given for a painful swelling called *jogu* were said to be deadly:

Once they jab you, there is no way out. It [*jogu*] doesn't match with injection. Because it is in your blood, it is within the system. It goes through the blood, and then, as soon as you have an injection, your blood clogs immediately, your heart will stop, and then you are dead. (Bierlich 2000:709)

Bierlich argues that injections carry meanings as the essence of the foreign system of biomedicine, while the illness called *jogu* is essentially Dagomba. *Jogu* represents aspects of social life (witchcraft, the antisocial: hidden human intentions and machinations) that may be dealt with through the local idiom of divination but which must not be touched by an external power such as biomedicine. (2000:712). Thus the danger of injections here has to do with the opposition between cultural categories construed as internal and external. We will return to this opposition towards the end of this chapter.

Women in Sri Lanka were particularly critical of 'English' contraceptives. The pill, because of its heating effect, burnt up their *dhatu*, a substance associated with vitality and strength. As a result the *dhatu* was no longer strong enough to create a foetus (Nichter and Nichter 1996:77). Another concern was that the pill made the womb dry. One woman said: 'A dry womb is like a dry field. If you plant seeds in a field which is not moist, the seed will not take to the soil. A womb which has become totally dry through continued use of birth control pills becomes useless' (1996:77). Similar fears about the effect of the contraceptive pill have been reported from all parts of the world. Costa and Chaloub (1992) heard from about 80 per cent of the women they interviewed in three Brazilian cities that they thought the pill was harmful and that they found it difficult to take the pill daily; 60–70 per cent of them reported side-effects, such as headaches, weight gain and dizziness.

In his study of 'heart distress' (*narahatiye qalb*) in Maragheh, Iran, Good (1977) drew up 'semantic networks' of complaints and problems which in the perception of the people were related to 'heart distress'. In one of the figures mapping out problems in female sexuality, the contraceptive pill takes a central position. It is linked to dirty blood, lack of blood, loss of vitality, infertility and growing old early. All these symptoms add up to the general disease of *narahatiye qalb*. For example, if menstrual blood is considered dirty blood which should leave the body, it is clear that the pill which reduces the menstrual flow is suspected of accumulating dirty blood in the body, thus causing sickness (see also Good 1980).

One Ayurvedic healer pointed at another negative effect of allopathic medicine. His critique reminds us of the remark by Britten's informant which opened this chapter: medicines are unnatural.

Allopathic medicines are like eyeglasses. They allow you to see but once you have put them on your eyes they do not improve. Your eyes become dim with continual use of glasses and you come to depend on glasses more and more. Eyeglasses are not bad. They are a good crutch, but if one does not need a crutch this may be a bad thing. One leans on the crutch and does not strengthen the leg, one wears the glasses and does not strengthen the eyes, one takes medicines and does not strengthen the body. To become dependent on the medicine bottle makes the company strong, but the body remains weak. (Nichter and Nichter 1996:211)

Rejection of biomedical products owing to cultural disagreement and – mutual – misunderstanding is vividly portrayed in a literary journalistic account of a dramatic case in California. Fadiman (1997) describes the clash between the staff of a small county hospital and a Hmong family from Laos over a child with severe epilepsy. Repeatedly it is discovered that the parents refuse to give their child the prescribed medicines or change the dose (not so surprising since the prescription had changed twenty-three times in less than four years). The medications had been prescribed in varying combinations, varying amounts and varying numbers of times per day. The parents had the feeling that the medicines were in fact *causing* the disease instead of curing it. It was an opinion that the American doctors were not used to. They *were* used to patients objecting to side-effects and had their answers to those complaints. But the Hmong parents had more fundamental objections that the doctors could not understand.

Natural treatment

One of the most common critiques of pharmaceutical drugs is that they are artificial and even poisonous. They are unfavourably compared to more natural forms of healing. Although we tend to think of the longing for naturalness in health and healing as part of a critique of contemporary civilization and science, this sort of 'cultural politics' has a long tradition in Western medicine. Medical reformers of early modern Europe opposed the expensive and complex Arabic medicines favoured by learned Galenic doctors. Arguing that God in his mercy had given to each nation the means of cure for its own diseases, they praised the simple remedies growing in the fields, free to the poor, and far better than the exotic ones sold by the apothecaries (Conrad *et al.* 1995:309–10). In late-eighteenth- and early-nineteenth-century Europe and America, challenges to medical orthodoxy often focused on drugs. Some reformers, like Samuel Hahnemann the founder of homoeopathy, and the American botanical practitioners, proposed a completely different system of using medicines. Proponents of natural healing were against the use of any drugs at all. Hydropathy, popular in Europe and the United States at this time, appealed to the belief in the inherently beneficial quality of natural things. It was based on the idea that health can be preserved by drinking large amounts of water to clean the bowels and kidneys, sweating, and taking frequent baths to expel morbid humours (Gevitz 1993).

The current 'renaissance' of herbal medicine and other natural products is a worldwide phenomenon. In low-income countries the choice of natural remedies implies both a critique of the high costs of manufactured products and a rejection of their damaging effect on the natural constitution of the body (Miles 1998a, 1998b; Tan 1999). In high-income societies the revival of natural medicines is mainly the expression of unease with the iatrogenic character of biomedical products and the popularity of 'back-to-nature' and 'New Age'-type movements. A national survey in the United States in 1990 revealed that one-third of the respondents had used at least one 'unconventional therapy' in the past year (Eisenberg et al. 1993). Those reporting the use of alternative medicine tended to have more education and higher incomes. We may assume that they represented the more critical part of the population. Unfortunately, reasons for their choice of other therapies were not included in the survey but – taking Britten's findings as a starting point – we may safely assume that preference for 'natural medicine' played a role. In a follow-up in 1997 the trend towards unconventional therapy had continued (Eisenberg et al. 1998).

Ideas of naturalness and aversion against toxicity in pharmaceuticals are frequently mentioned in studies of alternative medicine (e.g. Roth 1976; Aakster 1986). 'The principal cause of illness is an anti-natural life', remarks someone in Miles' (1998b) study of Ecuador. The concern about natural products does not limit itself to medicines, but has put its stamp on many other domains of life, food in particular. Tan (1999) devotes an entire chapter to medicinal plants in his study of the politics of medicines in the Philippines. Plants are safe. As one person remarks: 'You cannot get an overdose with medicinal plants. They are plants. Some of them are used as food' (1999:168). Their safety lies in their naturalness and their metonymic reference to other natural things.

The idea of nature is often conflated with national, class or ethnic consciousness and opposed to the foreign and artificial in a kind of medicinal politics of identity. Tan points out that medicinal plants in the Philippines have a national value. They are contrasted to 'Western' medicines (people use the English term). The Western medicines were associated with bad practices of Western countries such as dumping poor-quality and dangerous drugs. He quotes a mother in Hardon's (1991:123) study, saying that the drugs in the store are *not* good and *not* safe because they are 'not from our own country while medicinal plants are truly Filipino'. A similar quote is taken from Scheper-Hughes' study of North Brazil where she records excerpts from a skit.

Many of the drugs are toxic, they are poisonous, and they are given out to the poor without regard for their side effects...Don't put your faith in doctors and in drugs...We can begin to cure ourselves with the healing herbs that are free for the taking. We need to protect our forests and our healing herbs and not allow greed and the sugar plantations to choke them into oblivion. (Scheper-Hughes 1992:525–6)

The parallel with the early European opposition to Arabic drugs is striking. Herbal medicines can thus become symbols of resistance to oppression. Natural medicines, in short, are not only regarded as safer and better because they are from nature but also because they are familiar, 'our own'. This is a striking contrast with another – more common – phenomenon that we came across before (chapter 3), the attraction of drugs which are foreign.

Conclusion

The 'unorthodox accounts' that Britten collected from a handful of respondents in London represent a growing weariness and doubt about medicines among people everywhere. They have second thoughts about the pills and other substances that were first welcomed as indispensable tools to keep healthy and stay in control of their lives. From medicines they turn into poison, from tokens of care into signs of neglect, from helpers into enemies of nature, from comfort into threat.

Scepticism towards medicines occurs not only in high-income societies where consumers have become more demanding and critical of the quality of medical services. It exists also in poor communities in the so-called non-Western world, where people, in some situations at least, regard Western pharmaceuticals as harmful, too powerful, aggressive and in conflict with local concepts of health and healing. Doubts can derive from increased biomedical knowledge among consumers, but may also arise in the lack of such knowledge leading to cultural misunderstanding and suspicion.

We have suggested that these themes can be understood as a kind of incipient cultural politics, in which medicines are used to place oneself critically in opposition to something, whether it is the doctor, the medical establishment, biomedical technology, or the power of cosmopolitan (Western) ways. Expressing scepticism about pharmaceutical drugs can be a way of asserting (or constructing) a contrast: nature versus scientific technology; the ancient Ayurvedic tradition versus Western modernity; individual agency versus professional authority; or even, the people versus international capitalism. Medicines are a strategic point for formulating such oppositions because they are commodities in a commercial system, elements of biomedical technology, as well as personal products for use on and in individual bodies. They are part of everyday life and also of national and international economy.

Part III

The providers

6   Drug vendors and their market: the commodification of health

Pharmaceuticals are commodities and they go the way of all commodities – the market. The sale of medicines flourishes in many forms, from e-commerce on the internet to the hawker selling pills on a crowded African bus. Many kinds of drugs are legally sold over the counter (OTC) or by prescription in licensed pharmacies. But everywhere in the world, there is an informal market in medicines where nominally restricted drugs are sold without a prescription by people not authorized to do so. In many countries of the South, this weakly regulated trade is an enormous business.

The trade thrives because there is a growing felt need for medication. People worldwide increasingly believe that they need a pill for every ill. This eagerness for medicine assures demand. The globalization of pharmaceutical production and marketing assures supply, and also cultivates desire for drugs. As we saw in chapter 2, habitual use of medicines is encouraged by advertising and the experience of their broad efficacy in social life. It is important to note, however, that popular enthusiasm for biomedical pharmaceuticals is even found in places where advertising and promotion barely reach.

Commodification of health is the term often used to denote the increasing use of pharmaceutical products to restore and maintain health. Researchers and social analysts point to the way that the focus on commodities obscures the economic, political and environmental factors that influence health. They are also concerned that the lively business of medicines escapes official control, so that medicines are misused and people waste money. The underlying issue is whether the state should be, or can be, the guardian of its citizens, regulating medicines as public goods, and restricting their circulation as free commodities. In this chapter we examine the issue of commodification by looking at drug sellers and their customers in the West African state of Cameroon. We concentrate on their concerns, as a way of grounding these analytical considerations.

In Ebolowa, a provincial capital in southern Cameroon, pharmaceuticals go to the market quite literally, as they do in many African towns.

Fig. 6.1 A woman passes and asks the price of white Folkologo (chloramphenicol) in a Cameroon market.

In the marketplace, among the stalls offering vegetables and household supplies, are those displaying capsules, vials and tablets. Van der Geest (1987, 1988, 1991) studied the informal sale of medicines in Ebolowa in 1980 and 1983.[1] His field notes provide a lively picture of the marketing of those valued commodities.

Notes from a Cameroon marketplace

Mr D. is an old man who sells Western medicines in one of the three markets of Ebolowa. He had been a cocoa farmer, but since losing one of his legs after an accident on his farm, he has tried to eke out an existence by selling medicines. Some forty different Western drugs are spread out on a small table in front of him. Of some kinds of medicine, only a small supply appears available, of others much more is in evidence. Some are in their original packing, others are in jars and boxes without a label. I estimate some 75 per cent of his products would fall under the category of 'prescription-only'.

Many people are passing by, those who arrive in town and those who are waiting for a taxi. Some people leave their luggage with the old man while they do their shopping. The 'market' is a covered place about 10 metres wide and 30 metres long. It holds an estimated ten booths where one can buy snacks, drinks and daily necessities. In two booths medicines are sold. Between the booths are wooden benches where people sit down to eat or relax in the shade, waiting for transport, conversing, or taking a nap.

During one of my visits to Mr D. I see a young man, looking through the vials of injectable antibiotics on the old man's table. He finds Almopen, notices its date of expiration – 1978 (five years ago) – and finally chooses Pénextilline. When I ask why he needs it, his answer is elusive. 'It is an antibiotic, you can use it for all kinds of things, rheumatism for example.' 'But what will you use it for?', I ask. 'It is not for myself, it is for my brother, I don't know why he needs it.' I: 'Why are you buying it here? Isn't there a dispensary in your village?' 'Under construction', he advises me. 'Moreover', he adds, 'the nurse is hardly ever at his post.' I ask him, 'Is the Almopen not good because the date has expired?' 'You can't use it any more for an injection', he answers, 'but it is still good for sprinkling onto a wound.' When I discuss this conversation later on with a pharmacologist, he comments that the sprinkling is not a bad idea.

Another young man buys two penicillin tablets (each 500,000 units). I ask why he needs them. He is a prisoner (some prisoners move freely in town and can be hired for work by the town's notables for very low wages). Yesterday he visited a woman and this morning, when he urinated, he felt pain. So he thinks he has caught '*chaude pisse*' (gonorrhoea). I ask him if two penicillin tables are sufficient. His answer is no, but he has no more money. In any event, two are better than none. He asks if I can help him. I give him 200 francs and he buys another two tablets. The doctor with whom I discuss this conversation says that no venereal disease symptoms could appear so quickly. Furthermore, a dose of four such tablets is not sufficient for treating gonorrhoea.

A middle-aged woman who speaks in pidgin asks for a remedy for filaria. D. says that he doesn't have anything. He tells her to try the pharmacy. But she complains that she doesn't know which medicine to ask for. Once again, I become aware of the fact that many people are inhibited to go to the pharmacy. You can't casually look around, pick up medicines, and ask: 'Have you got anything for filaria?' There are all sorts of people who stare at you, and the people behind the counter are different from yourself. They are not patient and friendly. You do not feel at ease. It is a bit like a hospital.

When I arrive at the market, Robert, the other medicine seller, is busy making plastic covers for identity cards. A lucrative job: one for 450 francs. Today, he also sells bananas. When I want to buy four, he refuses to accept my money. In addition, he sells notebooks, sunglasses, trinkets, safety pins, key hangers and portfolios. A woman passes and asks the price of 'white Folkologo' (chloramphenicol). That is 30 francs for one capsule. She leaves without buying. When I ask him about the price he explains that the price may vary depending on how many there are at the market.

A few days ago, he explained to me the difference between red-yellow and white Folkologo. Only the red-yellow capsules are tetracycline, but the people call both types Folkologo. The white ones are chloramphenicol. They are stronger but help only against stomach ache and wounds. Tetracycline is effective against twelve diseases, for example diarrhoea, bronchitis, abscesses, menstrual pains and gonorrhoea. 'When you want to sleep with a woman who you suspect of the disease, you should first take a capsule. That is the most important function of tetracycline.'

A soldier buys six capsules of Ampicillin Totapen. It is his daily dose for gonorrhoea. The price of six is 900 francs. The man wants to reduce the dose to four per day, because he can hardly pay, but Robert convinces him that he should take six, otherwise he will not get healed properly. For one and a half hours the soldier is the only customer who buys medicines. Robert tells him that he should not have sex while taking the medicines.

A taxi driver, in a hurry, buys something which is not openly offered for sale. Robert takes it from below the counter and they argue about the price. With a razor blade Robert cuts a medicine strip into two. I recognize the product: little silver bullets, Hovotest, a popular medicine to increase the libido. I ask the driver how much he has paid. 'Too much', he says, '2500 francs for eight pills.' That's why he was arguing. Later on I ask Robert why he hides the Hovotest. 'Because it is forbidden.' Sometimes they come to check and when they find it, he is in trouble. He does not know why it is forbidden. In actual fact, most of his medicines are 'forbidden'. I suspect that he hides them because they are expensive and policemen will be more inclined to 'confiscate' them for private use.

A man buys fifty tetracycline capsules for a reduced price, 10 francs per piece. He says he has an 'autorisation' to run a school pharmacy in his village. He regards himself as a first aid person in his community. He will sell the capsules for 20 francs. Other medicines in his possession are Nivaquin, chloramphenicol, penicillin (tablets and injections), Vermox, piperazine, Combantrin and Solaskil. He buys them from Robert, the official pharmacy in Ebolowa and from the Ministry in Yaoundé.

These observations show the kaleidoscopic character of the informal (and in most cases also illegal) sale of medicines. A wide variety of medications were available to customers trying to take responsibility for their health problems. Medicine vendors made a living while offering a convenient, friendly service for which there was considerable demand. How are we to understand this example of medicines in the market? Two aspects of the context for drug marketing in Ebolowa provide a beginning: first, the realities of health problems; and second, the articulation of the formal and informal sectors of health care.

The context of drug vending in Cameroon

Ebolowa is the capital of the Province (*Division*) of Ntem. For the majority of the population who lived in the surrounding villages, agriculture was the most important means of subsistence. Ebolowa, with its 20,000 inhabitants, was not only the administrative centre but also the main place of trade, education, medical care and other services.

The health situation in the villages left much to be desired. There was a shortage of clean drinking water and sanitary facilities. Pigs, goats and other domestic animals wandered freely around; refuse disposal was insufficient; and the housing was often of bad quality. Certain food habits, whereby the best food was reserved for the adults, especially the men, formed an extra threat to child health and was a cause of infant protein calorie deficiency. About 20 per cent of the children under five years were malnourished and 5 per cent were anaemic. Malaria and intestinal helminthiasis were the most common diseases for which the people in Ntem consulted the medical services. They were followed by skin diseases, colds and influenza, rheumatic complaints, bronchitis and gonorrhoea. Measles with complications such as pneumonia, malaria or encephalitis was by far the most important cause of death among children. Child (under five) mortality was estimated to be 150 per 1,000 and infant mortality 86 per 1,000.

The health care system upon which people relied to deal with these problems was a composite one. In Ntem Province there were three hospitals offering 450 beds altogether. The two largest, with a total of 400 beds, were both situated in the capital Ebolowa, about 5 kilometres apart. In addition to this, there were forty-five health centres and only one officially recognized pharmacy. Other facilities, especially primary facilities such as herbalists, traditional midwives, informal medicine sellers, neighbourly help and of course self-help, could not be expressed in figures. The formal sector included those facilities operated by or authorized by the state, while the informal part of the health care system comprised all the rest, including Mr D. and his colleagues selling medicinal commodities in the marketplace.

In his publications, Van der Geest has argued that the informal trade was intrinsically connected to the formal sector and could not be understood unless that articulation was taken into account.[2] The public health services did not function as they should. They were often short of medicines and other materials, and many of their nurses and doctors felt frustrated about their jobs: they could not do their work because of these shortages, their living conditions were often poor and their patients blamed them for not being able to provide proper care. Medicines and treatment in the public services were officially free of charge, but often patients had to pay something in order to get help. Not infrequently patients also discovered that no medicines were available and they had to travel to the nearest shop or pharmacy to buy the prescribed medications. 'Nearest' could mean up to a day of travel, including the time spent waiting for transportation. Sometimes they did not even find anyone present at the health centre. In actual practice, therefore, the so-called free service often proved to be quite expensive because it forced people to pay for transportation and to buy their medicines elsewhere. It also cost them considerable time.

Solutions to these problems were available in the *informal* private sector where medicines were traded. Those taking part in this trade constituted a heterogeneous group. Most were ordinary vendors who sold general provisions, including medicines, in shops and kiosks. In Ebolowa there were approximately seventy-five such shops and kiosks where one could purchase at least one or two types of medicines. A second category consisted of market vendors who sold medicines alongside other products. A third group could best be referred to as 'hawkers'. They travelled from village to village during the cocoa harvest season when the villagers had some extra money at their disposal. These hawkers provided a variety of articles in addition to medicines. A fourth category consisted of traders like Mr D. who specialized in the sale of medicines and had a much larger assortment than the previously mentioned groups. In Ebolowa four such traders were encountered. They not only sold medicines but also gave medical advice when asked. One of them gave injections as well. A fifth group comprised medical institution personnel. Some of them privately sold medicines which were supposed to be provided to the patients free of charge.

Sellers of medicines in the informal sector mainly obtained their products from three sources: medicines were smuggled into Cameroon from neighbouring Nigeria and distributed throughout the country; they were purchased – without prescriptions – from legally established pharmacies and sold at a profit; and they were bought from medical service personnel who thus tried to earn some extra income.

These private services – both formal and informal – were living proof of the malfunctioning of public health care. They existed because and where the public services did not achieve their objectives. Van der Geest estimated that about half of all modern health care delivery in Cameroon occurred outside the public (state-owned) services. The informal circuit had acquired a crucial position in daily health care, next to the private hospitals and health centres.

There were at least four reasons why informal drug vendors responded better to the needs of poor people than the formal institutions. All four were related to availability and attainability. First, drugs from vendors were more affordable. Clients could purchase as little or as much as they needed for self-treatment at that moment. Second, drug vendors were geographically more accessible than other sources. A vendor could always be found within a radius of a few kilometres from where one lived, but a pharmacy or health centre with drugs might be 50 or more kilometres away. Third, most vendors were available day and night. Their shops only closed when everybody had gone to bed; even after 'closing', it usually was possible to buy medicines if necessary. This flexibility contrasted sharply with the strict time schedule to which the formal services adhered. The fourth reason for the drug vendors' popularity was that the social distance between provider and client was much smaller than in the formal sector. In a shop it was possible to look around, examine various products and ask questions about how they should be used. Such behaviour was not possible in a hospital or professional, well-regulated pharmacy where social distance between users and providers was pronounced.

However, there were also disadvantages in buying from a drug vendor. Clients knew, for example, that the products they bought were often of inferior quality. The choice of medicines was limited and vendors were known to have little medical knowledge. The preference for a drug vendor should, therefore, be viewed within the context of the total range of therapeutic choices. People with a medical problem would first try a treatment which cost them little. Only when this failed, would other, more costly and more inconvenient, steps be taken.

In the next chapter, we examine the structure of health care provision more closely, by focusing on pharmacists, both licensed and 'acting'. The point we want to make here is that the process of commodification should be understood within the context of a particular health care system.

The commodification of health

The thriving sale of drugs in Ebolowa has parallels in many African settings. In towns and rural areas, medicines are sold in shops and markets, by vendors in bus and lorry parks, and by pedlars who pedal their bicycles from village to village (Alubo 1987; Fassin 1987; Akubue and Mbah 1989; Senah 1997; Whyte 2001). In Asia and Latin America, the business of medicines is equally or even more lively. Biomedical drugs are even sold by 'traditional healers', and 'traditional' or natural medicines are packaged and sold on the model of biomedical commodities (Afdhal and Welsch 1988; Miles 1998a; Wolffers 1988). The increasing availability of medicines as products for sale has been called commodification – a term that has been used in a variety of ways. (The form 'commoditization' is used by some authors in preference to commodification.) We would like to suggest that it embraces two important sets of processes.

Making medicines common

The first set of concerns has to do with the way medicines are made *common*. The theoretical approach here starts with cultural economics and focuses on the way things are imbued with use and exchange values. Appadurai (1986:9) suggests a definition of commodity as 'any thing intended for exchange'. His methodological focus on 'the social life of things' makes it possible to ask questions about their 'commodity-hood' (1986:13) – that is, when and how their exchange potential is realized.

Kopytoff (1986) proposes that we understand commoditization in terms of a contrast between the singular and the common:

> To use an appropriately loaded even if archaic term, to be saleable or widely exchangeable is to be 'common' – the opposite of being uncommon, incomparable, unique, singular, and therefore not exchangeable for anything else. (Kopytoff 1986:69)

He suggests that categories of things may be more or less commoditized (that is, more or less freely exchangeable). Money, as a technology of exchange, tends to facilitate commoditization; Kopytoff writes of the 'drive to commoditization' – 'to extend the fundamentally seductive idea of exchange to as many items as the existing exchange technology will comfortably allow' (1986:73). Kopytoff sees commoditization as a pressure exerted against cultural tendencies to particularize value.

The conventions that restrict certain kinds of drugs to professional control provide examples of the tendency towards singularization. Prescription-only drugs are discriminated as having a particular value. In Appadurai's terms they are 'enclaved commodities' whose social life is restricted in that they are not meant to be made common through free exchange. However, that is exactly what has happened in Ebolowa and many other settings. Drugs that are supposed to be dispensed by trained health workers in authorized medical facilities are 'illegally' bought and sold in free markets. Appadurai and Kopytoff give us abstract analytical frames for asking about the general commodity status of categories of medicine. Ethnography, like that from Cameroon, reveals the historical circumstances in which drugs become common when the public formal system, with its conventions and restrictions, is weakened and intertwined with the informal system of drug vendors.

The 'fundamental seduction' of commoditization is evident in an increasing commercialization of medicine. More and more types and forms of medicines are commonly available for sale. But this fundamental seduction takes the form of particular attractions in specific situations. As Van der Geest suggested, the residents of Ntem Province were charmed by the availability and easy attainability of the medicinal commodities offered by the vendors, which they compared to the shortages and restrictions of medicine in the formal sector where its commodity career was more limited. They liked the convenience of time and place; they appreciated being able to buy according to their means; they were persuaded by discussions in which they could participate.

In so far as commoditization makes medicines common, it makes them all the synonyms of common: popular, general, ordinary, familiar. In the Ebolowa market people were able to examine and handle a large variety of drugs; as commonalities they were up for discussion, open to interpretation and easy to acquire. Tetracycline, chloramphenicol and ampicillin are treated like bananas and safety pins – as ordinary wares. The implications of this are enormous: the drive to commoditization is a motor by which substances – materia medica – become more and more popular as ways of understanding and managing health and illness.

Making health a commodity

That leads to the second set of concerns about medicines as commodities, the critique that health itself is being commodified through the business of medicines. Here we move beyond a focus on the social life of things, to ask about the cultural and social implications of medicines as commodities. Are they being used in an attempt to solve problems that should be addressed in other ways? Are people deceived into thinking that health can be attained through medicinal commodities?

In the Ebolowa market, one could say that sexual health had been commodified. The taxi driver who bought the little silver bullets known as Hovotest was buying sexual potency, he hoped. Others purchased anti-biotics to prevent and treat sexually transmitted infections (STIs). The prisoner who had visited a woman the day before and now feared gon-orrhoea was trying to ensure sexual health by means of a commodity. In principle, there are other ways. He could have refrained from visiting the woman. The state could distribute free condoms and offer an effective programme of information, education and communication about STIs. Hospitals and health centres could avail user-friendly free treatment that would bring down the frequency of STIs and obviate the need to go shop-ping for antibiotics in the market. In practice, the other alternatives were purely hypothetical for the vendors and their customers. The question is whether they would have been pursued if sexual health had not been commodified in this way.

These were issues powerfully raised by Scheper-Hughes (1992) in her study of the violence of everyday life for poor urban people in north-eastern Brazil. She showed how poverty, hunger and worry were defined as medical problems and treated with drugs, in an argument similar to the medicalization issue discussed in chapter 4. 'If hunger cannot be satisfied, it can at least be tranquilized, so that medicine, even more than religion, comes to actualize the Marxist platitude on the drugging of the masses' (1992:202–3). She speaks of the complicity and bad faith of health workers and pharmacists who supply drugs to people in far greater need of decent living conditions. But she also writes of people's own faith in drugs which have a 'lethal attractiveness' as a means to fortify bodies ultimately weakened by social injustice (1992:200).

Nichter, who did fieldwork in India and Sri Lanka, extensively discusses the popular belief that health can be obtained and maintained through the consumption of commodities, medicines (Nichter and Nordstrom 1989; Nichter and Nichter 1996). Buying medicines is viewed as a 'quick fix', the most convenient and cost-effective way of taking care of one's health for those who do not have the time and the means to live a truly healthy life. Nichter emphasizes the 'false consciousness' involved in this type of behaviour: 'a false sense of health security is fostered by the inflated claims of medicines' (Nichter 1989:235). He introduces the term 'phar-maceuticalization', a process that he regards as a form of 'fetishization' (cf. Ellen 1988), attributing power to medicines beyond their active ingre-dients. Like Scheper-Hughes, he emphasizes that the focus on medicinal commodities is promoted by the pharmaceutical industry and supported by those with political power who want to be seen as providing health. But it distracts people from recognizing and dealing with the sources of their problems: 'The false consciousness generated by health commodification serves to undermine the impetus to participate in ecological-environmental based popular health movements in a context where they are of crucial and immediate importance' (Nichter 1989:235).

Yet Nichter also points out that the commodification of health through pharmaceuticals cannot be explained simply as an invasion by drug companies or a deception perpetrated by the politically powerful. His rich ethnography continually shows that people as social actors make use of commodities for their own ends. While they may neglect the political-economic sources of ill health, they are using commodities to deal with other problems. Nichter's writings contain two tendencies that Miller (1995) finds in much of the anthropological work on consumption and commodities: on the one hand, an ethical (moralizing) stance that sees commodification as a danger to be resisted; and, on the other, a recognition that commodities may be actively appropriated for social projects.

The cases Nichter describes are mainly set in bustling Asian cities with stark contrasts between poor and rich inhabitants. For the worker who cannot afford to stay home sick, a wonder pill or injection seems the best alternative. Hardon (1991), too, describes how people in the slums of Manila, facing the dilemma of poverty and poor health, see no better choice than consuming drugs. What may be irrational and harmful from a medical point of view, makes sense in a particular social and economic context.

Several factors promote the commodification of health, according to Nichter. The hectic pace of life in the city and the harsh working conditions increase the demand for tranquillizers; and the polluted environment motivates the use of medicines which clean the blood, remove gas and improve digestion. The easy access to medication – a doctor's prescription is not required – further encourages a high rate of routine self-medication.

Especially in the eyes of the poor, having money seems the best guarantee for good health, because one can buy medicines. Nichter illustrates this graphically with the reaction of a young boy who had the chance to peek into his first aid kit: 'He sighed and told me that with such medicines one could go anywhere without fear' (Nichter and Nichter 1996:275). Medicines seem to offer the possibility of control, as suggested in chapter 4. If life is uncertain and dangerous, there is security in these little but powerful objects. The prisoner in Ebolowa market, worried about the health consequences of having visited a woman the day before, was trying to exert some control over his situation.

Rejecting this attitude as false consciousness, bad faith, complicity or deception is not entirely justified. For people living in a hostile and unhealthy environment, using medicines may be the only means left to keep going and maintain their self-respect. Medicines are not only placebos in a medical sense, they also have social and political effects, as we saw in chapter 2. They are a way of coping with situations of social and economic stress. Reeler (1996), who carried out fieldwork in rural and urban communities in Thailand, points out that money, however little, can be a crucial mode of empowerment in the struggle for health. It allows people to make an exchange, to choose a commodity without being dependent on an inconvenient, patronizing and demeaning formal health care system.

Conclusion

The contrast between the throbbing life of an Asian city and the sleepy atmosphere of a Cameroonian rural town may look great, but both have shown us conditions in which commodification and pharmaceuticalization of health seem to flourish. In both situations environmental health is poor, sex is dangerous, food expensive, work insecure and proper health care difficult to come by, while pharmaceuticals are easy to get in local markets and simple kiosks around the corner. It is true that Mr D.'s forty different drugs do not resolve the problems of sanitation and nutrition in Ntem Province. But there, as elsewhere, commodification is a solution to other immediate difficulties in accessing health.

Ironically, the exaggerated expectations of pharmaceuticals keep not only the customers but also – even more so – the drug vendors going. To them, pharmaceuticals are not so much products to alleviate suffering and improve health but first of all things to sell and, for that matter, valuable ones. They, too, need them to survive. Commodification proves salutary to buyers and sellers alike.

7 Pharmacists as doctors: bridging the sectors of health care

Through the anthropological literature on pharmacists, drugstores and other shops selling medicines in developing countries runs a theme of ambiguity. Researchers puzzle about the difficulties of placing these practitioners and their practices in the framework of roles, categories and sectors that usually form the basis for analysis of health care systems. Are they folk or professional practitioners? Providers of health care or commercial entrepreneurs? Purveyors of modern biomedical knowledge or of lay concepts of treatment?

Pharmacists and drugstores are a strategic vantage point from which to consider health care systems precisely because they do not quite fit. After all, the point is not to sort phenomena into appropriate pigeon-holes within a model of the health care system. Rather the analytical task is to grasp underlying principles and overall patterns by asking useful questions about the criteria for making distinctions. To this end, the transactions of medicines between drugstore attendants, their customers and their suppliers are instructive.

One of the reasons why the sale of drugs by pharmacists in retail outlets is so challenging to system frameworks is that there is extreme variation in the shops and their operators. Drugs are sold in specialized pharmacies or chemist shops, at pharmacy counters in supermarkets, at medicine shops, and in ordinary provision stores that carry pharmaceuticals together with food and household items. The person behind the counter may be an accredited pharmacist with years of professional training, or a pharmacy assistant trained on the job, or simply a shop attendant familiar with medicinal products. In a global perspective, the role of pharmacist is an elastic one.

This chapter, like the previous one, is about the buying and selling of medicines. But whereas commodification was seen in chapter 6 as a force that avails medicines to consumers, here we want to look more closely at the way it affects health care systems. A customer in the Ebolowa market could deal with health problems in an impersonal way by buying a commodity, an object. Now we turn to the way health care is personalized

Fig. 7.1 'Almost like a doctor' is the way a customer describes her pharmacist: a pharmacy in Colombia.

through social relations. The concrete interactions between 'pharmacists', their customers and their suppliers can be understood at a more abstract level in terms of health care as a social system. Words like bridging, mixing, intersecting, articulating, mediating and brokering provide metaphors for the patterns we want to describe.

The position of pharmacists in Latin American health care

Several studies from Latin America focus on the bridging role of pharmacists and drugstores in the provision of health care. They show many common features, as we shall see. But here, too, we need to attend to differences in contexts (for example between big cities and rural areas). Whereas a large urban centre has professional pharmacists in some neighbourhoods at least, they are rare behind the counters of drugstores in poorer rural areas. In small towns and country shops, there is less professional information about the biomedically recommended use of drugs.

Conflation of roles in a Mexican city

Casi como doctor – almost like a doctor – is the way a customer described her pharmacist in the northern Mexican city of Juarez. The phrase captured so well the overlapping of roles that Kathleen Logan (1988) used it as the title of her article on the place of pharmacies in health care. Like many other researchers working in Latin America, Logan found that treatment with drugs bought from shops was the preferred response to most common symptoms of illness. While some people went to pharmacies with prescriptions to be filled, the vast majority simply purchased drugs that they knew about or that were suggested by the pharmacist. The pharmacists of Juarez were almost like doctors because they recommended drugs for the symptoms their customers described. But they were not quite doctors because they did not unilaterally decide on certain medications. As Logan says: 'Through discussion the pharmacist and client come to agree on which medication the client will purchase... [pharmacists] give information to enable people to choose among similar products' (1988:114).

Ciudad Juarez was a city of a million people when Logan carried out her fieldwork in 1980. It was a major industrial and tourist centre with a better standard of living than many other parts of Mexico. Logan's research was in an inner-city area with a variety of health care options including private physicians, public hospitals and health centres, and herbal curers. But pharmacists were the health professionals most frequently consulted by the people in her study. There were 200 pharmacies in the city, ranging from large chain stores in the downtown area to small, neighbourhood, one-man shops.

Two aspects of the legal regulation of pharmacy were important for understanding the role of pharmacists. First, many were not professionals. Mexico had a shortage of university-trained pharmacists, and it was therefore permitted for people without professional degrees, who had trained as pharmacy apprentices, to operate stores in rural areas. This category of 'second-tier pharmacist' was by far the most common, and even in cities like Juarez they ran local pharmacies. The university-trained pharmacists were more likely to be found in the large downtown stores. Second, 'prescription only' drugs were commonly sold without a prescription.

So why were pharmacies so popular as sources of health care? From informants' explanations and her own observations, Logan derived a series of reasons. Most important, people valued the advice they received from pharmacists. In drugstores, they could get recommendations for treatment, as well as information about different kinds of drugs. Whether they came to purchase a specific drug, or, in effect, used the pharmacist to get a diagnosis and prescription, they were able to ask questions and get guidance. At the same time, they were able to maintain more control over their own treatment. People are customers and not patients in pharmacies. Ultimately, they decide what treatment to buy. Pharmacists must respect their customers and try to please them if they are to stay in business.

Other reasons for the popularity of pharmacies in Juarez are similar to those that bring people to buy drugs in the Ebolowa market (chapter 6). They are cheap, convenient and comfortable. Pharmacists charge only for the medicine they sell; their advice, unlike that of the doctor, is free. They are found in every neighbourhood and have long opening hours; there are no long waits, no forms to fill out, and no time-consuming examinations. There is a lack of social distance between buyer and seller. (This is always relative of course. Some customers in Ebolowa felt more at ease buying from a market stall than from a pharmacy. In Juarez there was a difference between neighbourhood drugstores and the professionally manned pharmacies.) Many of the Juarez non-professional pharmacists were from socio-economic backgrounds similar to those of their clients. They did not intimidate with professional jargon, and they accepted, and even shared, their customers' concepts of health care. Neighbourhood pharmacists were familiar with the living conditions and health problems of their customers; often they lived in the same area.

Combining knowledge traditions in a Salvadoran small town

In western El Salvador Anne Ferguson (1988) examined the commercial pharmaceutical sector in a small town (pop. 11,300) she called Ascunción. It had a government health post and a doctor in private practice, and there was a public hospital with twenty-two physicians in a nearby town. Four pharmacies, as well as medicine vendors, pharmacy clerks working from their homes and spiritists, provided drugs. Ferguson focused on the pharmacies, which were the most important source of care for the poorer inhabitants of the town. While the middle- and upper-income families resorted to private doctors most often, the poorer people preferred pharmacies – even though treatment at the Health Post was free (Ferguson 1988:29). They valued the courtesy and convenience of pharmacy service; they also liked the variety of brand-name medicines available, in contrast to the unlabelled drugs distributed at the Health Post.

In El Salvador pharmacies were supposed to be manned by licensed pharmacists or certified pharmacy clerks. In practice, those behind the counter in Ascunción had no formal training; they had learned on the job. Two of the seven pharmacy clerks in these four shops were illiterate. None had more than a sixth-grade education. One attendant was the ten-year-old nephew of the owner. The owners themselves did not, or could not, provide professional supervision: although one owner was a licensed pharmacist, he was occupied with other business interests; another was a doctor, but he was bedridden. The two other owners had no professional training, having only reached the fifth grade in local schools (1988:30).

What kinds of information and knowledge guided the transaction of medicines in these shops? Product information in the form of package inserts or reference books was almost non-existent. Ferguson notes that at the time of her research many multinational drug companies had stopped including inserts in their prescription-only medications in order to discourage over-the-counter sales and self-medication. (Price (1989:908) reported the same restriction mandated by law in Ecuador.) Lacking training and written information, pharmacy attendants relied on product information provided by sales representatives from the pharmaceutical companies and distributorships that supplied their shops. These people were somewhat better educated than the attendants, but their training focused more on marketing and sales than pharmacy.

The lack of professional information on the drugs left space for integrating them into local ideas about drug use. As Ferguson says:

In a sense, pharmacy personnel in Ascunción serve as interpreters between different medical care traditions, gleaning what they can from information they receive regarding Western medications and relying to a large extent on shared cultural understandings of the nature and treatment of illness. (Ferguson 1988:31)

For example, pharmacy attendants sold tetracycline for colds, and also advised their customers to avoid 'cold' fruits and drinks and bathing, in accordance with local ideas about chest colds.

Ferguson sees pharmacies as the most important element in what she calls the 'commercial pharmaceutical sector' (which also includes other non-professional sources of biomedicines). She defines this as: 'the popular sector of medical care that has developed in response to the penetration of Western manufactured drug products and the disarticulation of elements in the Western biomedical tradition' (1988:21). The pharmaceuticals have been separated from the information that was intended to guide their use, and from the control of authorized professionals such as prescribing physicians and trained pharmacists. In this sector, the practitioners are shop owners, pharmacy attendants, sales representatives, injectionists and vendors of medicine.

They are neither indigenous nor Western practitioners, but rather popular sector representatives who combine alternative and Western knowledge of disease process and cure and whose practices bridge the medical and business sectors of society. (1988:22)

The pharmacy as crossroads on a Guatemalan plantation

Sheila Cosminsky, who carried out research on a plantation in western
Guatemala in the 1970s with follow-up work in 1993, emphasized the
nodal position of the pharmacy in the title of her article: 'All Roads Lead
to the Pharmacy' (1994). She saw pharmacies as linked to the whole
range of health care providers in the area. Doctors in the nearby towns
wrote prescriptions to be filled at the pharmacy. So did spiritists like
Don Manuel who, when possessed by the spirit of an 'invisible doctor',
prescribed either herbal medicine or drugs to be purchased from the pharmacy (Cosminsky 1994:110). Lay injectionists and travelling medicine
vendors bought their supplies from the town pharmacy too.

For people living on the plantation, the most convenient source of
pharmaceuticals was Marina's store. Marina was a 'lay pharmacist' and
'lay injectionist'; she obtained her medicines from a pharmacist in town
who explained about how to use them. Such information was in turn
passed on in the advice she gave to the customers seeking drugs at her
rural shop. When Cosminsky returned to the area in 1993, she found
that people were, if anything, more dependent on shops and pharmacies
as sources of health care. Wages had not kept pace with the increase
in doctors' consultation fees, so many found it cheaper to seek health
care directly from the pharmacy. Folk healers continued to incorporate
pharmaceuticals from pharmacies in their practices, a process (which
Cosminsky termed 'sacralization') whereby medicines were included in
spiritual practices.

The pharmacies and shops in this part of Guatemala offered a range
of products from patent medicines to injectable antibiotics. They sold
'mixtures, elixirs, and oils' that were local remedies, including *cordial de
susto*, for the fright sickness that is part of popular concepts of illness.
Thus they not only shared local concepts of illness; they also offered
local medicinal products in addition to the synthetic pharmaceuticals
manufactured by the multinational drug companies.

Summing up the role of the pharmacist in Guatemala, Cosminsky calls
him/her a 'cultural broker':

> he is actually mediating three levels: the multinational drug companies and inter-
> national biomedicine, the national level and the community level. In Guatemala
> he is also mediating three different medical systems or traditions: biomedicine,
> Ladino popular medicine, and Indian popular medicine. (1994:112)

Regulation: quasi-legal shops and shadowy practices

The problem of analysing the role of pharmacists and drugstores is especially acute in countries where the legal regulation of pharmacy and drug

sales is lax, while need and demand for drugs are high. In such situations researchers have used terms like 'quasi-legal' to describe the operations of shops retailing drugs. One way of analysing a health care system is in terms of state control. The distinction between the 'formal' and the 'informal' sectors is based on the criterion of state recognition and authorization. Just as we speak of a second, informal or parallel economy that is not regulated directly by the state, so one can also point to the informal sector of health care.

The opposition between formal and informal is not necessarily a simple one. Anthropologists studying bureaucracy have long emphasized the informal in the formal; fixed structures of authority and procedure cannot actually survive without informal relations and methods that adapt ideals to reality. In the case of health care systems, particularly but not only where the state does not play a strong regulatory role, the articulation of the formal and informal is complex. The channels, activities and personnel through which drugs flow can be formal or informal or some combination of the two (Streefland and Hardon 1998).

As we saw in the case of Juarez, the issue of regulation concerns the classification of shop attendants, as well as their practices of drug provision. Like Mexico, El Salvador and Guatemala, most countries restrict the sale of prescription drugs to pharmacies manned by certified pharmacists. But where there is a shortage of such professionals, exceptions may be made in order to ensure the availability of drugs in peripheral areas. Sometimes a category of pharmacy assistant is recognized and allowed to operate shops in underserved areas. (Though, as in Juarez, they may extend their sphere to urban areas as well.) Often the person behind the counter does not have state-recognized qualifications, even when a pharmacist owns the shop or is supposed to be attending it.

Shops themselves are classified and allowed to sell certain categories of drugs. Those that are permitted to sell restricted drugs are supposed to require a doctor's prescription. But it is extremely common that they sell antibiotics and other prescription-only drugs on demand. Laurie Price (1989) spoke of pharmacies in Ecuador as constituting 'a shadow system of biomedicine' where prescription drugs were sold without prescriptions in what she termed 'no-doc sales'. Wolffers (1987) found that all of the twenty-eight pharmacies he studied in Colombo, Sri Lanka, sold the restricted antibiotic tetracycline to customers who asked for it. However, they were sensitive about it and about their lack of training when questioned by researchers. In contrast, such practices were so accepted in Quito when Price worked there that neither drugstore clerks nor customers seemed bothered by her recording of sales (half of customers buying prescription medicines showed no prescription.) As she remarks, 'Self medication is so much a part of the cultural fabric that

Ecuadorians do not regard it as a practice to conceal' (Price 1989: 909).

Almost like a doctor: social relations of therapy

In drugstores, medicines are transacted between providers and customers. One of the key analytical issues is the nature of the relation between these two parties. We have already seen that customers in Juarez valued pharmacists as providers of advice and treatment. To place this issue in a larger frame, let us consider the position of drugstore keepers and their customers within the model of the health care system proposed by Arthur Kleinman (1980:49–60).

Kleinman distinguished between the professional, folk and popular sectors of the health care system, on the basis of types of social relations and associated clinical realities. In the professional sector, patients consult authorized practitioners, who have undergone text-based formal training and obtained certification. As professionals they have some degree of organization; their training and regulation involve bureaucratic institutions that are characteristic of the professional sector. They are obligated to practise according to accepted technical and ethical standards. Their monopoly on esoteric knowledge and skills colours their relationships to their patients or clients. Folk practitioners, too, have specialized knowledge and skills, not available to lay people. But their training is not institutionalized, and their legitimacy rests on the recognition given them by clients, rather than on authorization by a state or professional bureaucracy (MacCormack 1986). They are thus more dependent on their clients/patients; they tend to share ideas and values with lay members of their communities and with what Kleinman calls the popular sector. Popular health care involves family members, neighbours and friends – non-specialists whose relations with one another are not defined in terms of needs for health care. They exchange knowledge and medicines as part of shared understandings of the world and ordinary social interchange.

Where national regulations are enforced and where there are sufficient numbers of trained pharmacists, transactions in pharmacies have many characteristics of the professional sector. Pharmacists act as gatekeepers, regulating access to prescription drugs, and dispensing doses of professional instruction together with medicines. They have their particular roles within the division of professional labour that characterizes health care. There is a certain formality in the relation between professional pharmacists and their customers that derives from the pharmacists' adherence to set procedures. The authority of the professional pharmacists is anchored in years of training and in their special relationship to doctors, who recognize their skills and rights. This authority may enhance social distance between them and their customers.

In the situations described above, however, the kind of health care provided by drugstores is less clearly within the professional sector. In these examples, pharmacy personnel are specialists, in that they are recognized by their customers as knowledgeable about drugs. But because their training is 'on the job' rather than based in educational institutions, they are more like folk practitioners. They are not so constrained by bureaucratic concerns or by the technical knowledge fixed in textbooks and authorized by a professional institution.

At the same time, we must bear in mind that the distinction between different categories of professional and folk practitioners, mandated by the state and used here as an analytical tool, is not necessarily recognized by local actors. As Price reported, many people in the community where she worked thought of drugstore clerks and pharmacists as physicians: 'it appears that many Ecuadorians operate with a different cognitive model of professional credentials than that held by professionals themselves' (Price 1989:908). They were not so concerned with which categories of professionals were authorized to do what. They valued the range of services on offer at drugstores – the combination of consultation, treatment and drug provision. So did the customers at retail pharmacies interviewed by Igun in Maiduguri, Nigeria. Documenting that they used the pharmacies as clinics, he concluded that

> pharmacy in Africa has encroached more and more into areas of activity that are legally the preserve of the medical profession – that of diagnosis and treatment. The utilization pattern demonstrates that the population sees nothing wrong with this encroachment . . . There may well be need to review the whole issue of division of labour in health care in the African context, given the realities demonstrated by this study. (Igun 1987:695)

Sometimes a drugstore actually has a professional doctor or trained health worker on the premises. Many urban drugstores in Nepal have a room where a physician holds consultations for a few hours every day. In Uganda, rural drugshops are often manned by medical assistants, nurses or midwives whose professional training is in the provision of health care rather than the dispensing of drugs. But more often, the person selling medicines takes on an expanded role for which he or she has not been trained. Injections and even intravenous drips may be administered in drugstores. Wounds may be dressed. Most important, customers consult drugstore personnel about their symptoms in order to get suggestions about appropriate medicines. And they discuss the medicine that they have been using or want to use – its suitability, qualities, effectiveness, side-effects, dosage and price. Because drugstore personnel are so orientated towards pleasing their customers, even trained health care professionals may behave more like folk practitioners in these settings (Whyte 1992).

Drugstore personnel are thus providers of health care for their customers. They are accessible specialists – whether folk or professional practitioners. More than that, they are also facilitators of popular health care. By furnishing medicines of whatever kind for people to take home and use, they provide input to the popular sector of health care, where people treat themselves and give each other medicines as family members and friends. Drugstores are also retail outlets where lay people can obtain the means to care for themselves.

Trying to think about shop transactions of medicines in terms of the sector model of the health care system raises the issues of authority, specialized knowledge and skills, and power relations. As Kleinman suggests, ultimate responsibility for health care lies in the popular sector in that decisions about seeking help are taken there. Acknowledging the authority of professionals may mean accepting their decisions about which drugs to take, why, when and how. In return one hopes to benefit from their specialist knowledge. Going to a drugstore to seek health care allows one to retain more control while still taking advantage of the knowledgeability of the retailer, whether certified pharmacist or experienced drugstore attendant.

The ambiguous and multi-faceted position of the drugstore in the health care system is being recognized in current policy discussions. In developed countries, pharmacists no longer compound drugs, nor do they count and package them. Pharmacists have become retailers who are 'overtrained for what they do and underutilised in what they know' (Gilbert 1995:126). 'Extended roles' for 'community pharmacists' are on the agenda. In South Africa, pharmacists serving the 'first world' part of the population discuss expanding their activities to health promotion, immunization, prescribing in acute cases, and administering injections (1995:128–9). The debate on 're-professionalization' through training for new roles would turn first world pharmacy in the direction drug retailing has already taken in many developing countries. There the problem is not retraining of pharmacy professionals, but providing some training for the many non-professionals staffing drugstores and selling drugs in provision shops (Kafle et al. 1992; Marsh et al. 1999). Such training entails a certain degree of official recognition, to which some professionals and policy makers object (Whyte and Birungi 2000).

More like a shopkeeper: commerce and medicine

If drugstores fit uneasily into the sector model of the health care system, they are ambiguous in another way as well. They are at once business enterprises and health care facilities. They should earn money while also providing effective help for people in need. Where pharmacies are operated by professionals, there is a potential conflict between professional and commercial roles; good professional practice is supposed to prevail over crude profit motives. Where professionalism is not so pronounced, the business aspect of pharmaceutical transactions shapes the way medicines move between people in drugstore settings. In fact, it is this commercial aspect that accounts for the way drugshop interactions slip across the professional, folk and popular sectors of health care.

Some researchers have focused attention on the way pharmacists maximize profit by selling many and inappropriate drugs and promoting drugs with high profit margins (Cederlöf and Tomson 1995). While anthropologists recognize this tendency, they draw attention to other aspects of the shopkeepers' practice as well. Retailers of pharmaceuticals must attract and keep customers. Even more than market vendors and travelling salesmen, drugstore retailers have regular customers whom they need to please. Sometimes this means accepting the customers' demands to buy fewer or cheaper drugs, or to give credit – practices that do not maximize profit in the short run, but may allow the shop to survive. Keeping customers requires treating them in a friendly manner, answering their questions and accepting their views. Sometimes it means selling what they want to buy even though the retailer does not think it is the best treatment. Thus satisfying the customer can undermine the specialist competence of the provider. This tendency is counterbalanced by the respect many customers have for the drugstore attendant's knowledge. Thus the interaction may take the character of a negotiation, as Logan noted in her study of pharmacies in Juarez.

Pharmacists and drugshop attendants have other kinds of interactions concerning medicines as well. For they must buy as well as sell pharmaceuticals. As we saw in the case of Ascunción, sales representatives from large pharmaceutical firms may be significant here. Anne Ferguson (1988:31) found two kinds of sales reps in this part of El Salvador; one category visited drugstores only, while another (somewhat better educated) visited physicians as well. Since all sales reps were highly dependent on commissions, they pushed their company's products with vigour. Ferguson emphasized the role played by the sales reps in providing information about drugs (information of dubious quality, she thought), and she also showed how their sales practices affected the pattern of retail drug provision to customers. Through promotion campaigns, incentives and special offers, the pharmaceutical companies influenced the prices and kinds of drugs on offer (1988:33–5).

One of the very few ethnographic studies of sales representatives was carried out in Bombay (Kamat and Nichter 1997, 1998). In this metropolitan setting, medreps (as they are called here) were primarily aiming at physicians. But Kamat and Nichter show that pharmacies were key links in their work. During the middle of the day, when physicians were not in their offices and trade was slower in the shops, the medreps worked the drugstores to find out which doctors were prescribing their firm's products and which products were moving well, and in general to do market research. The medreps recognized the way pharmacies linked physicians to consumers of medicines, and also the roles they played in selection of drugs by customers for self-medication. For the medreps, the pharmacies were not just retailers; they were also valuable sources of information about the market. Whereas Ferguson emphasized reps as providers of knowledge to drugstores, Kamat and Nichter showed that information also flowed the other way. Here, too, we see that drugstores and their personnel provide a bridge between health care (in this case the professional and popular sectors) and the world of business.

Drugstores are links in another way as well, for they are part of a chain of wholesale and retail that supplies drugs to many different niches. In developing countries, smaller shops purchase their medicines from larger ones, and 'informal providers' buy medicines from drugstores that may even be licensed. In the small town of Ascunción, two of the drugstores studied by Ferguson got their supplies from pharmacies in a nearby city. In the rural area of Guatemala where Cosminsky worked, not only shop-keepers like Marina but also travelling medicine vendors and injectionists bought their supplies of pharmaceuticals (including injectables and intra-venous fluid) from pharmacies in town. Thus retailers are also wholesalers for smaller-scale providers of medicines.

Conclusion

The unique position of the drugstore as a link between different sectors of the health care system, and as part of a chain of business connections, allows it to play a crucial role in the cultural dynamics of health care. In concluding this chapter, we can sum up the factors that facilitate processes of communication, integration and change.

Drugstore personnel communicate with their customers about drugs. As Nichter pointed out, it is often the chemist who educates the patients as to the purpose of multiple medicines, the importance of following a course of medication and the dangers of misusing a medication by tampering with dosage. It is the chemist who must reason with the patient within a set of economic constraints . . . the health education role of the chemist may prove as important, if not more important, than that of the practitioner. (Nichter 1989:224)

Because communication in a store is likely to take the form of a dialogue, it may be particularly effective. The retailer, more than a doctor, is likely to discuss price, alternative products and relative value, thus balancing purely clinical considerations with other concerns that are important to lay people. In a shop, customers can look at the range of products, pick them up, ask questions, check other shops and come back later. In this way too, they are good learning environments.

Because of the dependence of shops on their customers, personnel listen to them. They try to stock what customers want and they are aware of the values and meanings that influence customer choice. In some settings this leads to a product range that includes biomedical pharmaceuticals and medicines from other traditions, as Cosminsky found in Guatemala. Nichter (1989:191) noted a similar tendency in southern India, where drugstores stocked both Ayurvedic and allopathic medicines, and where customers were not necessarily concerned about the difference. Thus the mixing of cultural traditions of knowledge proceeds because the social situation of the store promotes integration. The drugstore attendant makes medicines accessible and relevant to the values and concerns of people's everyday lives.

Drugstores and their attendants are strong forces for the popularization of pharmaceuticals. In concrete terms, they provide the premises on which drugs and knowledge are transacted. They are user-friendly, and make access to drugs and advice convenient. In more abstract terms, they bridge and integrate professional and popular sectors of health care; they link local communities to international flows of products and ideas. Urban pharmacies, neighbourhood drugstores, and small rural shops are the channels through which popularization proceeds.

8   Injectionists: the attraction of technology

In popular English, the term 'technology' is commonly associated with tools and techniques. Upon reflection, however, it is evident that artefacts only have significance in the hands of people. Thus, at its Alma Ata conference in 1978, the World Health Organization defined technology as 'an association of methods, techniques, and equipment... together with the people using them'. The original Greek root of the word, *techné*, meant 'practical art', a concept that suggests intentions, uses and goal-directed projects. Technologies comprise people and objects in social relations expressed in purposeful activities (Pickstone 1994:14).

Recent approaches to technology go further in emphasizing that such complexes have a social history and social ramifications. The purposeful relations of people and things take on meaning and become routinized. Together they co-produce effects. This is not technological determinism in the old sense that archaeologists and social evolutionists once debated. Current studies of technology rely on participant observation and are keenly attuned to the implications of technologies for people's lives and their contested interpretations.

In this chapter we examine these matters through the example of the technology of pharmaceutical injections in Uganda. There, as in many developing countries, injections are enormously popular and widely used. They constitute a spectacular example of the dynamics of Western medical technology. The Ugandan story is fascinating, because it shows how medicinal technology was shaped by, and shaped, its particular cultural and social setting.

Injections in the changing Ugandan health care system

The hypodermic syringe was introduced in the 1850s by a Scottish physician, Alexander Wood (Howard-Jones 1971). It was rapidly accepted in Europe and America, by lay and medical people alike, and led to many new developments in materia medica (Haller 1981:1,678). Within a few decades the technique was passed into the hands of people on the frontiers

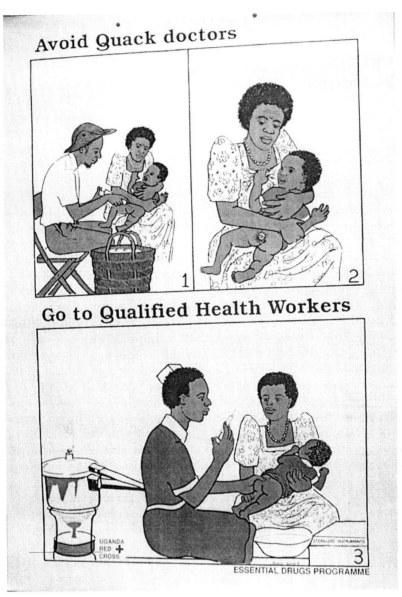

Fig. 8.1 Injections are iconic of biomedical pharmaceuticals. Uganda Red Cross poster for the Essential Drugs Programme.

of Western medicine. In 1899 Dr Albert Cook, the pioneer of biomedicine in Uganda, wrote about Semei Kasaja, a former patient whom he was training: 'He is very intelligent and quick at catching anything up. He takes the temperatures, night and morning marking off the decimal point quite correctly, and I have just taught him to give the hypodermic injections' (quoted in Iliffe 1998:21). Nearly a hundred years later, Harriet Birungi's research on injection practices in Uganda revealed that the majority of households had their own hypodermic equipment and that the technique that Dr Cook had imparted to Mr Kasaja was common knowledge. Injections had been domesticated, as Birungi showed with hard numbers and rich descriptions.

Glimpses of the early history of injections in Uganda show how they became standard practice within about thirty years. The earliest European practitioners of biomedicine there treated syphilis by mercury injection. By 1913, five 'deft, intelligent, patient' young Ugandan men had been trained to recognize venereal disease and give intramuscular injections of mercury (Iliffe 1998:33). With the discovery of Salvarsan, an organic arsenical compound effective against syphilis, and the spread of biomedical facilities in the 1920s and 1930s, 'heroic' (daring and risky) treatment became common in the form of 'rigorous course[s] of arsenical injections' (1998:52). A safer and cheaper bismuth compound for intramuscular injection against yaws was widely administered by African dressers (White 2000:101, 107–8). Quinine injections had been given to malaria patients since the early 1900s (Foster 1970:39), and injections were also used to treat sleeping sickness. In 1934 there were eighty-eight sub-dispensaries in rural areas of Uganda with 1.4 million attendances. 'The charge attendant is required to be capable of diagnosing common diseases, and to administer routine treatment by intramuscular, intravenous, or subcutaneous injection, or by the use of stock mixtures' (Thomas and Scott 1935:304–5). Thus even before the Second World War, many Ugandans were familiar with injections. After the war, injectable antibiotics like penicillin and antimalarials like chloroquine became available in East Africa. Treatment of tuberculosis involved daily injections of streptomycin for two months. Biomedical facilities dispensed great numbers of injections. No wonder that people came to expect them; nor is it surprising that people regarded them as strong treatment, since they were routinely given for serious diseases.

The colonial authorities in Uganda encouraged the training of African medical staff and the establishment of a system of government health care. Especially in Buganda, biomedicine was indigenized early on.[1] Mulago Medical School was the prestigious centre for training and research in East Africa right up until 1970. But alongside the formation of the medical profession, a struggle developed about ethics and control over injections. 'The problem was worst in Uganda, where from the mid-1930s the authorities campaigned against former medical staff who sold black-market drugs or, more seriously, gave injections' (Iliffe 1998:53–4). There were complaints that staff in government health facilities stole syringes and charged patients for injections. A medical student was expelled in 1947 for giving illegal injections. In the religious revival of the late 1940s, several 'saved' health workers confessed to wrongdoing concerning injections. One doctor, who had a private practice in addition to his government job, regretted that 'Really I was an "injection-monger" and not a doctor for the poor and ignorant' (1998:85, see also 53).

Reports of disciplinary actions and heartfelt confessions of sin suggest a persistent effort to keep injections from becoming common commodities. But it was a losing battle. 'By the 1950s the repression of needle men and drug sellers was increasingly difficult, as can be seen from amendments to the law raising the penalties and specifically outlawing injections' (1998:134). By the late 1960s, when Whyte began her fieldwork in eastern Uganda, there were 'needlemen' (*ab'episyo*) in every neighbourhood, who had acquired hypodermic equipment and provided illegal injections of penicillin (Whyte 1982). Yet getting the vials of injectable medicine, and the needle and syringe, was still not so easy. There were no shops openly selling these items in the rural areas. Needlemen and government health workers providing injections privately had access to channels not open to everyone.

This situation changed radically during the 1980s. The years of political tyranny and instability (1971–86) saw the decline of government health services, and by the late 1980s Ugandans had worked out private health care alternatives. Small drug shops and storefront private clinics sprang up everywhere (Whyte 1991). Even as the government health system revived with major donor support, the parallel system continued to flourish. Complaints about government health workers were rife and they in turn were bitter and demoralized about their poor conditions of service and inadequate pay. To survive, they engaged in private income-generating activities, mostly selling drugs and services (Asiimwe *et al.* 1997). In fact, government employees owned many of the small drug shops and clinics. In this process, injection equipment and injectable medicines became ordinary commodities, sold in neighbourhood outlets as well as government facilities. Injections were more widely used than ever before.

The popularity of injections in Uganda

Harriet Birungi undertook ethnographic fieldwork on injections from 1992 to 1993. The health care system described above was one important context of her work. The other was the AIDS epidemic and the international, national and local reactions to it. Uganda has been rightly praised for its response to the epidemic, especially for its massive public education campaign. But Birungi shows an unplanned consequence of this admirable effort. The first warnings stressed the dangers of sharing needles, a mode of transmission that was well known from research in North America. Although the messages stated that sterilization made needles safe, there seems to have been widespread doubt about sterilization. Health workers and lay people alike fastened on the hazards of risky needles that had been used on anonymous patients with unknown diseases (Birungi 1994a:127). Interestingly, the popularity of injections did not decline. Instead people found other ways of managing the danger of this valued technology.

In a sample of 360 households, Birungi found that in 25 per cent at least one person received an injection within a two-week period. The figure was 34 per cent in the 120 urban households; people in remote rural areas regretted that they could not afford more injections. Of the injections received, slightly more than a third were given in the non-profit government health units. The rest came from private providers and 17 per cent were administered at home. For those who went to a treatment facility, the likelihood of being injected was high; a survey of 420 consultations in fourteen public and private treatment facilities showed that seven patients out of every ten received an injection (Birungi 1994a:49–52). Such high levels of injection use are striking, but not so unusual in injection-keen developing countries. What was truly unique about Birungi's findings was the proportion of homes that had their own injection equipment and injectable medicine. In eastern Uganda where she worked, 63 per cent of households possessed needles and syringes, while 21 per cent had vials of injectable medicine on hand. A parallel survey, in a slightly more affluent area of western Uganda, found that 83 per cent had equipment and 34 per cent had injectable medicine at home (Birungi *et al.* 1994:15). Birungi concluded that injections were household utilities (Birungi 1994b).

The medicines injected in eastern Uganda were almost exclusively chloroquine and penicillin, pharmaceuticals that are high on Uganda's essential drug list, given the heavy morbidity and mortality from malaria and bacterial infections. Some people (about 20 per cent in the survey) took these two drugs combined in one injection. But in general, and perhaps given the limited choice, there was not much interest in which drug to take. Examination and diagnosis were weak even in health centres, and drugs were suggested according to symptoms.

A father and 2-year old son visit the health center. The child has vomiting and diarrhoea with some blood stains. The Assistant then inquires from the father whether the faeces had any worms or whether they were stinking. The man replies that he was not so particular at his observation, but of course the faeces smelt badly. The Medical Assistant then prescribes 2 chloroquine injections and crystalline penicillin, six hourly injection (until vomiting stops). Later the Medical Assistant tells me that the majority of such cases with diarrhoea and vomiting, normally have *omusudha* ['fever'] or 'measles'. (Birungi 1994a:43)

When Birungi herself fell ill with fever and joint pains, she described her symptoms to the practitioner at a private clinic in a small town. 'Without any examination the doctor prescribed three quinine injections, claiming that "today's *omusudha* can only heal with an injection"' (1994a:44). The term *omusudha* was the most common illness label, covering a wide variety of symptoms, including those of malaria. And injections were the treatment of choice for *omusudha*.

Injections were said to go directly into the blood, unlike tablets that, like food, pass out through defecation and vomiting. Since many diseases were thought of as 'in the blood', injections were seen as a more direct treatment. Chloroquine for fever was the most common medicine, and for small children injections were easier to administer because the tablets were bitter and easily vomited. Although national policy encourages oral forms of medication, people did not see tablets and injectables as alternatives. Rather injectables were perceived as the strongest medicine, the treatment of choice when tablets did not suffice (1994a:55). They were the prototype of biomedical therapy to the extent that people who went to a health unit and did not receive an injection were heard to remark that they did not get treatment.

Injection technology and social relations of health care

Birungi was not simply interested in the meanings of injections themselves. As a student of technology, she wanted to see the equipment and technique in use between social actors. And this oriented her towards qualities of social relationships. She found a widespread mistrust of government health care institutions and the workers there who were seen as impersonal and uncaring. Knowing the health worker personally, or paying money for special attention, might ensure that care was taken, her informants said. But otherwise, there were many remarks about government health workers who cheated patients by injecting them with water or giving them an underdose. People did not have confidence in the reliability of sterilization procedures carried out by staff who were underpaid and not committed to their jobs.

Surprisingly, not even the health workers are confident in their own equipment . . . At a government rural health center, amidst patients, I was astounded to see a nurse decline an injection administered using one of the reusable needles and syringes provided at the facility. She insisted on returning home to collect her personal equipment. (1994a:114)

Injection technology had been caught up in a process of personalization. People assumed that what was public and belonged to no one in particular was not cared for; therefore they mistrusted it (1994a:107). They were reluctant to be injected with the reusable needles and syringes provided at the health unit. But personal attachment gave people a sense of control. Bringing their own needle and syringe to a government facility was one way of personalizing treatment there. One old man refused to accept 'government injections' ('We know you health workers, you are good at injecting others with AIDS'). Nor would he allow the staff to sterilize the disposable syringe he had brought from home in an old dirty cardboard box. It was his, given to him by his daughter, and he did not see why it could not be used as it was: 'This is my injection', he said. 'I know it, I have used it recently to inject PPF [penicillin] and it worked' (1994a:141).

Personalization also involved seeking treatment from someone known. This could be a relative or neighbour, a local injectionist, or the proprietor of a nearby drug shop or storefront clinic. Or it might be a nursing aide from a government health facility, such as Maama John, who administers injections at her home when she is off work. Since she also sells agricultural produce and homemade alcohol, her house is a sociable place where people chat about many things including their illnesses and treatment (1994a:87–8). The value of personalization was well captured by one student who wrote: 'When I get an injection from a relative I know it is good. It is a real person whom I know who has injected me ... the provider knows that we share the same blood, so he has to inject me with one heart' (1994a:121). The quality of the injection thus depended on who gave it. This was sometimes concretized in the notion that some injectionists have a 'good hand' – their injections were effective and did not develop abscesses. But most important was the familiarity and concern of the person. Mukama, a popular itinerant injectionist, was praised because: 'He knows us and understands our local disease.' One day he visited Monica, a girl suffering from *omusudha*. He boiled the needle and syringe provided by her grandmother and injected Monica with 150 mg of chloroquine. The old woman told Birungi: 'Mukama is such a wonderful man – he has a good hand at treating *omusudha* and has saved many lives in the village.' In the next home Mukama injected a man whose family he had been treating for ten years. When Mukama joked that the man might have AIDS, the patient responded: 'Let it come, you will help me fight it.' He knew he would feel better by evening because: 'With Mukama's injections you are sure of recovering fast' (1994a:110). The long-standing relationship with local families, and his friendly manner, instilled trust in Mukama.

The social relations of therapy were central to understanding the technology of injections in Uganda. But it is also important to recognize the social history of the equipment itself. The sheer number of needles and syringes in today's Uganda is enormous. While the policy of the Essential Drugs Programme and the Extended Programme of Immunization is to supply reusable (fully sterilizable) equipment to the government health units, curative treatment is often with disposable needles and syringes. During the 1980s, relatively cheap disposables became widely available in Uganda. Patients are encouraged to buy their own, either at the unit, where they are sold privately, or from one of the many shops carrying them. Once patients have been injected, the equipment is given to them to take home. They can bring it again next time, or use it to have an injection from someone they know. Practically all disposable needles and syringes are reused. Bringing one's own injection equipment fits with the general development of a do-it-yourself ethos at government health units. Patients are expected to supply their own requirements – a plastic sheet for childbirth, paper for writing the diagnosis and prescription, and often the drugs for their treatment. So the fear of contracting AIDS from 'public' needles fitted into a situation where public provision of equipment and supplies was already declining. The widespread home ownership of needles and syringes must be understood in this light.

The cultural appropriation of technology

The popularity of injections in developing countries has been attested for a long time in reports of administrative and medical officials. The theme entered anthropology as a topic when Cunningham (1970) published an article about 'injection doctors' in Thailand – specialists in injecting who provided the service for people at home. Since then, there have been numerous references to injection in the anthropological literature on medicines and health care, as well as one edited collection (Bloem and Wolffers 1993) and several more programmatic overview articles about the challenges that this topic poses to anthropologists working in non-Western cultures (Reeler 1990, 2000; Whyte and Van der Geest 1994).

What are these challenges? Injections are iconic of biomedical pharmaceuticals; as smoke indicates fire, injections stand for the powerful substances and procedures of biomedicine. They are forms of technology in the sense proposed by Pfaffenberger (1988:249): 'Technology, defined anthropologically, is not material culture but rather a *total* social phenomenon in the sense used by Mauss, a phenomenon that marries

the material, the social and the symbolic in a complex web of associations.' 'It has a legal dimension, it has a history, it entails a set of social
relationships and it has a meaning' (1988:244). Thus the challenge is not
simply to explain the popularity of injections, but to analyse them in their
interlinked dimensions.

As students of culture, anthropologists ask how people themselves
make meaning of the equipment and procedure. Piercing the body to
introduce a healing substance (or to remove a 'sickening' object) is a
technique that is widespread in the world. Making a cut, or several small
incisions, with a knife or razor blade, and then rubbing in medicine, is
still common in many African settings. Injections do elegantly something
that was already known. Moreover, they do it more thoroughly, in that
they go deeper into the body. If, as in Uganda, certain sicknesses are
thought to move in the blood, then injections put medicine where it can
attack the sickness directly. So injections can be related to perceptions of
the body and bodily processes. These kinds of considerations draw our
attention to the ways in which cultural organization of experience may
predispose towards the acceptance of injection technology.

As students of technology, we must also ask how injections shape experience. Their popularity strengthens a view of illness as localized in
the flesh and blood – rather than, say, in the person as a whole, or in
the environment or social relations. In this sense, the metaphoric work
of technology is to help conceptualize the 'it' of illness, just as medicines
do in general (see chapter 4). Injections do this supremely well because
they *mark* the treatment by pain. 'Anthropologists have noted that the in-
fliction of physical pain in some cultures is "pedagogic" in that it stamps
forcefully in the victim's experience that which must be noted and re-
membered. In the same way, the pain of an injection makes the patient
know intensely that treatment has been given' (Whyte and Van der Geest
1994:149–50). The painful insertion of medicine through a needle shapes
the experience of disease as something in the body that can be controlled.
But how does this come to seem reasonable to people?

Some researchers have emphasized an historical approach that assumes
that cultural perceptions and desires change on the basis of people's experience with the outcome of specific kinds of therapy. Wyatt (1984)
suggests that it was the massive use of injections in campaigns against
yaws and kala-azar that established the injection as the pre-eminent therapy in places as widespread as Ghana, Brazil and Ceylon. The experience
of dramatic relief of symptoms after a single injection was evident, as well
in the early use of quinine for malaria and antrypal for sleeping sickness.[2]
In the 1950s penicillin injections also seemed miraculous in their effects.
Wyatt quotes a variety of historical examples to illustrate his argument:

On the Gold Coast intravenous and intramuscular injections of Salvarsan and its derivatives began in 1920: 'so spectacular were the results achieved with this form of treatment that all types of patients began to clamour for injections and most of them refused other forms of orthodox treatment – the Injection Age had truly arrived'. (Wyatt 1984:913 citing C.E. Reindorf)

The argument is that efficacy provides evidence that changes the culture of health.

The routinization of technology

The historical perspective is a good start, but insufficient to explain how experiences that are beyond living memory for most people still influence relations to injections today. Thinking of injections as technologies of biomedicine gives a clue. One of the early contributions to the ethnography of biomedical technology showed the importance of routinization in the social life of medical procedures and equipment. Koenig (1988) underlined the importance of the 'technological imperative' – the impetus to adopt a technology once it is available. For one thing, newer, more advanced technologies allow the provider to charge more for services. But even more fundamentally, the existence of a technical solution is tempting; once it is available, it is difficult to choose not to use it in the struggle to deal with problems. And once its use becomes widespread, the technological imperative becomes a moral one. 'The moral tone derives from the sense of social certainty experienced by health professionals. The standard of care becomes a moral, as well as a technical, obligation' (1988:485–6). Koenig argues that the meaning of a new technology derives from its use over time in particular social contexts. As it becomes a routine, it becomes an expectation, and even a moral right and obligation. As we saw in chapter 2, routine treatment has social efficacy in that it shows that the 'right' thing is being done, in a way that is commonly understood by those involved.

Part of the charm of medical techniques is their ceremonial aspect. Just as medicines offer a concrete response to the diffuse feeling of illness, so technical procedures offer a fixed and measured set of steps for application to the uncertainty of illness and treatment. They discipline the patient and the provider of therapy, and instil a sense of control. The establishment of such procedures, which Koenig compares to ritual, not only has the existential effect of suggesting control; it also is part of the social process of routinization. The same routines do not obtain in every setting, but they tend to be consistent over time within a setting (1988).

Injections in Uganda became routinized as biomedical services spread and consistently offered injections for various kinds of complaints. The procedure – almost a ritual – became known to providers and users alike: the needle is fitted to the syringe, the vial of medicine is shaken, the needle inserted into the vial, the medicine drawn up into the syringe. In southern Ghana, Senah (1997:163) noted the attention people gave to the rituals of injection: tapping the filled syringe three times and spurting a little bit of the medicine out before inserting it into an identified spot on the body. The repetition of these steps has become part of the habitus, the unspoken practice, of health care in many settings. The technique has become a 'natural' way of responding to illness – familiar and obvious. 'The technical aids become extensions of the human body, which one learns to use just as unthinkingly as the body itself' (Van der Geest 1994:1).

As the Ugandan example shows, the routinization of a technology has a social history and a political economic context. Injections were introduced as something powerful and special. Their value was assumed and communicated by the Europeans who first provided them. Access to the technology, including knowledge and skills, was restricted. Injections were 'enclaved', in the terms of Appadurai (1986), in that the authorities tried to limit their provision to certain people and settings. They were not supposed to become common commodities. But the effort was doomed to failure. As the value and power of injections became established within the growing biomedical health care system, health workers themselves began to sell them in order to supplement their salaries. Lay specialists (the needlemen) carried forward the process of commodification. But it was the combination of a weakened health care system, the response to AIDS, and the influx of medicines and disposable syringes that made injections ordinary wares. With the changes in the social relations of health care, the technology was transformed. It was routinized in settings such as homes, drug shops, small private clinics. As the ownership of private needles and syringes became widespread, more and more people learned the ceremony of administering injections.

It appears that in some countries, intravenous infusions have a similar social history. Senah (1997:163–4) describes how they have become 'the latest craze' among villagers in southern Ghana, who learned from experience at the hospital and now have infusions administered at drug stores. Reeler (1996:89–90) reports that the rice miller in the village where she worked in north-east Thailand was an informal provider of both injections and infusions.

Power and danger

Much of the discussion of biomedical technology in Europe and North America concerns the potential risks it entails. By risks we mean not only statistical probabilities but also, and more generally, unintended negative consequences. The dangers of technology can be envisioned as social, political, economic, environmental and medical, as well as personal and existential. The recognition of such danger is simultaneously an acknowledgement of power. A technology that is not seen as capable of producing effects poses no threat.

Public health researchers have been particularly concerned to point out the medical risks in injection technology as it is currently practised in developing countries. A recent review article concludes that about 95 per cent of these injections are given for curative, rather than preventive, purposes, and that most of them are unnecessary. The prevalence of unsafe injections is estimated at 50 per cent in developing countries (Simonsen *et al.* 1999). Most of the risk is associated with the use of unsterilized equipment that may transmit bloodborne pathogens, such as HIV, Hepatitis B and Hepatitis C, from one patient to another (Kane *et al.* 1999).

The World Health Organization responded to evidence about the widespread use of unsafe injections (in part presented by anthropologists like Birungi) by calling for the development of strategies for safe immunizations and therapeutic injections. It is remarkable how much attention is given to the equipment itself. The merits and costs of sterilizable, disposable and auto-disable (self-destructing) equipment are evaluated (Battersby *et al.* 1999a, 1999b), as well as the problems of technology transfer in adopting auto-disable syringes for immunization (Lloyd and Milstien 1999). The contributors to this discussion realize that technology, and its dangers, depend on its users.

No single technology will render injections safe; only diligent health workers who understand and carefully follow correct procedures will achieve safety, and only as long as the entire system (including disposal) is funded and managed adequately and used correctly. (Battersby *et al.* 1999a)

Yet for these writers technology is primarily equipment and procedures. The risks of unsterile injections are identifiable diseases that threaten the public and have economic implications for the country as a whole.

In contrast to this public health view of risk, anthropologists describe locally situated perceptions of the power and danger of injections.[3] In Uganda injection technology was more than equipment and procedures. Its meaning included the social relations in which it was embedded. Mistrust of anonymous government health workers made injections in their hands seem dangerous. Personal relations were more important than standard of sterilization for many people. And the danger was not only that health workers 'might inject people with AIDS'; they might cheat by diluting the medicine, or injecting water. Moreover they might not be there to give an injection when a child was feverish and vomiting and potentially at risk of dying. Ugandan users of injection were concerned about a wider and more experiential range of problems than bloodborne pathogens. They heard the warning about the dangers of needle-transmitted HIV, but they responded in terms of the total social phenomenon that injection technology constituted for them at that point in their social history.

Studies of injection technology in other settings show different local understandings of power and danger. Although much emphasis has been given to the worldwide popularity of injections, they are not always seen as desirable for every person or condition. Kristvik reports from Bhojpur in Nepal that injections are believed to be more powerful than pills and tonics – too strong for such as her four-year-old neighbour, who was partly paralysed after being treated in the hospital. As an informant explained: 'You know they gave her 25 needles . . . they ought to understand it is too much for such a small body' (Kristvik 1999:89). Injections are thought to be particularly risky if given for a condition caused by Jangali, the goddess of the forest, without first letting a traditional healer deal with the situation (1999:97). This may parallel the example we saw in chapter 5, in which injections were contraindicated for the Dagomba disease called *jogu*. The danger of injections in that case had to do with the opposition between cultural categories construed as internal and external, indigenous and foreign.

Conclusion

Injections, like the pharmaceuticals with which they are associated, are excellent examples of technology as a total social phenomenon. Needles and syringes take on cultural force as they are associated with techniques and procedures that shape people's experiences of illness, bodies and healing. Routines (which may or may not include sterilization) become natural and expected – perhaps even morally imperative. They take on social consequence as they are enclaved or diverted, as particular social groups have access to them. Technologies do not determine social and cultural processes. But they facilitate them. The common availability of injection technology in Uganda is a factor in the commoditization and popularization of biomedical health care. It has undermined the position of health workers as gatekeepers at the same time as it has promoted a sense of agency among the users of injections. Lay people are now able to control their own use of injections to a far greater extent than ever before.

9   Prescribing physicians: medicines as communication

Prescribing is speaking without words, through medicines. This chapter focuses on the prescriber as a broker in the dispensing of medicines, but it is not the practical act of prescribing and providing medicines which interests us. Prescribing is also a symbolic act; it is an effective style of communication. In the prescription the doctor signals to the patient who he is. Rarely is the division of roles between doctor and patient clearer than in the act of writing a prescription. Through the prescription the doctor tells the patient that he understands his problem and can do something about it. The communication is, however, circuitous. The prescriber may not really have a good diagnosis and may hide his uncertainty behind the medication. Prescription may precede, replace and forestall diagnosis. For most – not all – patients the prescription is a proof of the doctor's concern and competence.

Misunderstanding as therapy

Mark Nichter has written extensively about the commodification of health (see chapter 6). Health, in the perception of consumers, can be bought in the form of pharmaceuticals from drugstores and pharmacies. The doctor is often bypassed, because what really counts is the taking of a medicine. 'Pharmaceuticalization' is another term he uses for this phenomenon. Interestingly, the same author has also observed an opposite development in people's perception of illness and healing. During research among Sinhalese people in south-western Sri Lanka, he and his co-author Carolyn Nordstrom came across a strong feeling of dependence on the healing hand of the doctor. Whether a medicine works is not so much the result of its therapeutic substance but depends on the person who prescribes it. '[M]edicine is imbued with the qualities and intention of the giver' (Nichter and Nordstrom 1989:379). The authors introduce the concept of *Behet Aharawa* ('Medicine Answering'). A medicine 'answers', is effective, when the practitioner who prescribes it is sympathetic to the patient in a social as well as a physical sense. The medicine thus

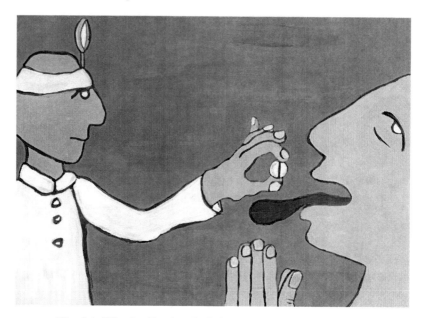

Fig. 9.1 'The healing hand of the doctor reaches the patient through the prescription and the medicine.'

becomes a vehicle between the person of the patient and the person of the practitioner. During an illness a patient will look for a doctor who is sensitive to his particular physical and social circumstances, a practitioner who has *afgunaya* for them. *Afgunaya* refers to the gift of healing a practitioner is credited as having (1989:377). The authors translate this concept as 'the power of hand'.

Patients looking for 'the power of hand' accept the medicine they receive as wholesome because it comes from that hand. The authors quote an informant who emphasizes that the same medicine may be effective in one case and ineffective in another: 'You see, even though it is the same medicine, it answers better if it is given by a person who has the gift of healing for you' (1989:383).

Lisbeth Sachs, a Swedish anthropologist, who also did research among Sinhalese villagers in Sri Lanka, wrote an article in the same year with the enigmatic title 'Misunderstanding as Therapy'. She, too, focused on the communication between patient and practitioner and the role of medicines in that communication. At first, her conclusions seem contrary to those of Nichter and Nordstrom, because she stresses the absence of communication. At a closer look, the insights provided by the two articles begin to fuse, however.

Sachs did her research in a rural health unit in central Sri Lanka. The health centre had a ward with thirty beds. Every day about 300 to 400 people visited the out-patient department. One medical officer and three female assistant practitioners were attached to the centre. The doctors were of high-caste families and carried enormous authority in their roles as practitioners. The patients, who were of low caste, were mainly rice field workers or brick-makers.

Sachs followed fifty patients before, during and after their encounter with the doctor. During the encounter, the communication between patient and doctor was monitored. Before the consultation the researcher discussed with the patient his/her complaint. The practitioner was given a card with three questions: (1) Patient's complaint? (2) Tentative diagnosis? (3) Drugs prescribed? The doctor filled the card and returned it to the researcher at the end of the consultation. The researcher followed the patient when he went to collect his medicines from the centre's pharmacy.

From the observations before, during and after the consultation Sachs made a remarkable discovery. Doctors and patients hardly communicated with one another. The practitioner did not hear the patient's complaint and the patient did not understand the doctor's diagnosis, but miraculously both parties felt satisfied about the encounter, which always ended in a prescription.

In the interview before the encounter with the doctor, patients described their problems in Ayurvedic terms, mentioning symptoms like heat escaping from the body, dry phlegm, yellow vomit and loss of semen, but during the consultation many of these symptoms were never mentioned. Instead of 'burning feeling' or 'heat behind the eyes' the patient would just say 'fever', and instead of 'too much phlegm' he would say 'cough'. The doctor, who had very little, if any, time for communication, would immediately make a biomedical diagnosis and prescription which were 'committed to paper without any evidence . . . of an examination, few spoken words and little, if any, eye or body contact' (Sachs 1989:342). Then the next patient was called.

The prescriptions were generous. '[The doctors] believed that every patient at the OPD was in constant need of vitamins, some kind of pain reliever and antibiotics or worm treatment. Their illnesses were multifactorial in origin, and it was seen as positive to prescribe several drugs' (1989:345).

Interestingly, the patients usually did not feel neglected or misunderstood; their respect for the doctor's expertise made them accept the doctor's verdict as the right decision, and the doctor in turn felt that she had done a good job. Sachs writes:

The mutual confidence of practitioners and patients in the medicines helps prevent the misunderstanding of each other's beliefs from being uncovered. This confidence imbues the medicines with a magic, symbolic aura, giving the practitioners as well as the patients a feeling that they contribute in their way to solving the acute health problem...Within the therapeutic encounter then, there exist two different systems of knowledge through which the effectiveness of these medicines is integrated. The contradictory symbolic meanings of the medicines remain unrevealed, allowing patients and practitioners to communicate in a satisfactory manner. (1989:345)

Sachs' description of prescribing medicines as an act which creates the illusion of communication and which results in satisfaction among both patients and doctors reveals five facets of prescription which will be discussed in this chapter. First, prescribing medicines, as we just saw, is a way of dealing with uncertainty; the doctor and the patient do not know the exact nature of the complaint or what to do about it. Yet prescribing a medicine alleviates that uncertainty and gives both parties a feeling of having dealt with the problem.

Second, prescribing is a token of concern on the part of the doctor. It shows that the doctor is a good doctor. Far from being an anonymous commodity, the medicine becomes a symbolic representation of the person of the doctor. Such a positive reception of medicine creates an ideal condition for recovery.

Third, prescribing is the prerogative of doctors. It is an act in which they express and reaffirm their authority over patients and over professional colleagues such as nurses and pharmacists. For the doctors in Sri Lanka, who have hardly any time to lose owing to the large number of patients, prescribing is a ritual and effective way to manage the length of the consultation firmly by cutting it off.

Fourth, the prescription itself, a tiny hand-written document, deserves our attention. It shares with other types of scripts the capacity to objectify, concretize and visualize and at the same time to hide subjective experiences. The prescription is one of the most cherished paraphernalia of the doctor expressing his superior knowledge and authority, but as an inscription, it is highly significant for the patient as well.

A final issue raised by the Sri Lanka example is the quality of prescribing from a biomedical point of view. Here we turn from the communication aspects themselves to their consequences for public health. If doctors allay their uncertainty by prescribing, we may ask if their prescription meets the standards of their own profession. Perhaps 'biomedical irrationality' is a side-effect of communicating through prescription. An additional question concerns the commercial interests doctors may have in dispensing medicines. Is such communication also a way to further, while disguising, the economic stakes of the doctor?

Silent communication: the magic of prescribing

Magic, in its popular conception, is what works but cannot be explained in the accepted terms of science, an effect which does not fit in common conventional causative thinking. Anthropology points at the importance of symbols in magic. Human acts, words and objects bring about certain effects, not through what they literally are, but through what they are believed to be; not through instrumental effectiveness, but through their symbolic meaning. In that sense, one could say that the act of prescribing and the piece of paper called 'prescription' do magic work on people, on their mental and emotional state, on their health and on their position in society.

Smith (1980:166–70) lists no less than twenty-seven 'latent functions' of the prescription – that is, effects which could be called 'magical' in the above-mentioned sense. The 'side-effects' of prescribing discussed below cover most of Smith's 'latent functions'.

Dealing with uncertainty

In an article on medical uncertainty, the sociologist Renée Fox remarks that the progress in medical science and technology 'has helped to reveal how ignorant, bewildered and mistaken we still are in many ways about health and illness, life and death' (Fox 1980:1). If science and technology do not eliminate uncertainty but rather produce more (and more difficult) questions, doctors still have the possibility of resorting to reassuring symbols of communication.

Prescribing medicines is one such symbol. Medical consultations are – almost by nature – highly ambiguous situations. Patients' complaints, which may have a long and twisted history, are summarized in a few words and have to be 'deciphered' by a doctor who cannot feel what the patient feels. The subjectivity of the illness experience and the limited scope for communication often creates an acute situation of uncertainty. One way of getting out of that situation is to shift the uncertainty to someone else and refer the patient to a specialist for further examination. Another way is to brush away the many questions by prescribing medicines. The concreteness of the prescription, which is soon to be exchanged for even more concrete therapeutic substances, overshadows the abstractness of the unanswered questions. The prescription becomes a magic item which symbolically deals with a difficult situation that cannot be dealt with directly in technical terms. The medicine is the materialization of a comforting word. As we have seen in the Sri Lankan case, the belief in the knowledge and kindness of the doctor adds to the reassuring effect of the medicine.

But the prescription – and subsequent medication – does not only allay the patient's anxiety; it also works for the doctor. That focus on solving his own problems is strikingly expressed in (the title of) a brief article by Wyndham (1982): 'My Doctor Gives Me Pills to Put Him out of My Misery...'. Comaroff, who studied prescribing behaviour by general practitioners in South Wales, calls their prescribing 'magic and medical optimism' and 'responses to situations of practical uncertainty and emotional concern' (1976:79). She compares these responses with the ritualization of optimism expressed in the magic Trobriand Islanders apply to their canoes to deal with the dangers of the sea. The magic of prescription thus works two ways: it restores the patient's confidence in recovery and the doctor's confidence in his own competence.

One could say that doctor and patient are linked in a kind of 'conspiracy'. Both may be at a loss and resort to the concreteness of medicines. The mutual feeling of being at a loss is particularly acute when 'patients' bring non-medical complaints to their physician: an unhappy marriage, loneliness, insecurity at work, problems with children or old age. The 'worried women' in chapter 4 who were given tranquillizers are a case in point. In such circumstances medication constitutes the silent language between doctor and client. It offers the opportunity to look away from the problems and think of more hopeful prospects. Wyndham remarks:

The drugs...may decrease the amount of misery, anxiety or unhappiness of the individual and – perhaps more importantly – decrease the amount of trouble the miserable person is causing others by her unhappiness...Indeed, attention is taken away from the unfavourable social and interpersonal arrangement which generated the anxiety or distress. (1982:22)

Prescribing a medicine reassures both doctor and patient that 'something' has been done about the disease. Comaroff quotes a doctor saying: 'I always provide a prescription in liquid or tablet form, even after a session of psychotherapy. Of course, it is not strictly necessary in medical terms, but at least, when they go home, they feel they have something to cling to' (1976:87). Pellegrino writes: 'prescription fits the impulse of modern man to control his own destiny, to take the problem in hand and conquer it with technology' (1976:626).

Token of concern

That medicines are tokens of the doctor's concern and that, reversibly, the concern fills the medicines with therapeutic power was beautifully shown in the Sri Lankan cases which started this chapter. When medicine is seen as the essence of medical practice, prescribing is the main thing

expected from a doctor. A non-prescribing physician woul
contradiction. Refusal to prescribe, which sometimes might b
from a biomedical point of view, would be irrational by lc
criteria. Doctors, in such situations, are encouraged to prescr
to overcome their uncertainty, as we have just seen, but also tc
patients and increase their reputation.[1]

The prescription, and later on the medicine, is a metonymic extension
of the doctor. There is, as it were, a dose of doctor in the medicine. The
healing hand of the doctor reaches the patient through the prescription
and the medicine. The prescription and the medicine are the material
proof that doctor and patient are still connected to one another. The
confidence awakened in the patient by the doctor is recaptured in the
concreteness of prescription and medicine.

The idea that the power of a medicine derives from the hand which
prescribes it (*agunaya* in Sinhalese), has been observed by several students
of medicine. De Graaf (1988) followed medicine use in ten Guizinga
families in northern Cameroon. To her surprise, the people emphasized
that medicines were good if a good person had dispensed them. They
called this the 'good word' which was added to the substance of the drug.
The 'good word', they explained, was spoken by a doctor or nurse who
cared about you.

Gould (1977), physician and anthropologist, writes that the inhabitants
of the north Indian village where he did his research began to ask him
for medicines, after they had got to know and appreciate him. His good
relationship with the people also made his drugs acceptable. Trust in him
was extended to his medicines.

The belief that the power of medicine is not inherent to the medicine
but is added to it by the prescriber or dispenser is relatively rare in
biomedicine but not uncommon in local medical traditions. Healers
sometimes claim that the therapeutic efficacy of a plant does not lie in
the plant itself, but that they give the plant its medicinal power through
a ritual act such as a prayer or a blessing. Yoruba healers in Nigeria,
for instance, awaken the power of a plant by incantations. The incan-
tation is not directed to the patient (who cannot understand it) but to
the medicine (Buckley 1985). Without the magical formula the medicine
would not work. Similarly, in Burundi, for 80 per cent of herbs used by
specialist healers, the efficacy is added to the herb by the healer. The healers emphasize that it does not matter *which* herb they use; the only thing
which counts is that *they* make it into a medicine (Baerts and Lehmann
1993).

Studies of placebo effect have shown that the prescriber's demon-
stration of concern and competence enhances the reception of the

medication and the patient's chance of recovery. The placebo effect, Pellegrino (1976:628) writes, 'is closely related to the aura which surrounds ingestion of any chemical substance properly invested with healing powers by the ritual of prescribing'.[2] Attributing the effect of medicine to a 'healing hand' or 'good word' is a cultural translation of the concept of placebo effect.

Establishing authority

Writing a prescription is a doctor's job, although exceptions can be found where doctors, owing to work pressure, delegate this to 'lower' professionals. In writing a prescription, the doctor communicates who he is. He exercises his professional authority and distances himself from the layman, who is not able to write – or often to read – a prescription. The patient is not even supposed to ask for a prescription – 'is not supposed', but, as we have seen (chapter 4) and will see in a moment, patients are not always passive receivers of prescriptions. Doctors often write prescriptions *because* patients request them and, conversely, patients may be sceptical and decide to do other things with a prescription than the doctor intended (chapter 5).

The prescription distinguishes the doctor from colleagues who are not doctors. To the insider the difference between a nurse and a doctor may be visible in their dress, or other attributes, but it is in the act of prescribing that the doctor can be identified without any doubt.[3]

The unequal relationship between doctor and pharmacist is – almost painfully to the pharmacist – demonstrated in the function of the prescription: it conveys the orders of the doctor to the pharmacist. Not surprisingly, the prescription has become a focal point in the fight over professional competence between pharmacists and doctors (Smith 1980: 164; Britten 2001). Pharmacists may regard themselves as more competent with regard to drugs than doctors, but it is still a doctor who writes the prescription for the pharmacist to fill. The prescription embodies the authority of doctors over pharmacists. The prescription, according to an old definition (Smith 1980:164), is 'an order written by a physician . . . directing the pharmacist to compound and dispense medication for a patient, and usually accompanied by directions for its administration or use'.

The prerogative to prescribe also gives the doctor a very specific power in the clinical encounter with the patient. By taking his pad and starting to write a prescription, the doctor emits a tactful but definitive sign that the consultation is over. It forestalls further discussion and constitutes a kind of 'silent communication'. The positive appreciation of the prescription

does not only conceal the fact that hardly any communication has ta
place and that uncertainty still exists, as we have seen; it also papers (
the patient's disappointment about the shortness of the encounter. When
Whyte and colleagues asked patients leaving a Ugandan health centre
whether they had put any questions to the health workers, one person
replied: 'I was going to ask, but he was already writing on the paper.'
For the doctor, it is the most effective way to deal with the persistent
problem of shortage of time and the 'overload' of patients, especially in
low-income societies with extremely unfavourable doctor–patient ratios.
Writing a prescription can best be described as a closing ritual which is
intended – and often succeeds – to send the patient away with hope and
positive feelings towards his medical problem, himself and the doctor.
Moreover, it provides the patient with legitimation that he is really sick.
The doctor's authoritative signature on the prescription form says that
this person needs treatment.

The prescription as script

Finally, we should not forget the prescription itself, a piece of paper with
text, however brief and fragmented. Archaeologists have found that some
of the first signs of human writing were prescriptions and instructions
regarding illness and medicines. As script the prescriptions have contributed both to the religious aspect of medicine (Fainzang 2001) and to
the objectification and standardization of medical thinking (Spangenberg
n.d.). The prescription has led to what Jeffrey Spangenberg has called 'the
scripturalisation of medicine'. Writing makes speech 'objective' by turning it into an object of visual inspection, according to Goody (1977:44).
The receptor shifts from the ear to the eye, the most authoritative sense
for establishing truth (Ong 1986:85). Writing also 'freezes' the fluidity
of speaking and makes it possible to pass messages as static objects. A
written text makes it possible for people to communicate without meeting
one another. In Denmark, the doctor can fax the prescription to the pharmacy so that the patient can pick up the medication at her convenience.
Space and time distances do not matter anymore. The reuse of old prescriptions in self-medication and the issuing of repeat-prescriptions are
striking examples of this objectification effect.

Historically, the power that lies in the written text made writing an
enviable art and the privilege of the political elite. In writing, the higher
class demonstrated its power over the illiterate, as doctors show their authority over patients in the production of prescriptions. It is no wonder
that written texts, and prescriptions in particular, are invested with magical powers and became themselves medicines. The prescriptive value

and the therapeutic value of the prescription, Fainzang (2001:29) writes, are sometimes difficult to distinguish. Samuel Butler wrote in one of his Notebooks: 'I read once of a man who was cured of a dangerous illness by eating his doctor's prescription.' The man's fortunate mistake parallels a common therapy in Islamic folk medicine: drinking the sacred words of the Koran after their ink has been dissolved in water (El-Tom 1985).

Yet the script is not just a powerful and relatively enduring object in itself. In some situations it can play an important role in the on-going communication through face-to-face visits, physical examinations and spoken words. Just as writing may cut short a consultation, so may it also fit into a continuing exchange. In her studies of traditional Chinese medicine in urban China Judith Farquhar has given an example where prescriptions, with their objectifying power, serve as 'discussion papers' in a rich process of communication. At the hospitals affiliated with the Guangzhou College of Traditional Chinese Medicine in the 1980s, every out-patient received a prescription for herbal medicines which was written into a case record book retained by the patient and onto a prescription form delivered to the pharmacy. Farquhar describes the consultation as a process of communication moving from concreteness and verbosity through writing to abstraction and silence, and back again through the written word to materiality and speech (Farquhar 1994a:205). The patient is invited to explain the symptoms in detail, while the doctor examines the pulse, tongue and appearance. In the next phase, spoken words and observations are transformed into writing as the doctor records the list of illness signs. Then comes the moment of silence and abstraction as the doctor considers the syndrome, mentally relating it to the vast archive of professional knowledge. Communication proceeds as the doctor writes out a list of four to sixteen herbal ingredients that correspond in detail to each and every illness sign inscribed on the same page. This paper is then exchanged for eminently discussable (1994a:202) materia medica, packed in parcels, one for each daily dose, to be decocted at home.

Farquhar explains that the prescriptions have different significance for doctors and patients. The rich body of professional literature includes an enormous collection of published case histories that resemble the notes in a patient's case record book and always include the exact herbal prescription. This is so important that Farquhar remarks: 'If the great interest of my teachers in Guangzhou in the evaluation of drug formulae is an index, then much of the intellectual life of Chinese medicine revolves around the reading and writing of prescriptions' (1994a:190). While professionals (silently) appreciate the underlying principles of diagnosis and treatment, 'patients see only a certain aspect of their illness and a manifestation of the treatment written down' (Farquhar 1994b:476).

Inscription has another part to play in this Chinese example. Prescriptions are generally written for three days, after which the patient must return so that the prescription can be adapted to changes in the symptoms. Those with chronic conditions may even visit the clinic several times a week (Farquhar 1994a:44). The term for a consultation means 'looking at illness' and this is a joint endeavour for the patient and the practitioner. The objectification of the signs of illness and the elements of treatment in the prescription, rewritten regularly, have the effect of encouraging the patient to attend to symptoms in detail in order to report them at the next visit, when they will be inscribed together with a new order for materia medica (Farquhar 1994b:480–1).

Communication and irrational prescribing

Anthropologists may be keen to point out that prescribing makes sense in a social and cultural context, even if it entails 'misunderstanding', as we have seen in the Sri Lanka example. However, biomedical observers have a completely different view and are concerned about the poor quality of prescribing. The literature on 'irrational prescribing' fills libraries, but it suffices here to sketch briefly the social and cultural implications of biomedically poor prescribing and of the attempt to improve the quality of prescribing.

In the introduction to a special issue on 'Inappropriate Distribution of Medicines by Professionals in Developing Countries' (1996), James Trostle remarks that inappropriate medicine use is usually attributed to patients. More than 8,000 articles were published in English between 1986 and 1995 on patient (non-)compliance, suggesting that 40 to 60 per cent of patients fail to take their medication as prescribed. Far less attention, however, has been devoted to faulty prescribing by professionals. There are many explanations, he writes, for doctors' inappropriate prescriptions: Doctors use pills 'to signal the end of a therapeutic encounter, create additional income, maintain professional prestige, and increase patient loyalty' (Trostle 1996:1,117). Additional reasons may be lack of information on drugs and absence of diagnostic technology leading to drug prescription as diagnostic tool. However, one of the contributions to the special issue, reporting a study of doctors in Lima, Peru, suggested that physicians' prescribing practices were more influenced by social expectations of patients and caretakers than by their knowledge of biomedical rules (Paredes *et al.* 1996). That is, doctors were more concerned to communicate well with their patients than to relate diagnoses to standard treatment guidelines.

Schwartz and colleagues (1989), who held open interviews with 141 physicians in the United States, report that almost half of the physicians indicated that patient demand was the most common reason for them to prescribe medication, and 24 per cent said their prescribing was based on the intentional use of the placebo effect. About the same percentage told the researchers that they were led in their prescribing by their own clinical experience, even if this contravened evidence from the professional literature.

The discussion in this chapter reveals ample reasons for prescribers to divert from their professional rules and standards. The social and cultural context often encourages medication where this is not warranted from a biomedical point of view. 'The powerful symbolism compels both the patient and the doctor to use a drug where scientific therapeutics would indicate none' (Pellegrino 1976:627).

One situation leading to overprescription, however, has not yet been discussed here: the commercial advantage that doctors derive from dispensing medicines. That is particularly likely to occur where prescription and sale of medicines are in one hand, a situation which policy makers try to prevent, but which still prevails in the private sector of many low-income countries. The low income of the doctors themselves is also likely to drive them to increase their fees by overprescribing. There is psychological wisdom in this marketing strategy as consumers are more willing to pay for the substance of medicines than for the fleeting minutes with the doctor.

Inappropriate prescribing is a double problem because doctors are trendsetters for informal prescribers, such as drugstore keepers and hawkers and for people practising self-medication (Hardon 1987; Van Staa 1993). The providers of drugs, who have been the subjects of this section of the book, are all to some extent influenced by the doctors themselves as authoritative role models.

Conclusion

Prescription, as we have seen, is more than brokering the dispensing of medicines; it is communication through symbols.

The medication indicates the doctor's concern; it enables him to communicate with patients with lesser education, different values, or different socio-economic status; it can forestall lengthy discussion of symptoms and their meaning...it is an effective device for parcelling out the limited time a physician can allot to a patient... Giving a prescription is also a major source of satisfaction to the physician, since it may be the only way he can 'do' something for the patient. (Pellegrino 1976: 627)

This said, however, we must recognize that communicating through medicines is a practice that has to be seen in a broader perspective as well. Prescribing practices are influenced by strategists such as drug manufacturers and policy makers, to whom we now turn.

Part IV

The strategists

10 Manufacturers: scientific claims, commercial aims

This chapter deals with the culture of manufacturers of pharmaceuticals, in which scientific research, medical concern and commercial interest are blended. Its theme, one could say, is 'cultural economy'. Drug manufacturers both *appeal to* common values and *create* them. Science, care, tradition, morality and rights to health come together in the production of medicines. In addition, the chapter deals with the lack of understanding of the culture of manufacturing owing to the scarcity of anthropological research in the world of pharmaceutical companies. It attempts to account for this gap in the anthropology of pharmaceuticals and discusses a number of alternative approaches to explore the perspective of the manufacturers and their sales representatives. These approaches include the study of advertisements and drug information provided by the industry, nomenclature and the activities of sales representatives ('reps'). The research carried out by Maarten Bode among representatives of some big Indian companies that produce Ayurvedic and Unani medicines is one of the rare examples of anthropological research on drug manufacturing.

The manufacture and marketing of Indian indigenous medicine

Bode was intrigued by the ambiguity surrounding indigenous medicines in Indian society. Casual observations and conversations with members of the Indian middle class revealed on the one hand a strong drive for modernity and keen involvement in the global economy and on the other an equally strong resistance to values and products imposed upon them by that globalization process.

That ambivalence is strikingly manifested in the production, marketing and use of the local medications referred to as Ayurvedic and Unani. Advertisements of these products emphasize both their ancient Indian heritage *and* the high tech and modern standards of research on which they are based. They seem to both welcome and reject modernization. In order to get a better understanding of this cultural ambivalence, Bode

Fig. 10.1 'The ideas and practices of the drug manufacturer remain largely inaccessible to ethnographic research': A pharmaceutical laboratory in Iran.

concentrated his research on the companies that manufacture these products and on the way they promote their products through advertisements and scientific publications.

Traditionally, Ayurvedic and Unani medicines were produced by local scholars and physicians and carried their stamp of knowledge and wisdom. Personal contact between the healer and his clients guided the production, administration and use of the medication. That ancient tradition of 'hand-made' medicine is, however, giving way to industrial production in modern laboratories owned by large companies. Nichter and Nichter quote an Ayurvedic medicine seller who finds himself between the old and new traditions.

I feel badly that I am selling this inferior quality medicine, but that's what people are interested in . . . Now I am like other chemists. I sell the company which makes me the most profit. So I stock 200 ml. bottles of commercial *ashoka arishta* which I sell for Rs. 7 and I make Rs. 3 profit . . . Business has never been better. (Nichter and Nichter 1996:294)

In 1995 Ayurvedic and Unani medicines comprised about 15 per cent of the 4 billion dollar Indian drug market. The mere size of this industry was a good reason for research, as Leslie (1989) remarked some years ago.

Bode studied the promotional material of three large companies and had interviews and more casual meetings with some of their representatives. He visited their offices, libraries and clinics, took lunch in their canteens, and attended their conferences. He did not, however, conduct fieldwork in the 'orthodox' anthropological way, in the sense of spending a long period of time with one company to observe the daily routines and local culture during that period.

The companies are run in a modern way. They subject their products to scientific tests and publish the results in journals financed by themselves. They claim the same scientific rigour as the laboratories of Western pharmaceutical companies and employ that image of high tech to promote their products. Their medicines are increasingly delivered in the form of pills and capsules, which can be precisely measured, as is the case for Western pharmaceuticals.

Monograph 5 of the Hamdard National Foundation (Hamdard is a company that holds 70 per cent of the market of Unani medicines) illustrates the scientific image the industry wants to create for itself. The publication reports on studies of the safety and efficacy of an oral rehydration solution derived from *Rooh Afza*, an Unani 'herbal polypharmaceutical drink'. *Rooh Afza* is India's best selling Unani tonic, responsible for 40 per cent of the company's profit. The tonic is not mentioned in the old canons; it was first developed in 1907 by the man who founded the company. The editor of the monograph thus summarizes the 'most scientifically dynamics' of the medicine found in the research (Arora 1991):

1. It produces decreased heart rate and increased cardiac output by its cardiotonic activity... Besides... the blood supply to ventricles is also increased. All these actions were more marked with sugar free extract from medicinal plants. An antispasmodic effect could be detected which was more expressed with sugar free extracts from flowers and smelling substances. This speaks of using the total preparation.
2. It was also shown that in dehydration it corrects the electrolyte balance and can be used in the maintenance of acid base balance in oral rehydration therapy in diarrhoea and in thirst.
3. Rooh Afza increases the Hb per cent of blood.
4. It increases the Ca^{+2} in serum.
5. It has got an androgenic activity as shown by its role of inducting nitrogen balance.

Such a text certainly plays on the discourse of Western science.

At the same time, in a beautiful illustration of the medicinal politics of identity discussed in chapter 5, the companies distance themselves from biomedical products and emphasize that *their* medicines are natural and without side-effects. Modern drugs, remarks a brochure of an Indian company, 'have played havoc with the natural power of resistance of the human system'. Slogans instil in consumers fear of the aggressiveness and counter-productivity of modern medicines. A marketing manager of one company compared using modern pharmaceuticals to 'printing money to fight inflation . . . [they] cure on the one hand and make you sick on the other'. Western pharmaceuticals are said to focus only on the symptoms whereas indigenous medication fortifies the immune system and works 'from deep within'. It regulates digestion and blood formation and thus takes care of the production of healthy humours and tissues. It 'balances' organs, 'lubricates' tissues and 'cleans' canals (Bode 2002).

In the industry's claims, medical messages fuse with moral ones. The naturalness of their products embodies traditional Indian values like purity, non-violence and harmony with the environment. Bode writes,

Metonymically Ayurvedic pharmaceuticals refer to the glorious age of the Vedas when people adhered to the rules for diet and social conduct. This mythical era is typified by the absence of disorder and corruption and the omnipresence of peace and purity. Being symbolically linked to this period will generate power for facing the strains of life in a corrupted world. (Bode 1998:367)

Indigenous medicines satisfy the demands of the new Indian elite who combine modernity with adherence to Indian identity. A brochure shows a traditional sage sitting in a test tube while preparing herbs. The products share in the prestige of high technology but retain their naturalness. They 'offer an antidote against the somatic and mental toxins which invade urban professionals. Their lives are after all marked and marred by the consumption of fast food, hard liquor and Western medicines, as well as by fear and stress due to severe competition.' They 'neutralize the venom of modernization' (Bode 1998:367). These medicines, combining the good of both tradition and modernity, symbolically represent what modern Indians want to achieve for themselves. The indigenous pharmaceutical industry, according to Bode, thus opens a window on present-day Indian culture, caught between two worlds.[1]

Towards an anthropology of manufacture

Bode's anthropological study on producers of pharmaceuticals is exceptional. Probably the Indian companies hoped to gain recognition by allowing a researcher on their premises. For the same reason (concern about their reputation) 'Western' producers of pharmaceuticals have done the opposite and closed their doors to social scientists. They have – to the best of our knowledge – never allowed anthropologists to study their companies. The remainder of this chapter will, therefore, not discuss and analyse the fruits of such research, but sketch (1) why anthropological research on the cultural economy of medicine manufacture is desirable; (2) why it has not taken place; and (3) how researchers have tried to make up for the inaccessibility of the manufacturers.

Market, culture and medicine

Market, culture and medicine are concepts which usually are placed in three different study domains. The market belongs to the economists, anthropologists claim culture and medical scientists take care of medicine. Here, however, we want to demonstrate their linkages. Evans-Pritchard, in his classic about Azande witchcraft (1937), wrote that witchcraft, oracles and magic are like three sides of a triangle. They suppose each other's presence. The same could be said about market, culture and medicine. Market and medicine only exist in the context of a culture. Conversely, culture is shaped by trading and health practices.

Value, the core concept of economy, is a cultural construct. Only what is *perceived* as valuable will become an item fit for exchange and trading. Nothing has value by its nature alone. Products which are regarded as exquisite food in one place, will be thrown away with disgust elsewhere. Thomas More illustrated the cultural arbitrariness of value in his *Utopia*, where gold had no value and children played with jewels until they realized how childish this was. While Utopia was fantasy, Malinowski observed the same thing on the Trobriand Islands, where parents would throw pearls to their children to play with. A few years later they saw 'White men straining all their forces in competition to acquire as many worthless things as they can' (Malinowski 1922:351).

Once a product has been given its value, it turns around and starts shaping the culture it belongs to. In the same classic study Malinowski describes how old dirty necklaces and armshells, which the islanders think are the most precious objects on earth, move them to undertake hazardous journeys to exchange these valuable objects with distant friends. Those journeys necessitate the building of canoes and the creation of magical rituals and inspire them to singing and dancing. Culture is the creation of human interests, the result of what people need, or, more precisely, what they think they need. Health and medicines are likely to be part of those needs.

Health has, indeed, a cultural and economic meaning. Good health, a Dutch saying goes, is one's most precious property. Indeed, more money is spent on the maintenance and restoration of health than on anything else in life. The money value of health can be read from the bills which hospitals send to insurance companies. A liver transplantation costs 100,000 dollars in the Netherlands, a kidney transplantation

25,000 dollars. The price of one day in the hospital is 500 dollars on average; in Ghana one would pay the equivalent of 2.5 dollars. These examples show that health is good business but they also suggest that the money value of good health varies enormously from country to country.

The production and marketing of medicinal substances fit this general picture. As we have seen in the previous chapters, medicines are popularly regarded as indispensable for keeping healthy. As commodities they are extremely lucrative; they are small, easy to transport (and ideal to smuggle), and the demand is constant and nearly without limit. Their usefulness in life cannot easily be disproved, or – to say it more bluntly – their uselessness is rarely unequivocally proven. Consumers do not have the technical know-how to measure the pharmacological effects of a medicine. This inability to measure efficacy leaves room for the most divergent ideas about medicines, varying from 'chemical poison' to 'miraculous power'.

'Drugs are manufactured by commercial organizations for the same reasons as any other product: to make a profit. The primary reason for the existence of any incorporated business is to benefit its shareholders' (Melville and Johnson 1982:4). A good medicine in the culture of the market is a drug that is a commercial success. Ethical codes drawn up by or for drug companies are first of all a matter of enlightened self-interest. The only thing that really counts is the profit. Famous is the quote by a representative of the drug industry: 'Multinational companies... are not bishops, they are businessmen' (quoted in Melrose 1982:27). Manufacturers are rarely so candid about their deeper motivations. 'Ethnographic data' on their cultural convictions are practically non-existent. It does not seem unreasonable to assume that profit-making constitutes the core value of the culture of medicine manufacture and marketing; but does it?

To understand the culture of the medicine market we not only should study the perceptions and values of consumers and sellers as in the previous chapters; we also need to know how producers of medicines conceive the commercial and medical value of their merchandise. The construction of meanings embodied in medicines starts in the laboratory. Missing those first moments in the life of drugs hampers a contextual understanding of how medicines assume their role in society. Anthropologists have not even been able to scratch the surface of the culture of manufacturing. Why?

The unknown manufacturer

The near non-existence of anthropological fieldwork in the pharmaceutical industry should not come as a surprise. First, there is the reluctance of anthropologists to enter the complex and highly technical world of industrial manufacturing. Most still prefer the relatively simple and conveniently arranged local community to conduct their fieldwork. The very term 'fieldwork', it should be noted, continues to convey Arcadian feelings.

More important, however, is the refusal by manufacturers to allow social scientists in their midst, most likely because our studies do not serve the interests of the industry. In addition, anthropologists anticipate that refusal and do not even try. Industries are defensive about their commercial aims. They practise what Goffman (1971) has called 'impression management'. Products which are supposed to alleviate human suffering are surrounded by a 'money taboo' (Stein 1990:155ff). Drug advertisements, for example, will avoid every reference to price or profit; they portray the ideal image of medicine: the concern of the physician, nurse or parent for the suffering patient. Healing and earning money are kept separate as much as possible.

If the *raison d'être* of the drug industry, profit-making, is so much in conflict with the ideal image of its products, it is indeed wise to close its doors to inquisitive social scientists who will certainly focus their attention on what the industry is not showing to the outside world: profit strategies, informal and illegal practices, unwarranted claims, conflicts, power struggles, politics and myth-making. Anthropologists have been concentrating on such issues in African villages and Asian slums and there is no reason for them to diverge from that tradition when it comes to industrial companies. The study by Latour and Woolgar (1979) on daily life in an American laboratory, which shows how traditions and politics in the laboratory contribute to the shaping of scientific achievements, supports this view.

Another ethnographic account of a laboratory, Rabinow's (1996) study of the invention of the polymerase chain reaction (PCR), has an historical character. The invention took place in the 1980s at Cetus Corporation in the USA. PCR is considered one of the exemplary inventions in biotechnology in the past decades. Rabinow's 'fieldwork' consisted of the study of documents and interviews with some of the key actors in the invention. He attempts to describe the culture of biotechnology and focuses on the configuration of science, politics, business and legal issues. As a matter of fact, historical studies, which have much in common with the anthropological approach but lack the opportunity of participant observation, seem more acceptable to industrial companies than the direct observations requested by anthropologists.[2]

In the 1970s and 1980s, when the marketing practices of the pharmaceutical industry caught the attention of social – and socially oriented –

scientists, that attention turned into almost exclusively critical publications on improper behaviour (e.g. Medawar 1979; Melrose 1982; Muller 1982; Silverman *et al.* 1982; Braithwaite 1984; Chetley 1990). In view of this development, it would be highly unlikely for any pharmaceutical company to welcome social science research. When one of us sent an article on drug promotion to two pharmaceutical companies and asked for their comments – and possibly corrections – he never received a reply. A Dutch anthropologist who studied medicine use in South Africa found no representative of the pharmaceutical industry willing to participate in an interview (Heilbron 1999). The favourite method of anthropologists, to enter a village somewhat casually – through the backdoor as it were – does not work in the case of the industrial 'village', with all its gates carefully watched. The only possibility would be to do undercover research.[3] We are not aware of any such attempt.

The result of all this is that the ideas and practices of drug manufacturers remain largely unknown and that crude stereotypes of the shrewd and unscrupulous entrepreneur continue to exist.[4] Having no access to the actors themselves, social scientists have had only one alternative: to study the publicly visible results of their activities.

Alternative research on promotion and information

The manufacturing and marketing of medicines consists of various phases. Drug discovery, testing and the actual manufacturing are the most difficult to observe. The marketing and sale/distribution are easier to see. As a result, studies of manufacture and marketing have concentrated on drug advertisements, information provided by the industry on inserts about proper use of medicines, scientific publications sponsored by the industry, name-giving to pharmaceuticals, and practices of sales representatives. Most of these studies were carried out by economists, medical scientists and journalists.

The *Journal of Drug Issues* brought out three special issues on drug advertising and promotion (Price 1974; Hargraves 1976; Rachin and Montagne 1992). These issues describe a process of increased state control of drug advertisements in American society. Dubious advertisements may lead to inappropriate prescribing and use of drugs, and medicalization by way of unnecessary drug taking. Sorofman (1992) discusses the effects on self-medication, while Montagne (1992) draws attention to the promotion of medication for social and personal problems. Lexchin (1992) describes the situation in the 'Third World' where control of promotion activities is often lax and the companies are allowed to put unwarranted claims on the efficacy of their products in the advertising to the general public. He refers to a 'double standard' in drug promotion between the rich and the poor countries.

Tan, one of the few anthropologists to study drug manufacturers, has paid considerable attention to advertisements in his country, the Philippines (Tan 1988, 1999). About 25 per cent of the cost of drugs is spent on their promotion, which includes advertising on television and radio and in print. Medicines are advertised on the Philippine radio in the following ways:

Honey, I've got a meeting but I have a cough and a cold.
Take Tusseran capsule to be sure, for all kind of cough.
For my cold too?
Yes even for headache and fever, doctors know that.
Tusseran, when your doctor wants to be sure.

Tennis tonight? I'm tired.
Not me, I take Enervon everyday.
But I take vitamins too.
My doctor says Enervon is different. You get 24 hours energy and body resistance.
It has the anti-stress formula not found in other brands.
Enervon. It's number one. (Tan 1988:126–7)

In 1993 more was spent on the advertisement of medical products than of food products, cigarettes, beverages or home-care products (Tan 1999:40–1). Advertisements make frequent and unqualified use of the word 'safe', have a predilection for superlatives, and fail to mention side-effects, precautions and contraindications. Kahane (1984:181–2) vividly describes the claimed omnipotence of medicines in advertising in a study from Taiwan:

Dizzy. Your eyes don't see clearly. Use Green Oil. It will help stimulate your energy. It will help wake up your head. It will help you work with more vitality.

Do mosquitoes and worms make you itch? Put on Green oil. Stop itching and stop swelling. It is a good medicine for travel and home. Prepare Green Oil.

Vuckovic and Nichter (1997), who describe drug advertising in the USA, point out that advertisements encourage people to ask their doctors for specific medicines. If they do not receive them, they may look for another doctor who *will* satisfy them. Drug advertisements create an awareness of risk which impels people to purchase medicines to obviate the risk or undo its consequences. Advertisements for oestrogen replacements and calcium supplements affect women's views of menopause (see also Lock 1993). 'At riskness', Vuckovic and Nichter (1997:1,293) write, 'has become a state, like illness, to be managed by medicine.'

Nichter and Nichter describe a conversation with a young man in India who studied advertisements attentively. 'Claims of medicine efficacy were often accepted quite literally.' The young man had used advertisement 'knowledge' to collect the following medicines:

a tonic to give him increased strength through better digestion, a blood pu-rification medicine, a glucose solution named Electrose which he describes as 'electronic solution' for tiredness... flatulence tablets to take when travelling, liver tablets for giddiness, and other assorted products. (Nichter and Nichter 1996:274)

But, the authors remark, advertisements also influence members of the medical profession. They quote a doctor who admits that he let himself be 'fooled' by the companies.

In a study on medicine distribution in rural Thailand, Sringernyuang (2000:162) remarks that 'irrational' drug use is encouraged by the 'culturally sensitive' marketing technique of the industry. The same ten-dency, promoting pharmaceuticals in terms and images that fitted local popular illness concepts, was observed in Taiwan (Kahane 1984), the Philippines (Tan 1999) and South Africa (De Wet 1998a, 1998b), and in India in the study of Ayurvedic and Unani companies which started this chapter (Bode 2002).

An international organization, Medical Lobby for Appropriate Market-ing (MaLAM) monitors the promotional activities of the pharmaceutical industry. Its aim is to put pressure on companies to provide adequate scientific information on their products. In 1987 MaLAM reported 462 advertisements as lacking correct information. In 1985 four independent pharmacologists undertook a review of advertisements in Australian and New Zealand medical journals and prescribing guides. They found that 53 per cent of a total of 138 advertisements did not meet the standards (Chetley 1990:55–6).

Package inserts tell a similar story of double standards and biased information (Silverman *et al.* 1982; Osifo 1983). Medawar and Freese (1982) present extensive information and documentation on the pro-motion of an anti-diarrhoeal drug for children in developing countries and on the debate between the company and a British consumer group. For the company, not only its sale profits but also its good name were at stake. In the years that followed this case, some companies reacted more diplomatically to consumer criticism in order to preserve their good name.

From inserts to scientific claims is only a small step. Abraham (1995), a sociologist, has examined research carried out by the pharmaceutical industry and governmental drug regulatory measures in Great Britain and the United States. He comes to the conclusion that the in systematically ignores unfavourable scientific results from it; research.

Abraham presents case studies of five medicines against arthritic diseases in which scientific uncertainty about efficacy and toxicity is effaced to serve the interests of the industry. One is the drug benoxaprofen. The therapeutic claims of the drug, shows Abraham, were not substantiated by scientific research, but the company managed to manipulate the research data to such an extent that the American FDA gave it permission to sell its product on the market. When, later on, the drug proved harmful and caused serious damage, the company tried as long as possible to prevent it from being banned. Abraham quotes a former employee at a drug company saying: 'Scientists who work for the pharmaceutical industry get steeped in corporate culture and slip into biases in favour of their own drugs' (Abraham 1995:2). Abraham himself emphasizes that he makes no attempt to determine whether that bias is conscious or not. He cannot, because he has not been able to meet the employees of drug companies and observe them in their natural environment. The assumption seems reasonable, however, that people involved in the manufacture of drugs largely fail to recognize their bias in their information on their products. Culture has its blind spots. Outsiders notice what is taken for granted by the natives. 'Corporate bias...is a problem, but it should not be reduced to matters of personal integrity', he concludes (Abraham 1995:257). But as long as participant observation in the industrial community remains impossible, that assumption, however plausible, remains unsubstantiated.

Anthropological research *is* sometimes possible at the fringes of the manufacturing world. Sales representatives ('reps') visiting hospitals, health centres, private doctors and pharmacies constitute the most visible part of the culture of pharmaceutical production and marketing. Kamat and Nichter (1997), who followed and interviewed fourteen reps in the Indian city of Bombay, describe their dual – if not contradictory – role. On the one hand they should promote the product they are selling; on the other hand, they are supposed to 'educate' doctors on drug prescription. It is clear from their study that promotion takes precedence. One rep explained his '3Cs' strategy as follows.

My strategy is first to 'convince' the doctor to support the product. If this doesn't work, I try to 'confuse' the doctor by filling him with unnecessary technical details. If nothing else, this at least generates some curiosity in him about the product. If I don't succeed in this too, then I try to 'corrupt' him. A generous quota of samples, expensive gifts, invitation to cocktail parties and 'what not' from the company often does the job. (Kamat and Nichter 1997:131)

Sales representatives operate both in low-income countries with a limited control over pharmaceutical trading and in the rich countries of 'the West'. According to Chetley (1990), more than 50 per cent of the promotional budget of pharmaceutical companies in the UK and Canada went to reps in 1983. In the UK, at the time, there was one rep for every eight general practitioners. Chetley quotes one rep saying: 'I don't think reps mislead doctors as a general rule. I think they are just reflecting the training they received. They are given selective information themselves because companies, in order to maintain motivation, only want them to know the real positives' (1990:58).

A more subtle strategy to promote one's own products lies in the art of naming them. Pharmaceutical companies have given attractive short and easy-to-remember names to their drugs, which contrast sharply with the long and difficult generic names of the same products. The generic names, which are used for drugs provided more cheaply (for example, in essential drug programmes), have been coined by the same company! The result is that both prescribers and clients remember the names of the expensive brand drugs better than those of the generics. The following examples of brand-names (with their generic counterpart) between brackets speak for themselves: Algesal (diethylaminesalicate), Atarax (hydroxyzin), Buscopan (butylscopolamin), Fansidar (sulphadoxine-pyrimethamine), and Ritalin (methylphenidat).

Ironically, the fact that anthropologists have not succeeded in studying the industry has not kept the industry from 'studying anthropology'. Some pharmaceutical companies have defended their promotion of useless medicines with anthropological arguments: it would be paternalistic and ethnocentric to withdraw a product, which the clients want and find beneficial, even if 'our' scientific research proves it to have no effects. Culture over science.

Conclusion

All this leads us back to a point raised earlier in this chapter: it is probably too simple to reduce the exaggerated claims and dubious marketing practices by drug manufacturers to shrewd commercial tactics and fraud. An anthropological research would likely produce a more nuanced insight into their professional culture, where commercial, medical and scientific concerns are fused. Medicines are constructed as good, valuable and indispensable objects. The manufacturers, who were the main figures of this chapter, live up to their name; they manufacture not only medicines but also the meanings of medicines and the need for them. Anthropological research into the culture of manufacture would lead to a better understanding of the inflated optimism regarding the efficacy and safety of medicines. That overconfidence could perhaps be called a form of ethnocentrism which exists in every culture and subculture.

Unfortunately, anthropologists have contributed hardly anything to the study of the culture of drug manufacturing. Reasons for this neglect lie with the anthropologists who showed little interest in choosing a modern industry as a setting for their fieldwork, but more so with the companies that refused to open their gates to critical observers.

That is not to say that little has been published on the manufacturing and marketing of pharmaceuticals. Most of this research focuses on promotional activities and is based on written and pictorial materials produced by the industry. Direct interviews and observations on the shopfloor of companies is not available. It should further be noted that most social science publications on drug manufacture and marketing take a critical if not hostile view of the industry which further aggravates the mutual animosity.

The main public concern about the role of pharmaceutical companies is that commercial gains and not medical needs determine their production of medicines. As a result, non-profitable but effective drugs against widespread serious diseases in poor societies are not produced. A recent editorial reads:

We cannot accept that the dearth of effective drugs for tropical diseases is simply the consequence of a global market economy. Drugs for neglected diseases do not belong in the free market; they require a centralized, public, nonprofit approach. Drugs are not a consumer commodity. (Veeken and Pécoul 2000:310)

The problem, however, is that drugs *are* commodities. Policy makers working for a more equitable distribution of medicines should take this into account. The challenge is how to reconcile commercial interests with public justice. A better understanding of the minds of manufacturers would help to meet that challenge.[5]

11   Health planners: making and contesting drug policy

While drug manufacturers work to widen the market for their commodities, another category of strategists, the public health planners, are concerned to control it. They aim to develop drug policies that limit public expenditure on drugs, while achieving maximum health benefits and meeting public health needs. Policy making tends to be described by health planners as an objective activity whose purpose is to promote efficiency and effectiveness in public health. An analytical gaze reveals two key aspects of this endeavour. One is the use of 'expert knowledge' which allows the health planners to recast their aims in the neutral language of science. The other is the assumption that interventions and knowledge developed centrally are applicable in diverse local contexts. As anthropologists we study policy making and policy implementation as sites for contentious political debates between parties with conflicting or diverging interests (Shore and Wright 1997). We see policy formulation and implementation as a process that is constantly reshaped by conditions encountered as policies move from the central to the local levels where they are implemented, and by political dynamics at all levels.

In this chapter we examine a visionary attempt to formulate a global policy on essential drugs that would ensure economy, safety and effectiveness in pharmaceutical supply and use. Global health planners design essential drugs policies and programmes assuming that 'all else is equal', and that all nations for whom a policy is intended have similar favourable conditions – the same 'level playing field' upon which to play out programmes (Manderson and Whiteford 2000). They develop guidelines for the formulation of national drug policies, ethical criteria, instruments for estimating drug requirements, and all kinds of other procedures for adoption at national levels. These are ideal-type models, which mainly exist on paper. We focus not on the ideal models, but on actual intervention processes. In our view the process of policy making and implementation is not only 'top-down', as is usually implied (see also Long 1992). Initiatives come from below, as much as they come from above. In fact, as we will see, national-level policy makers played an important role in

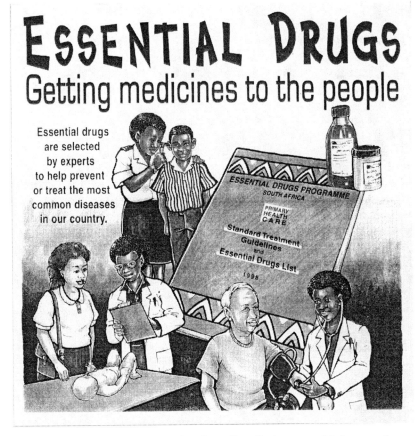

Fig. 11.1 Poster promoting the policy of using essential drugs and standard treatment guidelines.

developing the essential drugs concept, and prescribers and patients living in remote communities in developing countries, because they proved to be reluctant to adopt the essential drugs principles, have contributed to policy changes. Policy making and programme implementation are in our view best conceptualized as interactive processes, shaped by negotiations between networks of actors.

Studying drugs policy

As is the case with manufacturers, there is hardly any anthropological research that does systematic ethnography of health policy making. Judith Justice, one of the few medical anthropologists who has studied health planning, notes: 'In attempting to study the culture of a health planning bureaucracy, one enters terrain largely unexplored by anthropologists' (Justice 1986:4). Global and national policies tend to be defined by anthropologists as 'context', or macro-structures that influence people's lives. Sometimes, however, anthropologists who have worked as consultants on policy issues can reflect on their 'participant observation' in the world of health planners.

In the late 1980s two of us were involved in the evaluation of the World Health Organization's Action Programme on Essential Drugs. The study, later published in the book *Drug Policy in Developing Countries* (Kanji *et al.* 1992), examined the impact of ten years of global drug policy. Since the early 1990s we have participated in the implementation of essential drugs programmes in various ways; we draw on this experience in our analysis of drug policy making. We specifically focus on the emergence of a new public drug policy paradigm, the essential drug concept, which emerged in the 1970s and has guided drug policy making since.

The World Health Organization (WHO), as a global health institution, is a main actor in this story. It is governed by the World Health Assembly, a meeting of member states held annually in May, in which progress is discussed and plans are adopted. It thus functions as a transnational institution. In practice, policy making and implementation are influenced by networks of global and national planners, scientists, industry representatives, activists, Non-Governmental Organizations, and public and private donors. And the policies are affected by globalization processes that undermine the implementation of equity-oriented public health policies. These processes include the increased privatization of health care services, and the implementation of liberalized trade policies that define medicines as commercial goods, protected by intellectual property rights.

The birth of the essential drugs policy

Thirty years ago modern health technology had just awakened and was full of promise. Since then, its expansion has surpassed all dreams, only to become a nightmare. For it has become over sophisticated and over costly. It is dictating our health policies unwisely; and what is useful is being used for too few. Based on these technologies, a huge medical industry has grown up with powerful vested interests of its own. Like the sorcerer's apprentice, we have lost control, social control over health technology. (WHO 1978)

These words from WHO's director general, Halfdan Mahler, in his report to the 31st World Health Assembly in 1978, represent the movement for radical rationalization of the pharmaceutical sector that WHO developed in the late 1970s. At the time, several developing countries had worked out national policies to rationalize their purchase of medicines. The measures they took ranged from stepping up local production of drugs to bulk purchasing of a limited number of essential drugs in their generic form.

Sri Lanka, for example, faced with a chronic foreign exchange problem and a 40–50 per cent increase in drug prices, found that the 1970 allocation of foreign exchange could buy only half the drugs purchased by the 1965 allocation (Wickremasinghe and Bibile 1971). Sri Lanka was one of the first countries to implement a national drugs policy, which included the formation of a State Pharmaceutical Corporation to centralize imports of a limited list of 600 essential drugs (Lall 1979). The policy called for a process of re-education of prescribers on the rational use of these drugs.

Until the late 1970s, the WHO had largely concentrated policy on the safety and efficacy of specific drugs. As a global health institution, it was mainly concerned with technical and normative functions. Within the Organization only one unit, Pharmaceuticals (PHA), had a responsibility for drugs issues. It produced the International Pharmacopoeia, and it developed a certification scheme to help countries ensure the quality of pharmaceutical products. In his 1978 report to the World Health Assembly cited above, Director General Mahler proposed to broaden the scope of WHO's work in the area of drugs by setting up a global Action Programme on Essential Drugs (APED). The primary purpose was

strengthening the national capabilities of developing countries in the selection, supply and proper use of essential drugs to meet their real health needs and in the local production and quality control, wherever feasible, of such drugs. The immediate objective is to make essential drugs and vaccines available under favourable conditions to governments of the less developed countries in order to extend essential health care and disease control to the vast majority of the population. (WHO 1978:3)

The adoption of the essential drugs concept and the setting up of APED reflected a shift in WHO's concern in the late 1970s, away from a mainly technical approach that focused on the eradication of specific diseases, to a more comprehensive health policy (Walt and Rifkin 1981), which aimed at providing basic health services, especially in neglected rural and peri-urban communities. WHO's policy was summarized in its 'Health for All by the Year 2000' aim, which was to be achieved through the Primary Health Care approach. Access to affordable basic health care was considered a basic human right.

APED aimed to put into practice the first model Essential Drugs List, which had been formulated by a committee of pharmacological and public health 'experts' invited to WHO headquarters in Geneva for a round table discussion in 1977. They characterized the essential drugs concept as follows:

> While drugs alone are not sufficient to provide adequate health care, they do play an important role in protecting, maintaining and restoring the health of people... It is clear that for the optimal use of limited financial resources the available drugs must be restricted to those proven to be therapeutically effective, to have acceptable safety and to satisfy the health needs of the population. The selected drugs are called 'essential' drugs, indicating that they are of the utmost importance and are basic, indispensable and necessary for the health needs of the population. (WHO 1977)

The list included around 200 drugs and vaccines that were considered to be safe, effective and affordable. Most of these drugs were no longer protected by patent rights, and were available at low cost in the form of generics.

Implementing the essential drugs concept

It took some time for APED to begin operation because of confusion among the WHO staff managing the programme on what they should be doing. They were unsure whether they should take a lead in putting the essential drug concept into practice in developing countries, or whether they should only provide technical assistance on demand. And they were intimidated by the extremely hostile reaction of the pharmaceutical industry, which sought to limit its applicability to the less developed countries that lacked foreign exchange and hence needed to ration drug imports.

In 1983 a new programme manager was appointed to lead APED, Ernst Lauridsen, a Danish medical advisor who had been involved in the implementation of essential drugs programmes in Afghanistan and Kenya. Under his leadership APED evolved into a proactive programme, which promoted the essential drugs concept and channelled support directly to developing countries that demonstrated the political will to implement a national drug policy. APED generated funds from development assistance budgets of industrialized countries for the purpose of making essential drugs available in basic health care services in the least developed countries.

Between 1983 and 1985, APED concentrated on the supply side of drugs in collaboration with UNICEF's supply division. This division bought essential drugs in bulk from generic suppliers, ensuring high quality, and packaged the drugs in kits that were designed to meet the drug needs of basic health units in African countries. APED used the Kenyan and Tanzanian essential drugs programmes as models, because they had proved the applicability of the essential drugs concept. The programme further promoted the essential drugs concept by developing a wide range of tools, guidelines and training materials for national health planners who intended to implement essential drug programmes (Walt and Harnmeijer 1992).

The essential drugs concept: a contested site

While concentrating on the implementation of essential drugs programmes in poor countries, WHO was being lobbied aggressively by consumer activists and industry. Consumer activists drew attention to the unethical marketing of medicines in Third World countries and were calling for a code of practice, similar to the 'breast-milk substitutes' code (regulating marketing practices of the infant formula producers) that WHO adopted in 1981. The International Federation of Pharmaceutical Manufacturers Associations (IFPMA), anticipating such action, developed its own voluntary code. At the 1982 World Health Assembly, the consumer activist organization Health Action International (HAI)[1] distributed a pamphlet with a detailed criticism of the IFPMA code, arguing that its provisions were inadequate, and that there was insufficient commitment to enforce the code.

WHO, concerned with the heightened politicization of its work in the area of pharmaceuticals, sought to prevent further controversies by organizing another expert meeting, the 1985 Nairobi Conference on the rational use of drugs. In his introductory statement to this meeting, Mahler reminded the participants that they were there not as representatives of interested parties but as experts. He went on to say that the aim of the conference was to ensure that people, particularly in developing countries, had access to the drugs they needed; it was not intended to be a battleground for the pharmaceutical industry and consumers to vent their interests (WHO 1985).

Despite this assertion, the following issues evoked considerable conflicts in the expert meeting:

the adoption of a WHO code on the marketing of pharmaceuticals, with consumer 'experts' arguing that the voluntary code was dysfunctional;

the universality of the essential drugs concepts – with industry representatives arguing that it should only be implemented in poor countries that cannot afford access to a wider range of drugs;

the adoption of a so-called 'needs clause', which had been implemented in the Norwegian drug policy stipulating that any new drug has to be shown to be *more* effective than those already on the market and that there should be a clear need for the new product.

Adoption of the needs clause would mean applying the essential drugs concept in selection of drugs for the private as well as the public health sector. That policy was advocated by consumer 'experts' on the grounds that it would contribute significantly to the more rational use of drugs (partly because it is easier to educate doctors and consumers on the proper use of a limited number of drugs). The industry was vehemently opposed, arguing that this would be detrimental to the development of new drugs.

In the end the conference upheld the essential drugs concept as a universal principle; it neither accepted a code nor endorsed the 'medical need' clause. Summing up the expert meeting, Mahler suggested that WHO establish expert committees to produce guidelines on ethical advertising and on developing national drug policies. The outcome of the meeting was presented by the WHO secretariat to the 1986 World Health Assembly, as 'the Revised Drug Strategy'. More than the earlier policy, the strategy stressed the need to make the *use* of drugs more rational throughout the world; ensuring supply was not enough. It required WHO to secure the co-operation of 'concerned parties', including governments, industry and consumer groups. This last point was clearly a way for the WHO to accommodate the diverging interests in the field.

The 1986 World Health Assembly endorsed the Revised Drug Strategy. Having accepted Mahler's summing up of the Nairobi expert meeting, neither industry nor consumer representatives could oppose the revised policy, and it was adopted unanimously. The US delegation voiced the industry position that the essential drugs concept should be confined to the public sector in poor countries. The US preferred to regard WHO as a technical support agency and disapproved of its advocating state intervention in and control of the health market. The Third World countries and the Nordic and Dutch delegations supported the consumer view that the essential drugs criteria – safety, efficacy, need and affordability – should be used to reduce the number of drugs on the market in all countries, as a necessary condition for rationalized distribution and use of drugs (Hardon 1992). It is noteworthy that material support for implementation of essential drugs programmes at the national level came from Danish, Swedish and Dutch government development agencies, countries with a relatively small pharmaceutical industry and governments with long-standing social democratic traditions that endorse state regulation of the private health market.

National-level essential drugs planning

Global policies make little difference if they are not adopted at the national level. Once Lauridsen took over leadership of APED, WHO staff started playing an active role in motivating national health planners to adopt the essential drugs concept in national drug policies. Some countries, like Sri Lanka and Kenya (where Lauridsen had worked), were far ahead. The experiences of these countries had in fact led WHO to develop the essential drug concept. In the early years of APED there was a rapid increase in the number of developing countries that adopted essential drugs lists and implemented essential drugs programmes. The 1989 APED evaluation found that essential drugs lists existed in all the thirteen countries[2] studied, but that in seven countries they applied only to the public sector. The success in adopting national essential drug policies was found to be limited, reflecting lack of political will of government to rationalize their pharmaceutical sectors, and lack of capacity of national health planners to mediate opposition locally. National essential drugs policies would limit the use of inessential drugs; attempts to introduce restrictive legislation were met with opposition from national industry associations and physician organizations.

The evaluation found that essential drugs at the primary level of public health care had increased as a result of the implementation of essential drugs programmes. In poor countries in Africa, with small, generally poor populations of limited commercial interest to the pharmaceutical industry, essential drugs programmes proved easiest to implement. For example, in Kenya an essential drugs programme was initiated in 1981. The objective was to supply essential drugs in ration kits to rural primary-level health facilities. The Danish and Swedish development aid agencies, DANIDA and SIDA, agreed to cover the costs of drugs, which were purchased through UNICEF, and later partially supplied by local producers. The Kenyan drug policy did not aim to rationalize the private sector, which accounted for around 70 per cent of the drug market (Kanji and Hardon 1992).

In contrast, Bangladesh did manage to adopt an essential drugs policy that covered both the public and the private sector. Interestingly, this was done in the context of a military coup, when Lieutenant-General and Army Chief of Staff H.M. Ershad seized power in 1982. In the new political environment he introduced a radical change in drugs policy. Within four weeks of the coup he established an expert committee of eight members to confront the problems in production, distribution and consumption of pharmaceutical products. Less than three months later the Bangladesh Ordinance of 1982 was issued as a Declaration by Ershad, based on a set of sixteen guidelines that would regulate the private pharmaceutical sector. The main aim of the Ordinance was to halve the 'wastage of foreign exchange through the production and/or importation of unnecessary drugs of marginal value' (Reich 1994). The drugs policy was to be applied to both private and public sectors and created a restricted national formulary of 150 essential drugs plus 100 supplementary drugs for specialized use. Over 1,600 drugs deemed 'useless, ineffective, or harmful' were banned. One of the expert committee members was Zafrullah Chowdury, a leading HAI activist, and director of a local company manufacturing generic drugs. The Bangladesh association of pharmaceutical manufacturers was not represented on the committee. It was argued that its presence would delay and distort the process of policy development (Reich 1994; Walt 1994). At the time, 75 per cent of the Bangladesh pharmaceutical market was controlled by eight multinational companies (Rolt 1985).

The Bangladesh case illustrates how powerful the forces are which oppose implementation of the essential drugs concept in the private sector. Immediately after the Ordinance was issued, ambassadors from the US, France, the UK, Germany and the Netherlands complained to the President about the restriction on free trade (Wolffers 1992). Since 80 per cent of development aid to Bangladesh came from these sources, their complaints could not be ignored (Reich 1994). The WHO publicly supported the policy and so did some international NGOs, including HAI.

As a result of the policy, local production of essential drugs increased dramatically. By 1986, 80 per cent were manufactured locally, as opposed to 30 per cent in 1981. Prices of essential drugs dropped by 75 per cent. National drug companies started supporting the policy. However, although initial gains were promising, internal logistical problems impeded full implementation. Banned and illegal drugs were smuggled into the country, and the resulting black market was difficult to control. In the mid-1980s Ershad made some concessions to the multinational industry and permitted the return of some banned drugs (Walt 1994:172).

Assessing achievements

The 1989 APED evaluation concluded that the programme had had considerable impact on increasing access to essential drugs in public health services, but limited impact on the actual use of drugs. Part of the explanation lies in the public sector bias in implementation of essential drugs programmes. Health planners have a blind spot for drug use outside the channels of health care that fall under their mandate. They assume that people use public health centres, and that they take medicines on prescription. In most developing countries, as we have seen, this is not the case. Despite the WHO adoption of the Revised Drug Strategy oriented towards better use – and not just better supply – of drugs, public health planners continued to put most emphasis on making sure medicines were available in primary-level health facilities in the public sector. Training on the appropriate prescription and use of essential drugs lagged behind.

It is significant that most countries working on an essential drugs plan seem to exclude the private sector. In that way, opposition is diminished from private doctors who wish to maintain their freedom to prescribe, and businessmen who want to maintain profits. In fact, they may even see advantages in the programme. The pharmaceutical industry is increasingly willing to support essential drug policies that do not restrict drug distribution in the private sector. Essential drugs programmes represent an expansion of the market for cheap generic drugs that are supplied to people who could not previously afford any pharmaceuticals at all. For local politicians the supply of valued goods to health centres in remote areas is attractive, as it gives the impression of active concern. Attempting to control the private sector would certainly be politically unpopular. (Van der Geest, Hardon and Whyte 1990:183)

Yet given the heavy reliance on private sources of drugs, it is there that rational drug use must be addressed.

It is unlikely that essential drugs plans will succeed if the reforms are limited to the public sector. Doctors will continue to prescribe non-essential drugs because they believe them to be better – or because they can make more profit from them. Obviously sellers of medicines, both pharmacists and informal vendors, will continue to recommend the more profitable pharmaceuticals, which may not include essential drugs. And clients will continue to buy non-essential drugs because they are made to believe that they are better and perhaps also because they are more readily available. (1990:183)

The APED evaluation concludes that, in its support for the essential drugs concept, WHO created an environment for change and provided a forum in which consumer groups could affect policy. WHO's advocacy of the essential drugs concept in the 1980s led to various international agencies, governments, professional bodies and NGOs accepting and promoting the concept. At the country level, WHO's APED had been important mainly as an agency providing technical support. WHO consultants and their tools for assessing country situations, estimating drug requirements, selecting and procuring essential drugs and developing national drug policies were instrumental in mobilizing donor support for essential drugs programmes in specific countries. In a final chapter of the evaluation report, we attempted to look forward to new horizons in the 1990s. One of the issues we highlighted was the acute need to consider the increased demands for drugs posed by the AIDS epidemic (Hardon and Kanji 1992).

AIDS activists challenge the essential drugs concept

Ten years later, the enormous problems of health care for people with HIV/AIDS became a new site for contentious debates between interested parties involved in essential drugs planning. The debates followed the introduction of life-saving anti-retroviral therapies (ARVs) in the North. These new therapies are unaffordable for most developing-country essential drugs programmes. AIDS activists and other consumer lobbyists started campaigning for access to AIDS medicines globally, drawing attention to the effect of neo-liberal inspired globalization processes on public health. They not only pressured the WHO to take steps to make AIDS medicines accessible, but also targeted the World Trade Organization (WTO) to consider public health needs in the adoption of intellectual property rights. Specifically, the activists called for the implementation of two WTO provisions which allow countries either to produce medicines locally in case of public health emergencies under 'compulsory licensing' or to import the drugs from countries where they are not granted a patent (parallel imports). Industry representatives strongly disapprove of the implementation of these WTO provisions to lower prices in developing countries, as they argue that they need to recover the research and development costs for the new therapies.

The AIDS activists called upon WHO to include ARVs in the essential drugs list in order to put pressure on industries to lower prices, arguing that there are no alternative life-saving therapies for AIDS patients. The WHO and other drugs programme planners opposed this idea, as the drugs do not fulfil the criterion of affordability, and are not sufficiently tested yet to ensure therapeutic efficacy and safety in resource-poor conditions. The international relief organization Médicins sans Frontières (MSF) finally took up the issue and organized a seminar with WHO policy makers to discuss it in September 2000. The result of this negotiation was the proposal to develop a supplementary list of drugs that are essential but not yet affordable (MSF 2000).

In its campaign to increase access to essential drugs, MSF not only aimed to include ARVs on the list of essential drugs; it also developed strategies to lower the price of the drugs to make them more affordable to developing countries; and thus more 'eligible' as essential drugs. In February 2001, it announced that the Indian generic drug manufacturer Cipla, would sell its triple-combination therapy for AIDS to MSF for $350 per year per patient and to governments for $600/year. The $350 price was a discount of 96.6 per cent off the price of the same combination in the US, which would cost about $10,400 per year. At the time, local production of cheaper AIDS drugs was also taking place in other countries such as Thailand and Brazil, countries which aimed at making AIDS drugs available to patients in their populations. These efforts of developing countries were opposed strongly by the manufacturers of patented AIDS drugs. They worried about diminishing markets in developing countries, and about the consequences in developed countries where such cheaper drugs could be imported parallel to the patented drugs supplied at high cost by the multinational companies.

The pharmaceutical industry opposition was most visible in South Africa, where thirty-nine companies sued the South African government, which in its Medicines Act of 1997 adopted a law that would allow the government to import drugs from sources (such as the generic manufacturers in India, Thailand and Brazil) other than the patent holder. The companies argued that the law was unconstitutional and violated their international property rights. The South African health minister charged that millions of South Africans were dying because the anti-retroviral drugs sold by the multinational patent holders were too costly; he claimed that he was obliged to seek alternatives in the interest of public health. The South African government was supported by the internationally operating AIDS advocacy movement, resulting in worldwide press coverage of the law-suit. MSF presented a petition with 250,000 signatories to the companies calling on them to back down. (*The Economist* 21 April 2001; Drug-induced dilemma.) The companies, in an unprecedented defeat, did so in April 2001, stating in a press release: 'the agreement announced today balances the health needs of the South African population, respect for intellectual property, and the Government's interest in preserving the option of taking advantage of the flexibility of the TRIPS agreement to address public health concerns' (IFPMA 2001).

Policies are constantly reshaped in response to changing conditions. The AIDS epidemic has been one such force. It has also forced global health planners and all other actors involved in drug policy making to rethink the essential drugs concept. How relevant is such a concept if its implementation excludes from essential drugs lists medicines needed by AIDS patients, because they are too expensive? To what extent can affordability as a criterion be upheld for diseases where there are simply no cheap alternatives available?

Multiple levels, divergent interests

Global policies like Primary Health Care or Essential Drugs can be usefully analysed in terms of the links between the multiple levels at which they operate. The multilevel perspective (Van der Geest, Speckmann and

Streefland 1990) requires that we methodologically distinguish the significance that a policy might have to the actors at any given level. What APED meant to the officials and experts meeting in Geneva and Nairobi to develop a global programme differs from what it might mean to any given national government or again to the health workers in a rural district or to local residents struggling to get treatment. But asserting that different perspectives exist is only a first step. The methodological challenge is to show the links between levels and interests: how one affects the others in intended and unintended ways.

In an article tellingly entitled, 'The King's Law Stops at the Village Gate', Craig (2000) examines local and global pharmacy regulation in Vietnam. He shows how global regulatory bodies (not only WHO, but also the association of pharmaceutical manufacturers, organizations of consumer activists and others) address national governments like that of Vietnam, which has its own bureaucratic style and characteristic positioning in relation to the private sector. The Vietnam government did adopt a national drugs policy and a plan of action, but only one of seventy-five planned activities focused directly on consumers. National pharmacy regulation does not easily penetrate beyond the village gate, where other more subtle forms of regulation occur. He shows how lay medication is guided by implicit self-regulation through concerns about compatibility (similar to the *hiyang* concept described in chapter 2) and through emphasis on the correct dose of medicine. Amazingly, his informants knew the names, indications for and dosages of a dozen different antibiotics (Craig 2000:106). What rational use of drugs meant to the mothers advising each other on what to give their children was very different from what the national committees had written into policy. But there was a common concern about accurate dosing (though there was less congruence in the matters of diagnosis and indications). Craig suggests that policy makers could tailor their activities to the practices and interests of local users in ways that might make it easier to get past the village gate.

Diversity in national context is always a challenge to global health planners. To accommodate difference, the planners subsequently develop guides for situation analysis and programme planning, which then are aimed to facilitate national-level adoption of global blueprints. Key characteristics of the culture of global health planners are that they believe in the 'do-ability' of health policies and programmes and that they think they can change the world by encouraging national planners to adopt and implement the policies.

What changes in practice? There is sufficient evidence from health service studies that the link between the global health planners and the national and local levels was important in increasing availability of essential drugs in the public sector. The global-level players give technical guidance and provide national policy makers with access to agencies such as UNICEF that supply essential drugs, and to donors who are willing to pay for them. Thus they contribute to the movement of essential drugs from producers dispersed over the whole world to remote public health clinics in Zambia, Kenya, Indonesia and Pakistan. Drug supplies are important to national and local politicians; they demonstrate that the government is doing something, even in peripheral areas. The same holds for the church-based health programmes, which cater to at least half of the population in many African countries. They have adopted the policy and supply essential drugs, too.

But at the level of local drug providers and consumers, other interests are at play, of the kinds we have seen in the preceding chapters. The powerful forces of commodification and the convenient way that drugstores bridge sectors in health care systems make drug use difficult to regulate, especially through policies focused so heavily on the public sector. The consumers' assumptions about the value and efficacy of medicines are based on habitual practices and ways of reasoning little appreciated by global and national policy makers.

Partly owing to the growing body of anthropological literature that has documented these realities, global essential drugs planners have paid much more attention to the rational use of drugs in the 1990s. A new network emerged, the International Network on the Rational Use of Drugs, which aimed to promote more rational prescribing. This Network conducted yearly training courses for national-level drugs planners and health workers on ways to promote rational drug use, with strong support from WHO's Drug Action Programme. More recently one of us supported the Drug Action Programme in developing a course on promoting rational drug use in communities. This course encourages health policy makers to assess first how people use drugs, where they obtain them and what criteria they have for using them, before developing interventions aimed at improving the use of drugs.

Conclusion

Anthropologists have been participant observers in the process of making drugs policy in the last couple of decades. We have played an important role in documenting drug use and distribution practices in diverse contexts, and in evaluating programmes and projects, and we have been involved in efforts to give end-users more voice in the implementation of essential drugs policies and programmes. In doing so we take an 'enlightened professional' stance (Whyte and Birungi 2000). Using the essential drugs concept as a tool in our intervention projects, we adopt biomedical criteria for assessing safety and efficacy of drugs, as well as medical need. But we do not do so uncritically. We problematize the knowledge of both consumers of medicines and specialists, and we try to facilitate increased understanding and dialogue.

Part V

Conclusion

12 Anthropologists and the sociality of medicines

In this book we have been following the social lives of medicines in the hands of different actors: mothers of children in Manila, villagers in Burkina Faso, women in the Netherlands, consumers in London, shopkeepers in Cameroon, pharmacists in Mexico, injectionists in Uganda, doctors in Sri Lanka, industrialists in India and policy makers in Geneva. One important category of actors has been left implicit, however: we ourselves, the authors of these chapters. For us, anthropologists, medicines have still another meaning and another type of life; in our hands and on our paper they are intriguing cultural objects. They embody anthropological ideas about the power things have over people, and about the power relations between people mediated through objects, about symbolization, about medicalization, and about the process of globalization.

If medicines are life-saving objects to mothers with children, symbols to explain the world to African farmers, profitable commodities to traders, pharmacists and manufacturers, and tokens of concern to prescribing physicians and their clients, they are first of all topics for writing and reflection to anthropologists; they are good to think and good to write about. In people's ways of dealing with medicines all facets of cultural reasoning and action come to the fore, as we have tried to show in these chapters. At the same time, however, medicines are not purely an academic issue for anthropologists. We too accept their power to alleviate suffering and their significance for the people with whom we work.

Anthropological lives with medicines

Each of us encountered medicines as worthy of research in situations that were as much 'everyday life' as 'anthropology'. During our research medicines 'struck' us as being of the utmost importance for survival to the people we were staying with. We *had* to focus our attention on them. Ignoring pharmaceuticals, we realized, was the result of an inverse type of ethnocentrism among anthropologists who were only interested in

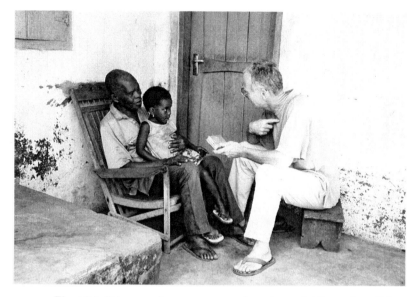

Fig. 12.1 Ethnography as an approach to the social lives of medicines: one of the authors during fieldwork.

'difference', in exotic phenomena, and who did not have to worry about access to medication when they were sick.

Sjaak van der Geest was first drawn to the study of pharmaceuticals when he was doing fieldwork on sexual relationships and birth control in a rural town in Ghana. During that research young people repeatedly told him that they used a certain medicine to prevent pregnancy and that they used the same medicine to terminate a pregnancy which they had failed to prevent. Students at the university, he soon found out, were using the same medicine for the same purposes. The name of the medicine was 'Alophen'; it was for sale in all drugstores he visited, in Accra as well as in rural towns and villages. Alophen, he discovered, was a purgative produced by a company in Detroit. How this product had come to play the role of most popular contraceptive for Ghanaian youth was a riddle. His curiosity – and concern – grew further when he found out that doctors and other medical professionals were unaware of the social life of Alophen; worse, they had never heard of it. The popularity and wide-spread use of foreign-produced medicines outside the knowledge and control of the professional medical world proved not only intriguing to him but also of life importance to those using them. Suddenly he began to see pharmaceuticals everywhere: in shops, at the market, in small kiosks and in private houses. Some of them were relatively harmless, others were dangerous prescription-only ones. A few years later he started his research on the distribution and use of pharmaceuticals in Cameroon.

Susan Whyte's anthropological life with medicines began with the realization that medicines from distant places formed a kind of alternative to the ritual treatments of misfortune she was studying in Uganda in 1970. She was intrigued with the way people attributed special power to medicines from the Indian Ocean island of Pemba, to amulets made of recycled cartridges and tin cans, and even to the fearsome 'batri', said to be extracted from the imported battery cells used in flashlights and radios. She also caught glimpses of specialists in another kind of foreign medicine, the lay injectionists who discreetly administered penicillin to their neighbours and earned a bit of money. Returning two decades later, she found there was nothing discreet about the booming business of 'European' medicines that had spread even in rural areas. Pharmaceuticals had become folk medicines. As Whyte explored the lively trade in pills, capsules and vials of injectable medicine, she was led to problems in the national health services as well as to local conceptions of the power of medicines. The fact that Denmark, where she lived, was supporting the Uganda Essential Drugs Programme challenged her to consider policy implications of what she was learning in ethnographic fieldwork. At the same time, commitment to a community she had known over many years, where infectious diseases continued to bring suffering and death, inspired her to think pragmatically. Together with a team of Ugandan researchers she became involved in the Uganda Community Drug Use Project with the purpose of contributing to improved use of those indigenized foreign medicines.

Anita Hardon was confronted with problems in the use of medicines when she was conducting fieldwork on the complex interactions between nutrition and infectious diseases in small children in a rural village in the Philippines. Mothers repeatedly asked her for advice on medicines, showing her prescriptions, usually with four or five different medicines, mostly unnecessary for common childhood coughs and diarrhoeas. She decided systematically to review treatments given to the children and found that 80 per cent of all children's illnesses were treated without health workers' advice. Trained also as a medical biologist, she was concerned about the risks of uncontrolled use of medicines in self-care and irrational prescribing by doctors. She was asked by a community-based health programme trying to educate consumers on the 'rational' use of medicines in self-care to assess why the interventions were not having much effect. This study resulted in her thesis, which describes how people confront ill-health in an urban slum in Metro Manila. It also impelled her to become an active participant in the international advocacy movement Health Action

International, which aims to increase access to essential drugs globally, to promote more appropriate drug use, to reduce the number of inessential drugs on the market, and to regulate advertising to prescribers and consumers. In her later work, Hardon has turned to the social construction of pharmaceutical technologies, specifically contraceptives. She has been part of the international women's health movement, which calls for reproductive technologies to be developed and provided more in line with women's needs.

Anthropologists handling medicines

The brief sketches above raise issues about how anthropologists studying medicines have positioned themselves in relation to kinds of knowledge and uses of knowledge. Medicines have intrigued us, and fuelled our anthropological imaginations, yet ideas and practices around medicines were not simply data to be analysed. We were concerned about health problems and we felt that what we had learned had implications for health professionals and policy makers. But we did not necessarily think that our knowledge should be used simply to facilitate their agendas. Rather we wanted to use it to interrogate public health paradigms and professional practice, to draw attention to blind spots and biases, including the neglect of consumer agency. We also wanted, at times, to go beyond analysis and critique, to engage ourselves in concrete projects of action. Reflecting on the ways we as anthropologists have handled medicines, we suggest that there are three distinguishable positions, although much anthropological writing straddles more than one (Whyte and Birungi 2000).

As a method of knowing, ethnography demands (preferably extended) periods of engagement in some empirical world of lived experience. Through 'the revolutionary move of joining people where they live' (Hart 1998), ethnography should richly describe the situated concerns of particular people using specific medicines for the problems they think are pressing. That kind of research practice, combined with the broad comparative perspective of anthropology, tends to give a view of all knowledge as contingent. What biomedical researchers believe about antibiotics is just one form of (ethno-)knowledge based in a certain kind of social practice. What customers in a Cameroon market believe about red and black capsules is equally legitimate and worthy of respect and understanding.

Such an approach could be called populist in its sympathetic portrayal of the lay users of medicines. At its best it unfolds lifeworlds and world-views; it shows how people experience symptoms and what choices and constraints guide their actions. Rational Drug Use? Users have their own form of rationality, as good ethnography reveals. The populist position

emphasizes the agency of consumers of medicines. It tends to d
their criticisms of the professional providers of medicine and ho
popularize it by obtaining medicines and knowledge on their own
A beautiful example is the citation of a statement made by an informant
in Sri Lanka:

> Medicine cures, doctors control the knowledge of medicines and we are made
> dependent. We do not receive health education about medicines, only about using
> soap, drinking boiled cool water, and taking immunizations – things from which
> there is no profit. There are many things we want to learn, but they teach us only
> what they want us to know. Yet we are not helpless. Just as we have learned to
> use *Sinhala Behet* (herbal medicines) so we will learn about *ingirisi* (allopathic)
> medicines through experience. (Nichter and Nordstrom 1989:367)

In the chapters of this book, the populist approach is strong. The sceptics
who do not take their medicine in London, the Ugandans going to a
trusted neighbour for an injection, the Cameroonians finding a way, when
the formal health care system lets them down: we are trying to understand
their reasoning in those situations.

The populist view valorizes consumers' capabilities and agency. In contrast, the 'enlightened' one doubts them. It reveals people's knowledge
of medicines as inadequate; their medication practices are irrational, and
they are likely to be victims of commercial interests. These criticisms are
based on an informed position against which popular knowledge is measured and found wanting. Much applied anthropology takes an 'enlightened' stance, almost of necessity. When we co-operate with biomedical
planners, policy makers and practitioners in projects whose aim is to improve health and health services, we often adopt biomedical standards for
evaluating medication practices. Although 'critical' medical anthropology
deplores the tendency of anthropologists becoming the 'handmaidens-
translators to biomedicine' (Morsey 1996:32), it also seems perverse to
refuse in principle to accept the knowledge of biomedicine when it has the
potential to save lives. There are high rates of self-medication in countries
where infectious diseases claim many children's lives. There is growing
microbial resistance to safe and cheap drugs for infectious diseases. In
these situations many anthropologists accept that it is important to com-
pare lay people's knowledge and use of drugs to biomedical orthodoxy.
But most would not focus only on the 'shortcomings' of lay people *vis-à-
vis* biomedical ideals of rational drug use.

A critical version of the 'enlightened' position problematizes the knowledge and practice of *both* specialists and lay people. The proliferation
of medicines is related to a transformation in consciousness whereby
professionals and lay people alike come to believe (or know) that

medicines are the answers to their problems. From this position, as we have seen, some speak of 'false consciousness' generated by health commodification – the belief that health can be secured through medicinal commodities (Nichter 1989:235–6). Notions of ideology, hegemony and complicity are invoked in discussing the medicalization and pharmaceuticalization of suffering. Health professionals play the role of intellectuals, 'sustaining commonsense definitions of reality through their highly specialized and validating forms of discourse' (Scheper-Hughes 1992:171). Lay people are 'complicit' in that their everyday knowledge and practice, indeed their bodily experience, are oriented towards medicinal commodities as solutions to their problems. The knowledge and practices of both users and providers of medicines are found wanting.

Against what standards are they measured? Neither Nichter nor Scheper-Hughes is explicit about this. But it seems safe to say that their criticisms are based on classic public health principles: recognition of the social/political/economic bases of health, social justice, disease prevention and health promotion, and rational drug use (pharmacological efficacy plus economic efficiency).

Much of the 'critical enlightened' view of medicines is directed against situations where people are using tonics, vitamins or other drugs deemed unnecessary, rather than taking steps to change the political economy of health. The critique is just as relevant to the use of 'indigenous' medicines. As Charles Leslie once wrote:

The bottom line in the discussions . . . is how much choice people in poor countries should have in spending their pennies. Of course health care planners believe that they should not buy tonics to prevent premature ejaculation, or to make their sons more intelligent. They should deal realistically with the terrible problems in their countries, with malnutrition and infectious disease. (Leslie 1988:xii)

At some point, this discussion gets uncomfortable for practising anthropologists. The public health concept of rationality and progress can be taken to imply that rituals, symbols and other concepts of efficacy are at best irrational, at worst deceptive. Where that point lies is highly debatable.

To what extent should anthropological research simply ignore biomedical judgements about rational use of drugs, in order better to engage the perspectives and practices of the consumers and providers? At what point, if at all, should they make judgements about 'irrationality', unwarranted medicalization, incompetence or exploitation? There is not going to be agreement on this question. In fact, individual anthropologists are not even consistent with themselves in this regard. But we want to point out that this question arises more insistently for an anthropology of materia medica than it does for anthropological studies in other domains of culture. Drugs are special commodities.

A third anthropological position is possible, one we have called pragmatic. It emphasizes the participation part of participant observation, and takes applied research as an opportunity both to work for limited change and to create knowledge through practical grappling with problems. The attraction of this position is that it is contingent and processual: it is oriented to the 'truths' of a given situation as they happen over time. It requires an appreciation of differentiated perspectives and interests; and it learns about them by trying to change them. But there are difficulties here, too. The action researcher has to make a decision – at least a tactical one – about what practices should be changed, and s/he has to make alliances with parties interested in altering them. In doing that, anthropologists place themselves in a social relation to medicines and to other actors. They handle them not only on paper, but in the strategizing and exchanges of social life.

An ethnographic agenda

However we choose to position ourselves in relation to the sociality of medicines, anthropologists have a unique contribution to make in the form of rich and careful ethnography. Let us conclude, therefore, by supplementing Nichter and Vuckovic's (1994) research agenda with some suggestions for field research that arise from the foregoing chapters.

To say that medicines are social is to remind ourselves of two sides of the same coin. First, medicines take on meaning through common social experience in the context of social relations. Second, their use in social life has implications, immediate and long term, for those relations. Stressing the sociality of medicines raises certain kinds of research questions to be answered through ethnographic research.

The logistics of meaning

The first set of questions has to do with how medicines come to mean for people in particular situations. We have seen that medicinal substances link conventional images from everyday life (tethered donkeys) or from imagined worlds (pure nature, scientific laboratories) to bodily experience. But how do those images get confirmed as meaningful? Answering that question requires attention to the ways people learn about medicines in the course of their daily lives. Researchers have been most concerned with what medicines mean and what people know about them. They are only now beginning to ask how people acquire different kinds of knowledge through social practice – and how they revise their knowledge.

Much of what people understand about medicines is learned at home from family, neighbours and friends. Children in Manila assimilate knowledge about cough medicine in the course of being treated by their mothers. Mossi women sitting around a cooking fire exchange advice about the ashes of forked sticks as medicine for fissures around a child's anus. But we have also seen how people learn through other kinds of relationships. Those Manila mothers saved the prescriptions they received from doctors, in case their child developed the same symptoms again. The authority of doctors, exemplified in that precious bit of script, was one among several social contexts for learning. Ugandans have learned about injections by going to the health centre, where injections have been the 'best treatment' for generations.

The growing forces of commodification have opened up new channels for getting to know medicines. The challenge for fieldworkers is to trace out empirically what kinds of social relations are involved. In some cases, familiarity and lack of social distance between seller and consumer seem to facilitate developing a common popular knowledge, as is the case with drug vendors and their customers in Cameroon. Advertising provides images to the public; but this seemingly anonymous communication may be personalized through discussions with the attendant in a neighbourhood drug shop about the merits of various brands. The commercial interests in manufacturing meanings for medicinal commodities present difficulties for this social logistics approach. But it is crucial to do ethnography along these lines in order to find out how images are formulated and communicated.

The social efficacy of medicines

A second set of research questions about the sociality of medicines concerns their social uses and effects. If we use the term efficacy, it is to raise the issue of whether the social workings of medicines are intended or seen as desirable. And by whom. Again, for ethnographers, these are empirical questions that require trying to understand the situated concerns of social actors as well as attempting to analyse connections of which the actors themselves may be unaware.

In an immediate sense, social efficacy is about what giving and taking medicines does for the social relationships of those involved. What are their intentions beyond getting rid of symptoms? Or rather, do the symptoms have social implications that are part of the problem? We have seen how complicated even these seemingly simple questions can be. Mothers in the Philippines were caring for their children in a context of high mortality where they might be blamed for negligence. Women Netherlands were trying to exert some control over their lives they could manage their jobs, children and husbands. Many Americans 'buy time' with medicines, in order not to miss work (Vuckovic 1999). Doctors may give medicines so as to end a consultation, please a patient or avoid having to listen to a lot of misery that cannot easily be helped.

How is the enactment of medication understood? Whatever the intentions of people interacting through medicines, the social meaning of offering and receiving medicine can differ. To be a compliant patient in a Dutch psychiatric hospital may be virtuous in the eyes of the staff and a total loss of autonomy in the experience of an 'inmate'. To reject biomedicine as artificial and turn instead to Bach Flower remedies is to perform a small statement about cultural politics. We have to enquire about the sense in which taking medicine is a social act as well as a medical one. Within relationships qualities like trust, authority, respect, concern and generosity are at stake. As a social actor, the consumer of medicines indirectly conveys something about his or her social identity as modern, enlightened, conventional, traditional, disciplined, critical or indifferent.

These kinds of research questions focus on direct interaction and immediate implications. But some of the most controversial aspects of social efficacy are about indirect and longer-term implications of medicine use for social relations. Like other forms of technology, medicines seem to be at the disposal of people; but people are also disposed by medicines to understand and deal with their problems in a certain way (Van der Geest 1994). This insight is the basis for the arguments that the mounting commercial availability of all kinds of medicines has far-reaching social effects. The growing presence of medicines creates an awareness of the need for medicines. This increases the wealth and power of those who supply them. And it also encourages people to define and manage their problems medicinally, emphasizing some kinds of social relations (with drug sellers and doctors) at the expense of others (such as environmental and social justice activists). We want to emphasize, however, that such conjectures about social efficacy should be subjected to empirical research in specific instances. That would mean examining the social effects of the composite, intertwined system of drug provision in general as we have sketched out in the cases of Cameroon and Uganda. Ideally ethnography on this topic would follow processes over time so that changes could be seen in historical perspective.

We hope that future anthropological work on medicines will produce ethnography on questions like these and thereby create a better basis for the development of theory and the application of knowledge.

Notes

2 MOTHERS AND CHILDREN

1. The explanatory model describes how illnesses are labelled, interpreted and treated. It is defined as 'the notions about an episode of illness and its treatment that are employed by all those engaged in the clinical process'.
2. Habitus, as defined by Bourdieu, is a useful concept in this regard. Habitus refers to: 'systems of durable, transposable dispositions, structured structures predisposed to function as structured structures, that is, as principles which generate and organize practices and representations that can be objectively adapted to their outcomes without presupposing a conscious aiming at ends (Bourdieu 1990:53). Habitus in terms of medication practices describes 'reasonable, common sense, behaviours' which are the result of past experiences and are bounded by the treatment options that exist in specific contexts.
3. Through an agency involved in the monitoring of advertisements Hardon was able to obtain data which revealed that out of the top ten brands in terms of advertising costs, six are available in the local grocery stores.
4. A similar relation between price and efficacy has also been described in India (Nichter 1980) and Brazil (Haak 1988).
5. Double blinding means that neither the person administering the medicine, nor the one receiving it, knows whether or not it is inert.
6. Helman (2000:136), citing Claridge, has pointed out that the effect of any medication on an individual (its total drug effect) depends on a number of elements in addition to its pharmacological properties:
    attributes of the drug itself (such as taste, shape, colour and name)
    attributes of the recipient of the drug (such as age, experience, education, socio-cultural background)
    attributes of the prescriber or supplier of the drug
    the physical setting in which the drug is prescribed or administered.
All these aspects can play a role in generating the 'meaning' response, because they can determine the confidence the patient has in the treatment and the expected outcome.
7. In this regard, it is interesting to note that, with the progress in the human genome project, differences in genetic and physiological makeup between people are more and more acknowledged in pharmacology. A new field of pharmacogenomics is pointing to such differences in pharmacological efficacy.

3 VILLAGERS AND LOCAL REMEDIES

1. This chapter draws on two earlier articles dealing with metaphors, metonyms and medicines (Van der Geest and Whyte 1989; Van der Geest and Meulenbroek 1993).
2. Lévi-Strauss (1963, 1966) emphasized the classificatory and thus intellectual and structuring potential of 'the logic of the concrete'. Plants and animals present themselves as concrete markers to divide the surrounding world into distinct categories. In totemic systems, differences among natural species are associated with differences among social categories. As totems they determine rules and taboos in various human domains such as eating and marriage. This insight led Lévi-Strauss to his most celebrated dictum:

   Their [the animals'] perceptible reality permits the embodiment of ideas and relations conceived by speculative thought on the basis of empirical observation. We can understand, too, that natural species are chosen not because they are 'good to eat' but because they are 'good to think'. (1963:89)

4 WOMEN IN DISTRESS

1. Issues of medicalization and women's responses to biomedical technology have been taken up in recent contributions that challenge the notion that women are passive objects of biomedical power (Lock and Kaufert 1998). While those contributions emphasize women's agency in relation to other forms of medical technology, we concentrate here on the uses of medicinal drugs.
2. Long-term users are defined as women who take the drug daily for at least one year. Former users are women who have stopped for at least six months after having used the drug according to the above pattern.
3. In a British study from 1979, Helman (1981) suggested that users of psychotropic drugs saw their medicines as tonic, fuel or food according to the extent to which they felt in control of their medicine taking. Such a classification tends to downplay the ambiguity of control, and the ways in which social actors change their notions of control over time.
4. A study in the Netherlands (Hardon and van Zorge 1998) found that young women had very few concerns about taking hormones for contraceptive purposes. They considered the contraceptive pill safe, and they used it to regulate their menstruation to fit with their holiday and weekend plans. To them the contraceptive pill was a welcome means for self-control in their lives. Around three out of every four seventeen- to eighteen-year-old girls in the Netherlands use the contraceptive pill. It is the norm.
5. The associations between humans and non-human entities has been elaborated by Latour (1993), who argues against a reductionism which creates boundaries between human agency and technology, culture and nature, subject and object. He argues for a 'symmetrical' approach which recognizes that both nature and society are to be explained. These ideas form the basis for what is now called actor-network theory, a form of relational materialism which takes as a point of departure that society is produced through the mutually constituting interactions of a wide range of human and non-human

entities. See also Prout (1996) for an illustrative example of the application of this theory in the analysis of the development and use of a pharmaceutical technology.

6. In the management of female ill health and mental distress, the women's health movement has been an important force for demedicalization, showing how medical practices have functioned as means of social control by reinforcing ideologies concerning women's ability to handle their emotions, as well as 'ideologies of women's appropriate role in work and the family' (Waitzkin 1991). This movement developed alternative ideas and treatment options for women's day-to-day health problems, including alternative means to deal with stresses and manage menopause (Boston Women's Health Book Collective 1998). It has contributed to an increase in self-care options for women and led to changes in medical practice. Most importantly perhaps, it has created space for women to discuss their experiences of health, ill health and therapy in their own terms.

6 DRUG VENDORS AND THEIR MARKET

1. The methods he used in his research were varied, and some could be characterized as 'investigative research' (Douglas 1976), a detective-like approach whereby the researcher assumes that the most relevant information is often being withheld while that which is said is meant to conceal what is really happening. Obviously, such concealment occurs when direct answers would be threatening to the informants. This was certainly the case for some unlawful practices in the field of drug distribution. In addition, many reports, minutes, accounts, and letters – some of which were confidential – were studied.

2. The formal sector also included private, mostly church-related, hospitals and health centres and commercial pharmacies. All of these functioned relatively well. They had a regular supply of drugs and their personnel were at their posts.

8 INJECTIONISTS

1. White (2000:89–121) argues that in colonial East Africa there was a fundamental ambivalence about biomedicine in general and injections in particular. But she emphasizes the enormous importance that the new technology had for people's imagination of bodies, skills and power relationships.

2. Lyons discusses the fear of needles in the first decades of the sleeping sickness campaign in the Belgian Congo (1992:188–9). She relates this to the widespread use of syringes and needles for painful lumbar punctures to extract spinal fluids for examination. Moreover, atoxyl, the drug used from 1906–20, was highly toxic and often caused blindness. A less toxic drug, tryponarsyl, was introduced in 1925. Injection centres were established where patients came for forty daily injections (1992:149, 152).

3. Lakshman and Nichter (2000) combine a public health concern about the risks of unsterile injections with an ethnographic documentation of perceptions and practices among practitioners and patients in Vellore, south India. Like Birungi, they emphasize the importance of patients' trust in

and personal relationships with the private practitioners who administered injections.

9 PRESCRIBING PHYSICIANS

1. Conversely, as we have seen in chapter 5, when patients are more sceptical about medicines, doctors are likely to be more reserved in writing prescriptions.
2. Using the placebo effect is not the same as prescribing a 'fake drug'. Many doctors regard a placebo as problematic; it may entail concern for the patient, but also disdain and deceit. If a patient finds out he has been given a placebo, his trust in the doctor will be broken.
3. In rural health centres in developing countries, however, nurses may take over the role of prescriber if a doctor is not around. The nurse becomes – sometimes literally – the 'doctor'. Sciortino (1992) describes such a situation for Central Java, Indonesia. She writes that nurses, more than doctors, conceal their uncertainty and lack of diagnostic and therapeutic knowledge through the prescription of medicines.

10 MANUFACTURERS

1. Another description of the ambiguous role of the Ayurvedic industry, meandering between globalization and localization, in this case between medicalization and moralization of senility in old age, can be found in Lawrence Cohen's (1998, see especially chapter 4) study of Alzheimer's and 'the bad family' in India.
2. Several historical studies of pharmaceutical companies have been carried out recently. Pieters (1999), by training a pharmacologist and molecular biologist, traced the fitful biography of interferon. Interferon started its life as a promising anti-virus medicine, then fell out of grace because it failed to fulfil its promises, but made a come-back a decade later as an anti-cancer medicine until that second promise also proved a disappointment. Pieters describes how industry, science and clinical workers had each other in a tight hold, each for their own interests. He points out that scientific claims got entangled with commercial aims and academic prestige. Pieters' sources were those of the historian – documents – but they also included in-depth interviews with some of the main characters of the events. Another example of a historical study of the pharmaceutical industry is by Galambos and Sewell (1995) about Merck, Sharp and Dohme. The study shows the crucial role of the market in shaping patterns of innovation in the production of vaccines over a period of 100 years.
3. 'Undercover' research violates the first article of the Statement on Professional and Ethical Responsibilities developed by the Society for Applied Anthropology: 'To the people we study we owe disclosure of our research goals, methods and sponsorships. The participation of people in research activities shall only be on a voluntary and informed basis.' Anthropologists disagree, however, as to how strictly and absolutely this rule applies (Bulmer 1982). Collecting information may be extremely desirable and important in just those situations where open research is not possible. People involved in illegal activities such

as drug dealers, pickpockets and sex workers are cases in point, but politicians, salesmen and medical doctors may also not tolerate an anthropologist in their midst. Another problem may be that the people under research will present a false picture of their ideas and practices once they know they are being 'watched'. In such situations researchers are likely to resort to a more liberal interpretation of their ethical code. 'Classic' examples of undercover research in medical anthropology are Caudill (1958) and Rosenhan (1973), who did fieldwork in psychiatric hospitals (before the professional code existed). Tomson and Sterky (1986) and Wolffers (1987) made their research assistants pose as clients in order to collect reliable information on sale practices by pharmacists and drugstore keepers. This technique of using 'simulated clients' is often used to study health providers, especially the relatively powerless small-time drug retailers in developing countries (Madden *et al.* 1997).
4. A recent thriller by the popular author John Le Carré (2000) is a scathing indictment of multinational pharmaceutical companies that use the people in Africa as unwitting research subjects for new and expensive medicines.
5. The conflict of interests between manufacturers, patients, insurance companies and policy makers emerged clearly in the case that the pharmaceutical industry brought before the South African court to prevent the country from providing cheap anti-AIDS drugs to its citizens. The industry eventually dropped the case (April 2001) because of the negative publicity it produced.

11 HEALTH PLANNERS

1. Health Action International is an umbrella of consumers organizations, which specifically aims to 'further the safe, rational and economic use of pharmaceuticals world-wide, to promote the full implementation of WHO's Action Programme on Essential Drugs and to look for non-drug solutions to problems created by impure water, poor sanitation and nutrition'.
2. Country case-studies were done in Colombia, Nigeria, Tanzania, Kenya, Zimbabwe, Mozambique, Burundi, North Yemen, South Yemen, Sudan, Bangladesh, Indonesia and Vietnam.

References

Aakster, C.W. 1986. Concepts in Alternative Medicine. *Social Science and Medicine* 22:265–73.

Abraham, J. 1995. *Science, Politics and the Pharmaceutical Industry: Controversy and Bias in Drug Regulation.* London: University College Press.

Ackerknecht, Erwin H. 1946. Natural Disease and Rational Treatment in Primitive Medicine. *Bulletin of the History of Medicine* 19(5):467–97.

1962. Aspects of the History of Therapeutics. *Bulletin of the History of Medicine* 36(5):389–419.

Adome, Richard Odoi, Susan Reynolds Whyte and Anita Hardon. 1996. *Popular Pills: Community Drug Use in Uganda.* Amsterdam: Het Spinhuis.

Afdhal, Ahmad Fuad, and Robert L. Welsch. 1988. The Rise of the Modern *Jamu* Industry in Indonesia: A Preliminary Overview. In *The Context of Medicines in Developing Countries: Studies in Pharmaceutical Anthropology,* edited by S. Van der Geest and S.R. Whyte. Dordrecht: Kluwer.

Akubue, P.I., and C.J. Mbah. 1989. Drugs and Treatment in Streetmarkets and Buses. In *Drug Distribution and Fake Drugs in Nigeria: Proceedings of an International Workshop,* edited by D. Pole. Basel: Institute of Medical Informatics.

Alland, Alexander. 1970. *Adaptation in Cultural Evolution: An Approach to Medical Anthropology.* New York: Columbia University Press.

Alubo, S. Ogoh. 1987. Drugging the Nigerian People: The Public Hazards of Private Profits. In *The Impact of Development and Modern Technologies in Third World Health,* edited by B.E. Jackson and A. Ugalde. Williamsburg, VA: Studies in Third World Societies.

Anderson, Robert. 1996. *Magic, Science and Health: The Aims and Achievements of Medical Anthropology.* Fort Worth: Harcourt Brace.

Appadurai, Arjun. 1986. Introduction: Commodities and the Politics of Value. In *The Social Life of Things: Commodities in Cultural Perspective,* edited by A. Appadurai. Cambridge: Cambridge University Press.

1990. Disjuncture and Difference in the Global Cultural Economy. *Theory, Culture and Society* 7:295–310.

Arora, R.B., ed. 1991. *Oral Rehydration Therapy with Rooh Afza.* New Delhi: Hamdard National Foundation.

Asiimwe, Delius, Barbara McPake, Frances Mwesigye, Matthias Ofoumbi, Lisbeth Ørtenblad, Pieter Streefland and Asaph Turinde. 1997. The Private Sector Activities of Public-Sector Health Workers in Uganda. In *Private*

Health Providers in Developing Countries, edited by S. Bennett, B. McPake and A. Mills. London: Zed Press.

Baerts, M., and J. Lehmann. 1993. *L'Utilisation de quelques plantes médicinales au Burundi.* Tervuren: Musée Royal de l'Afrique Centrale.

Basham, A.L. 1976. The Practice of Medicine in Ancient and Medieval India. In *Asian Medical Systems: A Comparative Study*, edited by C. Leslie. Berkeley: University of California Press.

Battersby, A., R. Feilden and C. Nelson. 1999a. Sterilizable Syringes: Excessive Risk or Cost-Effective Option? *Bulletin of the World Health Organization* 77(10):812–19.

Battersby, A., R. Feilden, P. Stoeckel, A. Da Silva, C. Nelson and A. Bass. 1999b. Strategies for Safe Injections. *Bulletin of the World Health Organization* 77(12):996–1000.

Bell, Susan E. 1987. Changing Ideas: The Medicalization of Menopause. *Social Science and Medicine* 24:535–42.

Bhatia, J.C., D. Vir, A. Timmappaya and C.S. Chuttani. 1975. Traditional Healers and Modern Medicine. *Social Science and Medicine* 9:15–21.

Bierlich, Bernhard. 2000. Injections and the Fear of Death: An Essay on the Limits of Biomedicine among the Dagomba of Northern Ghana. *Social Science and Medicine* 50:703–13.

Birungi, Harriet. 1994a. The Domestication of Injections: A Study of Social Relations of Health Care in Busoga, Eastern Uganda. Ph.D. dissertation, Institute of Anthropology, University of Copenhagen.

1994b. Injections as Household Utilities: Injection Practices in Busoga, Eastern Uganda. In *Medicines: Meanings and Contexts*, edited by N.L. Etkin and M.L. Tan. Quezon City, Philippines: Health Action Information Network.

1998. Injections and Self-Help: Risk and Trust in Ugandan Health Care. *Social Science and Medicine* 47:1455–62.

Birungi, Harriet, Delius Asiimwe and Susan Reynolds Whyte. 1994. Injection Use and Practices in Uganda. WHO/DAP/94.18. Geneva: World Health Organization.

Bledsoe, Caroline H., and Monica F. Goubaud. 1988. The Reinterpretation and Distribution of Western Pharmaceuticals: An Example from the Mende of Sierra Leone. In *The Context of Medicines in Developing Countries: Studies in Pharmaceutical Anthropology*, edited by S. Van der Geest and S.R. Whyte. Dordrecht: Kluwer.

Bloem, Maurice and Ivan Wolffers, eds. 1993. *The Impact of Injections on Daily Medical Practice.* Amsterdam: VU University Press.

Bode, Maarten. 1998. On the Consumption of Ayurvedic Pharmaceuticals in India: Extracting the Poison of Modernization. In *Uit de Zevende Hemel: Vijftig Jaar Politieke en Sociaal-Culturele Wetenschapen aan de Universitit van Amsterdam*, edited by A. Gevers. Amsterdam: Het Spinhuis.

2002. Indian Indigenous Pharmaceuticals: Tradition, Modernity and Nature. In *Plural Medicine: Orthodox and Heterodox Medicine in Western and Colonial Countries During the 19th and 20th Centuries*, edited by W. Ernst. London: Routledge.

Boston Women's Health Book Collective. 1998. *Our Bodies Ourselves for the New Century: A Book By and For Women.* New York: Simon and Schuster.

Bourdieu, Pierre. 1990. *The Logic of Practice*, trans. R. Nice. Stanford: Stanford University Press.

Braithwaite, J. 1984. *Corporate Crime in the Pharmaceutical Industry*. London: Routledge and Kegan Paul.

Britten, Nicky. 1996. Lay Views of Drugs and Medicines: Orthodox and Unorthodox Accounts. In *Modern Medicine: Lay Perspectives and Experiences*, edited by S.J. Williams and M. Calnan. London: University College Press.

———. 2001. Prescribing and the Defence of Clinical Autonomy. *Sociology of Health and Illness* 23:478–96.

Bruun, Birgitte. 2001. Service of the Engine: Pharmaceuticals, Moralities and Sex in a Malawian Fishing Village. Masters thesis, Institute of Anthropology, University of Copenhagen.

Buckley, A.D. 1985. *Yoruba Medicine*. Oxford: Clarendon Press.

Bulmer, M., ed. 1982. *Social Research Ethics: An Examination of the Merits of Covert Participant Observation*. London: Macmillan.

Bürgel, J. Christoph. 1976. Secular and Religious Features of Medieval Arabic Medicine. In *Asian Medical Systems: A Comparative Study*, edited by C. Leslie. Berkeley: University of California Press.

Burger, Alfred. 1988. *Drugs and People: Medications, Their History and Origins, and the Way They Act*. Revised edn. Charlottesville: University Press of Virginia.

Burghart, Richard. 1988. Penicillin: An Ancient Ayurvedic Medicine. In *The Context of Medicines in Developing Countries: Studies in Pharmaceutical Anthropology*, edited by S. Van der Geest and S.R. Whyte. Dordrecht: Kluwer.

Cambrosio, Alberto, Allan Young and Margaret Lock. 2000. Introduction. In *Living and Working with the New Medical Technologies: Intersections of Inquiry*, edited by M. Lock, A. Young and A. Cambrosio. Cambridge: Cambridge University Press.

Cassel, E.J. 1976. Disease as an 'It': Concepts of Disease Revealed by Patients' Representations of Symptoms. *Social Science and Medicine* 10:143–6.

Caudill, William. 1958. *The Psychiatric Hospital as a Small Community*. Cambridge, MA: Harvard University Press.

Cederlöf, Caroline, and Göran Tomson. 1995. Private Pharmacies and the Health Sector Reform in Developing Countries – Professional and Commercial Highlights. *Journal of Social and Administrative Pharmacy* 12(3):101–11.

Chetley, Andrew. 1990. *A Healthy Business? World Health and the Pharmaceutical Industry*. London: Zed Press.

Cohen, Lawrence. 1998. *No Aging in India: Alzheimer's, the Bad Family and Other Modern Things*. Berkeley: University of California Press.

Comaroff, Jean. 1976. A Pill to Swallow: Placebo Therapy in General Practice. *Sociological Review* 24(1):79–96.

Conrad, Lawrence I. 1993. Arab-Islamic Medicine. In *Companion Encyclopedia of the History of Medicine*, edited by W.F. Bynum and R. Porter. London: Routledge.

Conrad, Lawrence I., Michael Neve, Vivian Nutton, Roy Porter and Andrew Wear. 1995. *The Western Medical Tradition: 800 BC to AD 1800*. Cambridge: Cambridge University Press.

Conrad, Peter. 1985. The Meaning of Medications: Another Look at Compliance. *Social Science and Medicine* 20:29–38.

1992. Medicalization and Social Control. *Annual Review of Sociology* 18:209–32.

1994. Wellness as Virtue: Morality, and the Pursuit of Health. *Culture, Medicine and Psychiatry* 18:385–401.

Cosminsky, Sheila. 1994. All Roads Lead to the Pharmacy: Use of Pharmaceuticals on a Guatemalan Plantation. In *Medicines: Meanings and Contexts*, edited by N.L. Etkin and M.L. Tan. Quezon City, Philippines: Health Action Information Network.

Costa, M.A., and R. Chaloub. 1992. *Anticoncepcao oral: use e rumores: Fortaleza, Recife, Salvador*. Rio de Janeiro: CEPDD.

Craig, David. 2000. The King's Law Stops at the Village Gate: Local and Global Pharmacy Regulation in Vietnam. In *Global Health Policy, Local Realities: The Fallacy of the Level Playing Field*, edited by L.M. Whiteford and L. Manderson. Boulder: Lynne Rienner.

Crawford, Robert. 1984. A Cultural Account of 'Health': Control, Release and the Social Body. In *Issues in the Political Economy of Health Care*, edited by J.B. McKinlay. London: Tavistock.

Cunningham, C.E. 1970. Thai 'Injection Doctors': Antibiotic Mediators. *Social Science and Medicine* 4:1–24.

De Graaf, Karin. 1988. 'Het Goede Woord': Gebruik van Westerse Medicijnen bij de Guizinga in Noord Cameroen ['The Good Word': The Use of Western Medicines among the Guizinga in North Cameroon]. Masters thesis, Anthropology, University of Amsterdam.

De Wet, T. 1998a. Doepa after Dark: Protective Medicines for Infants in Soweto, South Africa. Ph.D. dissertation, University of Florida.

1998b. Muti Wenyoni: Commodification of an African Folk Medicine. *South African Journal of Ethnology* 21(4):165–72.

Douglas, J.D. 1976. *Investigative Social Research: Individual and Team Field Research*. Beverly Hills: Sage.

Douglas, Mary, and Baron Isherwood. 1979. *The World of Goods: Towards an Anthropology of Consumption*. London: Allen Lane.

Economist. 2001. Drug-Induced Dilemma. *The Economist*, 21 April.

Eisenberg, David M., R.B. Davis, S.L. Ettner, S. Appel, S. Wilkey, M. van Rompay and R.C. Kessler. 1998. Trends in Alternative Medicine Use in the United States, 1990–1997. *Journal of the American Medical Association* 280(18):1569–75.

Eisenberg, David M., R.C. Kessler, C. Foster, F.E. Norlock, D.R. Calkins and T.L. Delbanco. 1993. Unconventional Medicine in the United States: Prevalence, Costs, and Patterns of Use. *New England Journal of Medicine* 328(4):246–52.

El-Tom, A.O. 1985. Drinking the Koran: The Meaning of Koranic Verses in Berti Erasure. *Africa* 55(4):414–31.

Ellen, Roy. 1988. Fetishism. *Man* 23(2):213–35.

Estroff, Sue E. 1981. *Making it Crazy: An Ethnography of Psychiatric Clients in an American Community*. Berkeley: University of California Press.

Etkin, Nina L. 1988. Cultural Constructions of Efficacy. In *The Context of Medicines in Developing Countries: Studies in Pharmaceutical Anthropology*, edited by S. Van der Geest and S.R. Whyte. Dordrecht: Kluwer.

1992. 'Side Effects': Cultural Constructions and Reinterpretations of Western Pharmaceuticals. *Medical Anthropology Quarterly* 6:99–113.

1994. The Negotiation of 'Side' Effects in Hausa (Northern Nigeria) Therapeutics. In *Medicines: Meanings and Contexts*, edited by N.L. Etkin and M.L. Tan. Quezon City, Philippines: Health Action Information Network.

Etkin, Nina L., P.J. Ross and I. Muazzamu. 1990. The Indigenization of Pharmaceuticals: Therapeutic Transitions in Rural Hausaland. *Social Science and Medicine* 30:919–28.

Etkin, Nina L., and Michael L. Tan, eds. 1994. *Medicines: Meanings and Contexts*. Quezon City, Philippines: Health Action Information Network.

Evans-Pritchard, Edward E. 1937. *Witchcraft, Oracles and Magic among the Azande*. Oxford: Clarendon Press.

Fadiman, Anne. 1997. *The Spirit Catches You and You Fall Down*. New York: Noonday Press.

Fainzang, Sylvie. 1986. *L'Interieur des choses: maladie, divination et réproduction sociale chez les Bisa du Burkina Faso*. Paris: L'Harmattan.

2001. *Médicaments et société: le patient, le médecin et l'ordonnance*. Paris: PUF.

Fardon, Richard, ed. 1995. *Counterworks: Managing the Diversity of Knowledge*. London: Routledge.

Farquhar, Judith. 1994a. *Knowing Practice: The Clinical Encounter of Chinese Medicine*. Boulder: Westview Press.

1994b. Eating Chinese Medicine. *Cultural Anthropology* 9(4):471–97.

Fassin, Didier. 1987. The Illicit Sale of Pharmaceuticals in Africa: Sellers and Clients in the Suburbs of Dakar. *Tropical Geographical Medicine* 39: 166–70.

Ferguson, Anne. 1981. Commercial Pharmaceutical Medicine and Medicalization: A Case Study from El Salvador. *Culture, Medicine and Psychiatry* 5:104–34.

1988. Commercial Pharmaceutical Medicine and Medicalization: A Case Study from El Salvador. In *The Context of Medicines in Developing Countries: Studies in Pharmaceutical Anthropology*, edited by S. Van der Geest and S.R. Whyte. Dordrecht: Kluwer.

Ferguson, James. 1988. Cultural Exchange: New Developments in the Anthropology of Commodities. *Cultural Anthropology* 3(4):488–513.

Fernandez, James W. 1986. *Persuasions and Performances: The Play of Tropes in Culture*. Bloomington: Indiana University Press.

Foster, George. 1984. Anthropological Research Perspectives on Health Problems in Developing Countries. *Social Science and Medicine* 18:847–54.

Foster, W.D. 1970. *The Early History of Scientific Medicine in Uganda*. Nairobi: East African Literature Bureau.

Foucault, Michel. 1980. *Power/Knowledge: Selected Interviews and Other Writings 1972–1977*. Toronto: The Harvester Press.

Fox, Renée C. 1980. The Evolution of Medical Uncertainty. *Milbank Memorial Fund Quarterly* 58(1):1–49.

Frankenberg, Ronald F. 1986. Sickness as Cultural Performance. *International Journal of Health Services* 16(4):603–26.

Frazer, James G. 1957 [orig. 1890]. *The Golden Bough: A Study in Magic and Religion*. London: Macmillan.

Gabe, J., and M. Calnan. 1989. The Limits of Medicine: Women's Perception of Medical Technology. *Social Science and Medicine* 28:223–32.

Galambos, L., and J.E. Sewell. 1995. *Networks of Innovation: Vaccine Development at Merck, Sharp & Dohme, and Mulford, 1895–1995*. Cambridge: Cambridge University Press.

Gevitz, Norman. 1993. Unorthodox Medical Theories. In *Companion Encyclopedia of the History of Medicine*, edited by W.F. Bynum and R. Porter. London: Routledge.

Giddens, Anthony. 1984. *The Constitution of Society*. Berkeley: University of California Press.

Gilbert, Leah. 1995. The Pharmacist's Traditional and New Roles – a Study of Community Pharmacists in Johannesburg, South Africa. *Journal of Social and Administrative Pharmacy* 12(3):125–31.

Gish, O., and L.L. Feller. 1979. *Planning Pharmaceuticals for Primary Health Care: The Supply and Utilization of Drugs in the Third World*. Washington DC: American Public Health Association.

Goffman, Erving. 1971. *The Presentation of Self in Everyday Life*. Harmondsworth: Penguin.

Good, Byron. 1977. The Heart of What's the Matter: The Semantics of Illness in Iran. *Culture, Medicine and Psychiatry* 1:25–58.

Good, Mary-Jo DelVecchio. 1980. Of Blood and Babies: The Relationships of Popular Islamic Physiology to Fertility. *Social Science and Medicine* 14B:147–56.

Goody, Jack. 1977. *The Domestication of the Savage Mind*. Cambridge: Cambridge University Press.

Gould, H.A. 1977. Modern Medicine and Folk Recognition in Rural India. In *Culture, Disease and Healing: Studies in Medical Anthropology*, edited by D. Landy. New York: Macmillan.

Greenway, Christine. 1998. Objectified Selves: An Analysis of Medicines in Andean Sacrificial Healing. *Medical Anthropology Quarterly* 12:147–67.

Griffiths, Frances. 1999. Women's Control and Choice Regarding HRT. *Social Science and Medicine* 49:469–81.

Haafkens, Joke. 1997. *Rituals of Silence: Long-Term Tranquillizer Use by Women in the Netherlands: A Social Case Study*. Amsterdam: Het Spinhuis.

Haak, Hilbrand. 1988. Pharmaceuticals in Two Brazilian Villages: Lay Practices and Perceptions. *Social Science and Medicine* 27:1415–27.

Haak, Hilbrand, and Anita Hardon. 1988. Indigenised Pharmaceuticals in Developing Countries: Widely Used, Widely Neglected. *Lancet* 2:620–1.

Haller, John S. 1981. Hypodermic Medication: Early History. *New York State Journal of Medicine* 81(11):1671–9.

Hannerz, Ulf. 1987. The World in Creolisation. *Africa* 57:546–59.

1992. *Cultural Complexity: Studies in the Social Organization of Meaning*. New York: Columbia University Press.

Hardon, Anita. 1987. The Use of Modern Pharmaceuticals in a Filipino Village: Doctors' Prescriptions and Self-Medication. *Social Science and Medicine* 25:277–92.

1991. *Confronting Ill Health: Medicines, Self-Care and the Poor in Manila*. Quezon City, Philippines: Health Action Information Network.

1992. Consumers versus Producers: Power Play Behind the Scenes. In *Drugs Policy in Developing Countries*, edited by N. Kanji, A. Hardon, J.W. Harnmeijer, M. Mamdani and G. Walt. London: Zed Books.

Hardon, Anita, and Najmi Kanji. 1992. New Horizons in the 1990s. In *Drugs Policy in Developing Countries*, edited by N. Kanji, A. Hardon, J.W. Harnmeijer, M. Mamdani and G. Walt. London: Zed Books.

Hardon, Anita, and R. van Zorge. 1998. De Pil, Controle en Seksualiteit: Een Exploratief Onderzoek naar Pilgebruik onder Nederlandse Meiden [The Pill, Control and Sexuality: An Exploratory Investigation into Use of the Contraceptive Pill among Dutch Girls]. *Medische Antropologie* 10(1):19–32.

Hargraves, R., ed. 1976. *The Promotion of Prescription and Proprietary Drugs: Corporate Self-Interest versus Social Responsibility. Journal of Drug Issues.* Special Issue 6(1).

Hart, Keith. 1998. The Politics of Anthropology: Conditions for Thought and Practice. *Anthropology Today* 14(6):20–2.

Heilbron, G. 1999. Je Bent Wat Je Slikt: Enkele Biografieën van Modern Geproduceerde Traditionele Geneesmiddelen [You Are What You Swallow: Some Biographies of Modern Manufactured Traditional Medicines]. Masters thesis, Amsterdam Free University.

Helman, Cecil G. 1981. 'Tonic', 'Food', and 'Fuel': Social and Symbolic Aspects of the Long-term Use of Psychotropic Drugs. *Social Science and Medicine* 15B:521–33.

2000. *Culture, Health and Illness*. Oxford: Butterworth.

Homedes, Nuria, and Antonio Ugalde. 1993. Patients' Compliance with Medical Treatments in the Third World: What Do We Know? *Health Policy and Planning* 8(4):291–314.

Howard-Jones, Norman. 1971. The Origins of Hypodermic Medication. *Scientific American* 224(1):96–102.

Hunt, Linda M. *et al.* 1989. Compliance and the Patient's Perspective: Controlling Symptoms in Everyday Life. *Culture, Medicine and Psychiatry* 13:315–34.

Hunter, Myra S., Irene O'Dea and N. Britten. 1997. Decision-Making and Hormone Replacement Therapy: A Qualitative Analysis. *Social Science and Medicine* 45:1541–8.

IFPMA. 2001. 'Patients Are the Winners through Partnership', press release 19 April 2001. Geneva: IFPMA.

Igun, U.A. 1987. Why We Seek Treatment Here: Retail Pharmacy and Clinical Practice in Maiduguri, Nigeria. *Social Science and Medicine* 24:689–95.

Iliffe, John. 1998. *East African Doctors: A History of the Modern Profession.* Cambridge: Cambridge University Press.

Illich, Ivan. 1976. *Limits to Medicine. Medical Nemesis: The Expropriation of Health.* Harmondsworth: Penguin.

Iyun, B.V. 1994. Socio-cultural Aspects of Drug Use in the Treatment of Childhood Diarrhoea in Oyo State Nigeria. In *Medicines: Meanings and Contexts*, edited by N.L. Etkin and M.L. Tan. Quezon City, Philippines: Health Action Information Network.

Janzen, John. 1978. *The Quest for Therapy: Medical Pluralism in Lower Zaire.* Berkeley: University of California Press.

Jarcho, Saul. 1993. *Quinine's Predecessor: Francesco Torti and the Early History of Cinchona*. Baltimore: Johns Hopkins University Press.

Justice, Judith. 1986. *Policies, Plans, and People: Foreign Aid and Health Development*. Berkeley: University of California Press.

Kafle, Kamud, Ritu Prasad Gartoulla, Y.M.S. Pradhan, A.D. Shrestha, S.B. Karkee and Jonathan Quick. 1992. Drug Retailer Training: Experiences from Nepal. *Social Science and Medicine* 35:1015–25.

Kahane, J. 1984. The Role of the 'Western' Pharmacist in Rural Taiwanese Culture. Ph.D. thesis, Anthropology, University of Hawaii, Honolulu.

Kamat, Vinay R., and Mark Nichter. 1997. Monitoring Product Movement: An Ethnographic Study of Pharmaceutical Sales Representatives in Bombay, India. In *Private Health Providers in Developing Countries: Serving the Public Interest?*, edited by S. Bennett, B. McPake and A. Mills. London: Zed Books.

——— 1998. Pharmacies, Self-Medication and Pharmaceutical Marketing in Bombay, India. *Social Science and Medicine* 47:779–94.

Kane, A., J. Lloyd, M. Zaffran, L. Simonsen and M. Kane. 1999. Transmission of Hepatitis B, Hepatitis C and Human Immunodeficiency Viruses through Unsafe Injections in the Developing World: Model-Based Regional Estimates. *Bulletin of the World Health Organization* 77(10):801–7.

Kanji, Najmi, and Anita Hardon. 1992. What Has Been Achieved and Where Are We Now? In *Drugs Policy in Developing Countries*, edited by N. Kanji, A. Hardon, J. W. Harnmeijer, M. Mamdani and G. Walt. London: Zed Books.

Kanji, Najmi, Anita Hardon, Jan Willem Harnmeijer, Masuma Mamdani and Gill Walt. 1992. *Drugs Policy in Developing Countries*. London: Zed Books.

Keesing, Roger M. 1987. Anthropology as Interpretative Quest. *Current Anthropology* 28:161–9.

Kleinman, Arthur. 1980. *Patients and Healers in the Context of Culture*. Berkeley: University of California Press.

Koenig, Barbara A. 1988. The Technological Imperative in Medical Practice: The Social Creation of a 'Routine' Treatment. In *Biomedicine Examined*, edited by M. Lock and D. Gordon. Dordrecht: Kluwer.

Kopytoff, Igor. 1986. The Cultural Biography of Things: Commoditization as Process. In *The Social Life of Things: Commodities in Cultural Perspective*, edited by A. Appadurai. Cambridge: Cambridge University Press.

Kristvik, Ellen. 1999. *Drums and Syringes: Patients and Healers in Combat against TB Bacilli and Hungry Ghosts in the Hills of Nepal*, Bibliotheca Himalayica. Kathmandu: EMR.

Lakoff, George, and Mark Johnson. 1980. *Metaphors We Live By*. Chicago: University of Chicago Press.

Lakshman, M., and Mark Nichter. 2000. Contamination of Medicine Injection Paraphernalia Used by Registered Medical Practitioners in South India: An Ethnographic Study. *Social Science and Medicine* 51:11–28.

Lall, S. 1979. Problems of Distribution, Availability and Utilization of Agents in Developing Countries: An Asian Perspective. Paper read at Pharmaceuticals for Developing Countries, at Washington DC.

Latour, Bruno. 1990. Postmodern? No, Simply Modern. Steps Towards an Anthropology of Science. *Studies in the History and Philosophy of Science* 21(1):154–71.

1993. *We Have Never Been Modern*. Cambridge, MA: Harvard University Press.

Latour, Bruno, and S. Woolgar. 1979. *Laboratory Life*. Princeton: Princeton University Press.

Le Carré, John. 2000. *The Constant Gardener*. New York: Simon and Schuster.

Leslie, Charles. 1975. Pluralism and Integration in the Indian and Chinese Medical Systems. In *Medicine in Chinese Cultures: Comparative Studies of Health Care in Chinese and Other Societies*, edited by A. Kleinman *et al.* Washington DC: US Department of Health, Education and Welfare.

1976. Introduction. In *Asian Medical Systems: A Comparative Study*, edited by C. Leslie. Berkeley: University of California Press.

1988. Foreword. In *The Context of Medicines in Developing Countries: Studies in Pharmaceutical Anthropology*, edited by S. Van der Geest and S.R. Whyte. Dordrecht: Kluwer.

1989. Indigenous Pharmaceuticals, the Capitalist World and Civilization. *Kroeber Anthropological Society Papers* 69–70:23–31.

Lévi-Strauss, Claude. 1963. *Structural Anthropology*. Vol. 1. New York: Basic Books.

1963. *Totemism*. Boston: Beacon Press.

1966. *The Savage Mind*. Chicago: University of Chicago Press.

Lexchin, Joel. 1992. Pharmaceutical Promotion in the Third World. *Journal of Drug Issues* 22(2):417–54.

1995. *Deception by Design: Pharmaceutical Promotion in the Third World*. Penang: Consumers International.

Lloyd, J.S., and J.B. Milstien. 1999. Auto-disable Syringes for Immunization: Issues in Technology Transfer. *Bulletin of the World Health Organization* 77(12):1001–7.

Lock, Margaret. 1993. *Encounters with Aging: Mythologies of Menopause in Japan and North America*. Berkeley: University of California Press.

Lock, Margaret, and Patricia A. Kaufert, eds. 1998. *Pragmatic Women and Body Politics*. Cambridge: Cambridge University Press.

Logan, Kathleen. 1983. The Role of Pharmacists and Over-the-Counter Medications in the Health Care System of a Mexican City. *Medical Anthropology* 7(3):68–89.

1988. 'Casi Como Doctor': Pharmacists and Their Clients in a Mexican Urban Context. In *The Context of Medicines in Developing Countries: Studies in Pharmaceutical Anthropology*, edited by S. Van der Geest and S.R. Whyte. Dordrecht: Kluwer.

Logan, Michael H. 1973. Humoral Medicine in Guatemala and Peasant Acceptance of Modern Medicine. *Human Organization* 32(4):385–95.

Long, Norman. 1992. From Paradigm Lost to Paradigm Regained: The Case for an Actor-Oriented Sociology of Development. In *Battlefields of Knowledge: The Interlocking of Theory and Practice in Social Research and Development*, edited by N. Long and A. Long. London: Routledge.

Lupton, Deborah. 1997. Foucault and the Medicalisation Critique. In *Foucault: Health and Medicine*, edited by A. Petersen and R. Bunton. London: Routledge.

Lyons, Maryinez. 1992. *The Colonial Disease: A Social History of Sleeping Sickness in Northern Zaire, 1900–1940*. Cambridge: Cambridge University Press.

MacCormack, Carol. 1986. The Articulation of Western and Traditional Systems of Health Care. In *The Professionalisation of African Medicine*, edited by M. Last and G.L. Chavunduka. Manchester: Manchester University Press.

Madden, J.M., J.D. Quick, D. Ross-Degnan and K.K. Kafle. 1997. Undercover Careseekers: Simulated Clients in the Study of Health Provider Behavior in Developing Countries. *Social Science and Medicine* 45:1465–82.

Maehle, Andreas-Holger. 1999. *Drugs on Trial: Experimental Pharmacology and Therapeutic Innovation in the Eighteenth Century*, edited by C.J. Lawrence, V. Nutton and R. Porter. Clio Medica 53, The Wellcome Institute Series in the History of Medicine. Amsterdam: Editions Rodopi B.V.

Malinowski, Bronislaw. 1922. *Argonauts of the Western Pacific*. London: Routledge and Kegan Paul.

    1948. *Magic, Science and Religion and Other Essays*. Garden City, NY: Doubleday.

Mamdani, Masuma, and G. Walker. 1985. *Essential Drugs and Developing Countries: A Review and Selected Annotated Bibliography*. EPC Publication 8. London: London School of Hygiene and Tropical Medicine.

Manderson, Lenore, and Linda M. Whiteford. 2000. Introduction: Health, Globalization and the Fallacy of the Level Playing Field. In *Global Health Policy, Local Realities: The Fallacy of the Level Playing Field*, edited by L.M. Whiteford and L. Manderson. Boulder: Lynne Rienner.

Marsh, V.M., W.M. Mutemi, J. Muturi, A. Haaland, W.M. Watkins, G. Otieno and K. Marsh. 1999. Changing Home Treatment of Childhood Fevers by Training Shop Keepers in Rural Kenya. *Tropical Medicine and International Health* 4(5):383–9.

Martin, Emily. 1987. *The Woman in the Body: A Cultural Analysis of Reproduction*. Boston: Beacon Press.

    1994. *Flexible Bodies: The Role of Immunity in American Culture from the Days of Polio to the Age of AIDS*. Boston: Beacon Press.

Medawar, Charles. 1979. *Insult or Injury? An Enquiry into the Marketing and Advertising of British Food and Drug Products in the Third World*. London: Social Audit.

    1992. *Power and Dependence: Social Audit on the Safety of Medicines*. London: Social Audit.

Medawar, Charles, and B. Freese. 1982. *Drug Diplomacy*. London: Social Audit.

Melrose, Diane. 1982. *Bitter Pills: Medicines and the Third World Poor*. Oxford: OXFAM.

Melville, Arabella, and Colin Johnson. 1982. *Cured to Death: The Effects of Prescription Drugs*. London: Secker and Warburg.

Meulenbroek, A. 1989. Percepties rond Ziekten bij de Mossi in de Regio Basma, Burkina Faco [Perceptions of Illness among the Mossi in the Basma Region of Burkina Faso], Anthropological-Sociological Center, University of Amsterdam.

Miles, Ann. 1998a. Science, Nature, and Tradition: The Mass-Marketing of Natural Medicine in Urban Ecuador. *Medical Anthropology Quarterly* 12(2):206–25.

    1998b. Radio and the Commodification of Natural Medicine in Ecuador. *Social Science and Medicine* 47:2127–37.

Miller, Daniel. 1995. Consumption and Commodities. *Annual Review of Anthropology* 24:141–61.

Moerman, Daniel. 1991. Physiology and Symbols: The Anthropological Implications of the Placebo Effect. In *The Anthropology of Medicine: From Culture to Method, Second Edition*, edited by L. Romanucci-Ross, D.E. Moerman and L.R. Tancredi. New York: Bergin and Garvey.

——— 2000. Cultural Variations in the Placebo Effect: Ulcers, Anxiety, and Blood Pressure. *Medical Anthropology Quarterly* 14(1):51–72.

Montagne, Michael. 1991. The Culture of Long-Term Tranquilliser Users. In *Understanding Tranquilliser Use: The Role of the Social Sciences*, edited by J. Gabe. London: Routledge.

——— 1992. The Promotion of Medication for Personal and Social Problems. *Journal of Drug Issues* 22(2):389–406.

Morsey, Soheir A. 1996. Political Economy in Medical Anthropology. In *Handbook of Medical Anthropology: Contemporary Theory and Method, Revised Edition*, edited by C.F. Sargent and T.M. Johnson. Westport, CT: Greenwood Press.

MSF. 2000. Translating the Essential Drug Concept in the 2000's Context. Concluding Remarks of a Seminar Organised by MSF: Campaign for Access to Essential Drugs, 19 September 2000, Geneva.

Muller, Mike. 1982. *The Health of Nations: A North–South Investigation*. London: Faber and Faber.

Nederlandse Staatscourant. 1991. Wijziging besluit Farmaceutische Hulp aan Ziekenfondsverzekerden [Change of Decision concerning Pharmaceutical Help to Patients under National Health Insurance], 20 February, 36.

Ngubane, Harriet. 1977. *Body and Mind in Zulu Medicine*. London: Academic Press.

Nichter, Mark. 1980. The Layperson's Perception of Medicine as Perspective into the Utilization of Multiple Therapy Systems in the Indian Context. *Social Science and Medicine* 14B:225–33.

——— 1989. *Anthropology and International Health: South Asian Case Studies*. Dordrecht: Kluwer.

Nichter, Mark, and Mimi Nichter. 1996. *Anthropology and International Health: Asian Case Studies*. Amsterdam: Gordon and Breach.

Nichter, Mark, and Carolyn Nordstrom. 1989. A Question of Medicine Answering: Health Commodification and the Social Relations of Health in Sri Lanka. *Culture, Medicine and Psychiatry* 13:367–90.

Nichter, Mark, and Nancy Vuckovic. 1994. Agenda for an Anthropology of Pharmaceutical Practice. *Social Science and Medicine* 39:1509–25.

Oddens, B.J., M.J. Boulet, P. Lehert and A.P. Visser. 1992. Has the Climacteric Been Medicalized? A Study on the Use of Medication for Climacteric Complaints in Four Countries. *Maturitas* 15(3):171–81.

Ohnuki-Tierney, Emiko. 1981. *Illness and Curing among the Sakhalin Ainu: A Symbolic Interpretation*. Cambridge: Cambridge University Press.

Ong, W.J. 1986. *Orality and Literacy: The Technologizing of the Word*. London: Methuen.

Oppenheim, A. Leo. 1962. Mesopotamian Medicine. *Bulletin of the History of Medicine* 36(2):97–108.

Osifo, N.G. 1983. Overpromotion of Drugs in International Product Package Inserts. *Tropical Doctor* 13(1):5–8.

Oths, K.S. 1992. Some Symbolic Dimensions of Andean Materia Medica. *Central Issues in Anthropology* 10:76–85.

Panganiban, J.V. 1970. *Diksiyunaryong Pilipino–Ingles*. Manila: Bede's Publishing House.

Paredes, Patricia, Manuela de la Peña, Enrique Flores-Guerra, Judith Diaz and James Trostle. 1996. Factors Influencing Physicians' Prescribing Behaviour in the Treatment of Childhood Diarrhoea: Knowledge May Not Be the Clue. *Social Science and Medicine* 42(8):1141–54.

Parkin, David. 1995. Latticed Knowledge: Eradication and Dispersal of the Unpalatable in Islam, Medicine and Anthropological Theory. In *Counterworks: Managing the Diversity of Knowledge*, edited by R. Fardon. London: Routledge.

Pellegrino, Edmund D. 1976. Prescribing and Drug Ingestion: Symbols and Substances. *Drug Intelligence and Clinical Pharmacy* 10:624–30.

Pfaffenberger, Bryan. 1988. Fetished Objects and Humanised Nature: Toward an Anthropology of Technology. *Man* 23(2):236–52.

Pickstone, John. 1994. Objects and Objectives: Notes on the Material Cultures of Medicine. In *Technologies of Modern Medicine*, edited by G. Lawrence. London: Science Museum.

Pieters, T. 1999. Biology Meets Drug Development: The Biography of a 'Miracle' Drug, the Interferons. Ph.D. thesis, University of Maastricht.

Pool, Robert. 1994. *Dialogue and the Interpretation of Illness: Conversations in a Cameroon Village*. Oxford: Berg.

Price, Laurie J. 1989. In the Shadow of Biomedicine: Self Medication in Two Ecuadorian Pharmacies. *Social Science and Medicine* 28:905–15.

Price, T., ed. 1974. *Drug Advertising Hearings. Journal of Drug Issues*, special issue, 4:203–312.

Prout, Alan. 1996. Actor-Network Theory, Technology and Medical Sociology: An Illustrative Analysis of the Metered Dose Inhaler. *Sociology of Health and Illness* 18(2):198–219.

Prout, Alan, and Pia Christensen. 1996. Hierarchies, Boundaries and Symbols: Medicine Use and the Cultural Peformance of Childhood Sickness. In *Children, Medicines and Culture*, edited by P.J. Bush, D.J. Trakas, E.J. Sanz, R.L. Wirsing, T. Vaskilampi and A.Prout. Binghamton: Pharmaceutical Products Press, The Haworth Press.

Rabinow, Paul. 1996. *Making PCR: A Story of Biotechnology*. Chicago: University of Chicago Press.

Rachin, R.L., and M. Montagne, eds. 1992. *Drug Advertising and Promotion. Journal of Drug Issues*, special issue, 22(2).

Rasmussen, Zeba A., M. Rahim, Pieter Streefland and Anita Hardon. 1996. *Enhancing Appropriate Medicine Use in the Karakoram Mountains*. Amsterdam: Het Spinhuis.

Reeler, Anne. 1990. Injections: A Fatal Attraction? *Social Science and Medicine* 31:1119–25.

———. 1996. *Money and Friendship: Modes of Empowerment in Thai Health Care*. Amsterdam: Het Spinhuis.

2000. Anthropological Perspectives on Injections: A Review. *Bulletin of the World Health Organization* 78(1):135–43.

Reich, Michael. 1994. Bangladesh Pharmaceutical Policy and Politics. *Health Policy and Planning* 9(2).

Rekdal, Ole B. 1999. Cross-Cultural Healing in East African Ethnography. *Medical Anthropology Quarterly* 13(4):458–82.

Rhodes, Lorna A. 1984. 'This Will Clear Your Mind': The Use of Metaphors for Medication in Psychiatric Settings. *Culture, Medicine, and Psychiatry* 8:49–70.

Roberts, Alan H. 1995. The Powerful Placebo Revisited: The Magnitude of Nonspecific Effects. *Mind/Body Medicine* 1(1):1–10.

Rolt, Francis. 1985. *Pills, Policies, and Profits*. London: War on Want.

Rosenhan, D.L. 1973. On Being Sane in Insane Places. *Science* 179:250–8.

Roth, Jules A. 1976. *Health Purifiers and Their Enemies*. New York: Prodist.

Sachs, Lisbeth. 1989. Misunderstanding as Therapy: Doctors, Patients, and Medicines in a Rural Clinic in Sri Lanka. *Culture, Medicine and Psychiatry* 13:335–49.

Sahlins, Marshall. 1976. *Culture and Practical Reason*. Chicago: University of Chicago Press.

Scheper-Hughes, Nancy. 1992. *Death without Weeping: The Violence of Everyday Life in Brazil*. Berkeley: University of California Press.

Schwartz, R.K., S.B. Soumerai and J. Avorn. 1989. Physician Motivations for Nonscientific Drug Prescription. *Social Science and Medicine* 28:577–82.

Sciortino, Rolalia. 1987. De Genezende Kracht is van God, maar Hij Manifesteert Zich door/in de Dukun [The Healing Power is from God, but He Manifests Himself through the Dukun]. Masters thesis, Free University, Amsterdam.

1992. *Care-Takers of Cure: A Study of Health Centre Nurses in Rural Central Java*. Amsterdam: Het Spinhuis.

Senah, Kodjo Amedjorteh. 1997. *Money Be Man: The Popularity of Medicines in a Rural Ghanaian Community*. Amsterdam: Het Spinhuis.

Shore, Cris, and Susan Wright. 1997. Policy: A New Field of Anthropology. In *Anthropology of Policy: Critical Perspectives on Governance and Power*, edited by C. Shore and S. Wright. London: Routledge.

Silverman, Milton. 1976. *The Drugging of the Americas*. Berkeley: University of California Press.

Silverman, Milton, and Philip R. Lee. 1974. *Pills, Profits and Politics*. Berkeley: University of California Press.

Silverman, Milton, Philip R. Lee and Mia Lydecker. 1982. *Prescriptions for Death: The Drugging of the Third World*. Berkeley: University of California Press.

Simonsen, L., A. Kane, J. Lloyd, M. Zaffran and M. Kane. 1999. Unsafe Injections in the Developing World and Transmission of Bloodborne Pathogens: A Review. *Bulletin of the World Health Organization* 77(10):789–800.

Singer, Merill, and Hans Baer. 1995. *Critical Medical Anthropology*. New York: Baywood Publishing Company.

Smith, M.C. 1980. The Relationship between Pharmacy and Medicine. In *Prescribing Practice and Drug Usage*, edited by R. Mapes. London: Croom Helm.

Sorofman, B. 1992. Drug Promotion in Self-Care and Self-Medication. *Journal of Drug Issues* 22(2):377–88.

Spangenberg, J. n.d. Het Recept als Schrift: De Verschriftelijking van de Geneeskunde [The Prescription as Text: The Scripturalization of Medicine]. Masters thesis, Anthropology, University of Amsterdam.

Spiro, Howard M. 1986. *Doctors, Patients and Placebos.* New Haven: Yale University Press.

Sringernyuang, Luechai. 2000. Availability and Use of Medicines in Rural Thailand. Ph.D. thesis, Medical Anthropology, University of Amsterdam.

Stacey, M. 1988. *The Sociology of Health and Healing.* London: Unwin Hyman.

Stampfer, M.J. 1991. Postmenopausal Oestrogen Therapy and Cardiovascular Disease. *New England Journal of Medicine* 325:756–62.

Steffen, Vibeke. n.d. Challenging Control – Creating Uncertainty: Antabuse Medication in Denmark.

Stein, H.F. 1990. *American Medicine as Culture.* Boulder: Westview Press.

Stimson, G. 1975. The Message of Psychotropic Drug Ads. *Journal of Communication* 25:153–60.

Streefland, Pieter, and Anita Hardon. 1998. Medicine Markets and Public Health. In *Uit de Zevende Hemel: Vijftig Jaar Politieke en Sociaal-Culturele Wetenschapen aan de Universitit van Amsterdam,* edited by A. Gevers. Amsterdam: Het Spinhuis.

Sussman, Linda K. 1988. The Use of Herbal and Biomedical Pharmaceuticals on Mauritius. In *The Context of Medicines in Developing Countries: Studies in Pharmaceutical Anthropology,* edited by S. Van der Geest and S.R. Whyte. Dordrecht: Kluwer.

Tan, Michael Lim. 1988. *Dying for Drugs: Pill Power and Politics in the Philippines.* Quezon City, Philippines: Health Action International Network.

——— 1999. *Good Medicine: Pharmaceuticals and the Construction of Power and Knowledge in the Philippines.* Amsterdam: Het Spinhuis.

Taylor, Carl E. 1976. The Place of Indigenous Medical Practitioners in the Modernization of Health Services. In *Asian Medical Systems,* edited by C. Leslie. Berkeley: University of California Press.

Taylor, Christopher C. 1988. The Concept of Flow in Rwandan Popular Medicine. *Social Science and Medicine* 27:1343–8.

Taylor, Richard. 1978. *Medicine Out of Control: The Anatomy of a Malignant Technology.* Melbourne: Sun Books.

Temkin, Owsei. 1964. Historical Aspects of Drug Therapy. In *Drugs in Our Society,* edited by P. Talalay. Baltimore: The Johns Hopkins University Press.

Thomas, H.B., and Robert Scott. 1935. *Uganda.* London: Oxford University Press.

Tomson, G., and G. Sterky. 1986. Self-Prescribing by Way of Pharmacies in Three Asian Countries. *The Lancet* 2:620–2.

Topo, Päiva. 1997. Climacteric Hormone Therapy in Medical and Lay Texts in Finland from 1955 to 1992. *Social Science and Medicine* 45:751–60.

Trostle, James A. 1988a. Medical Compliance as an Ideology. *Social Science and Medicine* 27:1299–1308.

——— 1988b. Doctors' Orders and Patients' Self-Interest. In *Compliance in Epilepsy,* edited by D. Schmidt and I.E. Leppik. Amsterdam: Elsevier.

1996. Introduction. Inappropriate Distribution of Medicines by Professionals in Developing Countries. *Social Science and Medicine* 42:1117–20.

Tuchinsky, C. 1991. *Produktion, Handel und Konsumption nicht-westlicher Medikamente in Südost-Asien: Malaiische Jamu in Singapore.* Münster: Lit Verlag.

Turner, Bryan S. 1984. *The Body and Society.* Oxford: Basil Blackwell.

1987. *Medical Power and Social Knowledge.* London: Sage.

Turner, Victor. 1967. *The Forest of Symbols: Aspects of Ndembu Ritual.* Ithaca: Cornell University Press.

Unschuld, Paul U. 1988. Culture and Pharmaceutics: Some Epistemological Observations of Pharmacological Systems in Ancient Europe and Medieval China. In *The Context of Medicines in Developing Countries: Studies in Pharmaceutical Anthropology,* edited by S. Van der Geest and S.R. Whyte. Dordrecht: Kluwer.

Van der Geest, Sjaak. 1982a. The Efficiency of Inefficiency: Medicine Distribution in South Cameroon. *Social Science and Medicine* 16:2145–53.

1982b. The Illegal Distribution of Western Medicines in Developing Countries. *Medical Anthropology* 6(4):197–219.

1984. Anthropology and Pharmaceuticals in Developing Countries. *Medical Anthropology Quarterly* 15(3 and 4):59–62, 87–90.

1987. Self-Care and the Informal Sale of Drugs in South Cameroon. *Social Science and Medicine* 25:293–305.

1988. The Articulation of Formal and Informal Medicine Distribution in South Cameroon. In *The Context of Medicines in Developing Countries: Studies in Pharmaceutical Anthropology,* edited by S. Van der Geest and S.R. Whyte. Dordrecht: Kluwer.

1991. Marketplace Conversations in Cameroon: How and Why Popular Medical Knowledge Comes into Being. *Culture, Medicine and Psychiatry* 15:69–90.

1994. Medische Technologie in Cultureel Perspectief: Inleiding. In *De Macht Der Dingen: Medische Technologie in Cultureel Perspectief,* edited by S. Van der Geest, P.t. Have, G. Nijhof and P. Verbeek-Heida. Amsterdam: Het Spinhuis.

Van der Geest, Sjaak, Anita Hardon and Susan Reynolds Whyte. 1990. Planning for Essential Drugs: Are We Missing the Cultural Dimension? *Health Policy and Planning* 5(2):182–6.

Van der Geest, Sjaak, and A. Meulenbroek. 1993. Metaphors, Metonyms and Homeopathy: Terms of Illness and Therapy among Mossi People in Burkina Faso. *Curare* 16(3/4):285–90.

Van der Geest, Sjaak, Johan D. Speckmann and Pieter H. Streefland. 1990. Primary Health Care in a Multi-level Perspective: Towards a Research Agenda. *Social Science and Medicine* 30(9):1025–34.

Van der Geest, Sjaak, and Susan Reynolds Whyte, eds. 1988. *The Context of Medicines in Developing Countries: Studies in Pharmaceutical Anthropology.* Dordrecht: Kluwer.

Van der Geest, Sjaak, and Susan Reynolds Whyte. 1989. The Charm of Medicines: Metaphors and Metonyms. *Medical Anthropology Quarterly* 3(4):345–67.

Van der Geest, Sjaak, Susan Reynolds Whyte and Anita Hardon. 1996. The Anthropology of Pharmaceuticals: A Biographical Approach. *Annual Review of Anthropology* 25:153–78.

Van Dongen, Els. 1990. Middelen van Onderdrukking en Verzet: De Sociale Betekenis van Medicijnen in een Psychiatrische Afdeling [Means of Oppression and Revolt: The Social Meaning of Medicines in a Psychiatric Ward]. *Medische Antropologie* 2(1):39–50.

Van, Staa, A. 1993. Myth and Metronidazole in Manila. The Popularity of Drugs among Prescribers and Dispensers in the Treatment of Diarrhoea. Masters thesis, Anthropology, University of Amsterdam.

Veeken, H., and B. Pécoul. 2000. Editorial: Drugs for 'Neglected Diseases': A Bitter Pill. *Tropical Medicine and International Health* 5(5):309–11.

Verbeek-Heida, P.M. 1983. How Patients Look at Drug Therapy: Consequences for Therapy Negotiations in Medical Consultations. *Family Practice* 10(3):326–9.

Vuckovic, Nancy. 1999. Fast Relief: Buying Time with Medications. *Medical Anthropology Quarterly* 13(1):51–68.

Vuckovic, Nancy, and Mark Nichter. 1997. Changing Patterns of Pharmaceutical Practice in the United States. *Social Science and Medicine* 44:1285–1302.

Waitzkin, H. 1991. *The Politics of Medical Encounters: How Patients and Doctors Deal with Social Problems.* New Haven: Yale University Press.

Waldram, James B. 2000. The Efficacy of Traditional Medicine: Current Theoretical and Methodological Issues. *Medical Anthropology Quarterly* 14(4):603–25.

Walt, Gill. 1994. *Health Policy: An Introduction to Process and Power.* London: Zed Books.

Walt, Gill, and Jan Willem Harnmeijer. 1992. Formulating an Essential Drugs Policy: WHO's Role. In *Drugs Policy in Developing Countries*, edited by N. Kanji, A. Hardon, J.W. Harnmeijer, M. Mamdani and G. Walt. London: Zed Books.

Walt, Gill, and Susan Rifkin. 1981. The PHC Approach in Developing Countries. London: Ross Institute Publications, London School of Hygiene and Tropical Medicine.

Weatherall, Miles. 1993. Drug Therapies. In *Companion Encyclopedia of the History of Medicine*, edited by W.F. Bynum and R. Porter. London: Routledge.

White, Luise. 2000. *Speaking with Vampires: Rumor and History in Colonial Africa.* Berkeley: University of California Press.

WHO. 1977. The Selection of Essential Drugs: Report of a WHO Expert Committee. Geneva: World Health Organization.

—— 1978. Thirty-First World Health Organization: Background Document for References and Use at the Technical Discussions on National Policies and Practices in Regard to Medicinal Products, and Related International Problems. Geneva: World Health Organization.

—— 1985. Rational Use of Drugs: Cooperation Prevails at WHO Conference in the 'Spirit of Nairobi'. Press Release. Geneva: WHO/32.

Whyte, Susan Reynolds. 1982. Penicillin, Battery Acid and Sacrifice: Cures and Causes in Nyole Medicine. *Social Science and Medicine* 16:2055–64.

1988. The Power of Medicines in East Africa. In *The Context of Medicines in Developing Countries: Studies in Pharmaceutical Anthropology*, edited by S. Van der Geest and S.R. Whyte. Dordrecht: Kluwer.

1991. Medicines and Self-Help: The Privatization of Health Care in Eastern Uganda. In *Changing Uganda: Dilemmas of Structural Adjustment and Revolutionary Change*, edited by H.B. Hansen and M. Twaddle. London: James Currey.

1992. Pharmaceuticals as Folk Medicine: Transformations in the Social Relations of Health Care in Uganda. *Culture, Medicine and Psychiatry* 16:163–86.

2001. Creative Commoditization: The Social Life of Pharmaceuticals. In *Cultural Creativity*, edited by J. Liep. London: Pluto Press.

Whyte, Susan Reynolds, and Harriet Birungi. 2000. The Business of Medicines and the Politics of Knowledge in Uganda. In *Global Health Policy, Local Realities: The Fallacy of the Level Playing Field*, edited by L. Manderson and L. Whiteford. Boulder: Lynne Rienner.

Whyte, Susan Reynolds, and Sjaak Van der Geest. 1994. Injections: Issues and Methods for Anthropological Research. In *Medicines: Meanings and Contexts*, edited by N.L. Etkin and M.L. Tan. Quezon City, Philippines: Health Action Information Network.

Wickremasinghe, S., and S. Bibile. 1971. The Management of Pharmaceuticals in Ceylon. *British Medical Journal* 3.

Willems, D. 1998. Inhaling Drugs and Making Worlds: A Proliferation of Lungs and Asthmas. In *Differences in Medicine: Unravelling Practices, Techniques, and Bodies*, edited by M. Berg and A. Mol. Durham: Duke University Press.

Wilson, John A. 1962. Medicine in Ancient Egypt. *Bulletin of the History of Medicine* 36(2):114–23.

Wolffers, Ivan. 1987. Drug Information and Sale Practices in Some Pharmacies of Colombo, Sri Lanka. *Social Science and Medicine* 25:319–22.

1988. Traditional Practitioners and Western Pharmaceuticals in Sri Lanka. In *The Context of Medicines in Developing Countries: Studies in Pharmaceutical Anthropology*, edited by S. Van der Geest and S.R. Whyte. Dordrecht: Kluwer.

1992. *Health in Bangladesh*. Amsterdam: VU University Press.

Wyatt, H.V. 1984. The Popularity of Injections in the Third World: Origins and Consequences for Poliomyelitis. *Social Science and Medicine* 19:911–15.

Wyndham, D. 1982. 'My Doctor Gives Me Pills to Put Him Out of My Misery': Women and Psychotropic Drugs. *New Doctor* 23:21–5.

Zola, I.K. 1972. Medicine as an Institution of Social Control. *Sociological Review* 20:478–504.

Subject index

194

Index of authors